HOW TO COMPUTE YOUR DESTINY

The Secret of Astro-Numbers

D1638409

HOW TO COMPUTE YOUR DESTINY

The Secret of Astro-Numbers

by

Paul & Valeta Rice

THE AQUARIAN PRESS
Wellingborough, Northamptonshire

United Kingdom Edition first published 1988

First published in the United States of America
in 1983 by Samuel Weiser Inc., York Beach,
ME 03910, USA

British Library Cataloguing in Publication Data

Rice, Paul
How to compute your destiny
1. Symbolism of numbers
I. Title II. Rice, Valeta
133.3'35   BF1623.P9

ISBN 0-85030-676-0

*The Aquarian Press is part of the
Thorsons Publishing Group, Wellingborough,
Northamptonshire, NN8 2RQ, England*

Printed in Great Britain by Richard Clay Limited,
Bungay, Suffolk

1 3 5 7 9 10 8 6 4 2

CONTENTS

ABOUT THE AUTHORS

Paul and Valeta Rice have been interested in occult studies for nearly fifty years, starting with the receipt of a book about extra-sensory perception from Duke University. Their search for esoteric knowledge has carried them into Astrology, Reincarnation, Palmistry, Tarot, Colour, Music, the I Ching, ESP, Dream Analysis, the Qabala, Yoga, Structural Dynamics, meditation, visualization and healing, and many other sciences. Their Socratic and regression techniques have won the acclaim of their clients.

While their professions are different (Valeta is a minister and a psychic counsellor, Paul is a professional engineer), the Rices enjoy the co-operation that team teaching provides. Every summer they travel extensively across the United States to wherever they are invited conducting workshops and seminars about Name Analysis and Birthdate Analysis, as well as conducting private sessions by appointment. They have been travelling together for over twenty-five years and have written major works about Name and Birthdate Analyses which have been published in the USA.

INTRODUCTION

When shall I start my next project?
When should I ask for a raise?
When should I sign that contract?
When should I get married?
How will I feel when I retire?

How many times has a person looked for an answer to these questions? During this modern age the veil has been lifted on the ancient science of the vibration of the Numbers. This ancient science, known as the *metaphysical science of numerology*, was developed by Pythagoras, who lived in the sixth century BC.

The simplicity of Numerology is astounding. If you can count on your fingers you can use Numerology. It requires only a few hours' study before you can begin to use the basic facts that you have acquired. This knowledge will give you the opportunity to see yourself and your acquaintances in a better light. Apparently the reason Numerology was used less than other occult sciences in the past was its simplicity, and society today seems also to prefer complexity.

The knowledge of the numbers which govern your life will reveal many things that you already know, had suspected or had hoped were true. The Numerologist takes his place alongside the Astrologer, Graphologist, Palmist and the Tarot reader, who all believe that we came into this life, not by chance, but by choice, and from these arts or sciences much can be revealed about a person's life.

Numerology reveals the vibrations in many categories, including the numbers connected to the Birth Date, the Personal Year and the Personal Month; it also shows how the planet vibrations correlate to these numbers. Awareness of the numbers connected to these categories helps us follow a course which will make us happy and prosperous.

Many people would really benefit from learning to harmonize their birthdate vibrations with the timing of their decisions: We are constantly called upon to make decisions which may bring significant changes to our lives. Often we make the wrong decisions over family, friends, or in business, because our *timing* is off.

The simple system of the vibration of the numbers, how they pertain to your life and the timing of your decisions will help you to come to logically-deduced insights and, if carefully followed, will make you increasingly happy and prosperous throughout your lifetime.

Pythagoras, who lived twenty-five centuries ago, is considered the Father of Numbers. It is believed that he received his knowledge of the occult value of the numbers while in Egypt and Babylon. He taught these concepts and many more in his School of Occult Philosophy where the few who were allowed to attend learned how 'everything can be related to numbers'.

The Science of Numerology is not a quick way to happiness and achievement; it is only by becoming aware of your favourable number vibrations, and then changing the unfavourable ones, that you can smooth your pathway. Numbers live and numbers tell and through them everyone can become aware of their vibrations and their relationship to themselves.

We have explored the mundane and esoteric values of the numbers and their relationship to astrology with a lot of help from our guides. This knowledge we wish to share with you.

Finally, when making general comments we have used the pronouns 'he', 'him' and 'his' in order to avoid long-windedness.

MAHALO!
(Thank you!)

PART I: DESTINY NUMBERS

COMPUTING YOUR DESTINY

Your *destiny*, sometimes called the *life path*, is the road that you as an individual travel. It determines why you are here and what you should be doing in this life in order to fulfil your soul. The Number combined with your birth sign reveals your soul urge, your reason for incarnating into this lifetime. If you do not follow your destiny, you can become frustrated with unresolved goals.

Each month is represented by a number:

January	1	*April*	4	*July*	7	*October*	1
February	2	*May*	5	*August*	8	*November*	2
March	3	*June*	6	*September*	9	*December*	3

Write your birth date on your personal chart on page 286, using the *name* of your month—for example *November*—not the number of the month. Be sure to write the full year—1935, not '35, or 1960, not '60, or whatever is the year of your birth. We use the '1' in the year (1935, 1966, 1940) as well as the rest of the numbers.

On scrap paper add the number of the month, the day of the month and the year of your birth together; then reduce this number by constantly adding the numbers together until you come to a single digit or a Master Number (**11, 22, 33, 44, 55** and **66**).

$19+4+1956$

Example: October 25   1942 (1+9+4+2=16; 1+6 = 7)
               1   7   7 = 15; 1+5=**6**

Example: April   26   1940
               4   26   14   =**44** or **8**

$APril \quad 4$
$19+ \quad 1956$
(31)

In the first example, each component (month, day, year) is reduced to a single digit; in the second, just the year has been reduced, and then only to the first stage. Experiment with your birthdate and see if you can come up with a hidden Master Number.

We call this *Research and Discovery* since we have found a *hidden* Master Number. When the Master Numbers are hidden an unexpected talent lies in the direction of the vibration of that particular number.

Example:

May	26	1919	
5	8	2	= 15; 1 + 5 = **6**
May	26	1919	
5	26	2	= **33** or **6**

Every time you calculate your Destiny Number (or someone else's) try all these methods. Then you find out if you or another person is vibrating on the Master Number or the single digit. There are people who are content to vibrate and work on the single digit pulsation and put their talents to excellent use in that position rather than try for the esoteric vibration of the Master Numbers. This depends a lot on other numbers which concern several categories in numerology.

The main purpose of finding your Destiny Number is to realize where you are in life's stream and learn to flow with it.

The Destiny Number and your birth sign are two things that you cannot change. You were born on a certain day, month, and year, for you chose to be here at that time to experience what you have come to this lifetime to learn.

When experimenting with *Research and Discovery*, simply remember there are various ways of reducing the Numbers.

Example:

August	22	1917	
8	22	18	(1 + 9 + 1 + 7)
	4	36	(19 + 17)
		9	(1 + 8 or 3 + 6)

We always show the single digit that the Master Number reduces to in order to see which level a person vibrates on.

Once you have calculated your Destiny Number, simply consult that number under your Sun sign—or under other signs that appear in your chart—and discover the Real You!

ARIES

21 March to 19 April

The **Ram**

Ruler: **Mars**

People with the birth sign *Aries* have the qualities of the *ram:* leadership, fearlessness, charging ahead of the pack, and sometimes butting their heads against the challenges of life as they try to get through by sheer force. All of their energies are self-directed and self-oriented. They use the 'here I am' principle to assert their natural command of a situation, bringing their executive ability to bear on the solutions to life. They jump to the foreground impulsively knowing that they can take the initiative with courage to solve the problem.

These self-starters of the zodiac are there at the beginning of a project, but do not expect them to be in at the ending if there is no continual challenge, as they soon become bored with the status quo. They need to move with speed and so leave slower people behind. This involves motion as well as the workings of the mind and the spirit.

Arians are the pioneers, venturing forth with strength and purpose to begin their goals. Therefore arousing the Aries' interest is not a difficult thing to do—*keeping* their interest alive in one direction requires expertise. Arians want freshness and dynamism in their work which they prefer to do alone, or at least enough alone so that they can work out their own solutions without a hovering boss. And as they go along in their chosen profession they are interesting to watch, for they are aggressive, competitive and aspiring in their dealings.

When it comes to love relationships, Arians embrace their lovers with enthusiasm and fiery passion, which can be replaced with disinterest if the relationship begins to drag or become monotonous. So spouses, lovers and room-mates have to take heed and keep the partnership interesting and exciting if they wish to hold on to this dynamic person.

PARTNERS

A relationship with a person who has a stable *birth sign* and/or *birth number* can mediate the Arian energies so they can be focused on starting things, letting the partner see these creative drives through to completion. This vigour can be used constructively when the Aries ego is held in check and a little diplomacy is used.

MARS

This planet, the ruler of Aries, is a positive out-going drive that propels the Arian self outwards. Mars is responsible for the courage to accomplish the goals Aries people set for themselves. If Arians remember the energy and the ruler of their sign, they understand themselves better. With that knowledge, they can understand their restlessness and their impatience with slower-moving people.

CARDINAL

This is Aries' force aspect manifesting itself in matter. It indicates more energy, dynamic objectives, activity, directness and interest in what is going on.

FIRE

The element of Aries, the virtues we bring with us to assist us in this lifetime, is Fire. Here again is additional energy, ardour, emotion and the energy to originate new ideas.

NEGATIVE VIBRATIONS

Impatience, intolerance and lack of consideration for others, wasted energy on unimportant issues, and depletion of energy due to scattered viewpoints, are the negative vibrations the Arian should try to control.

NUMBERS

The *number* that is connected to the Aries birth sign increases or decreases the energy of Aries. The number can increase Aries' fire and energy or add patience and stability.

DESTINY NUMBER 1

Young in spirit and raring to go, number **1** gives you the creative urge to bring forth your many talents. Your original ideas must be put to work or you will be very frustrated. The ram wants to leap ahead, leap-frogging over obstacles that would stop a different and more conservative sign of the zodiac.

Your quick mind moves faster with **1**, leaving your slower-paced friends behind and in chaos. Perhaps you might have to slow them down just a little if you want to keep in contact with them. If you decide to follow your creative leaning then you will just move ahead at your own pace, out-stripping and out-distancing others like a runner at a Marathon.

Since you are eternally optimistic, running ahead of the pack you will not necessarily bother you. Develop a strength within yourself so that criticism intended to divert your attention from your goals does not preoccupy you. Turn your face toward the goal and get in step with yourself.

Your personal integrity is high and, since you do not want to take the time to manoeuvre others, your friends and associates will respect you.

1, the ram, Aries and Mars all combine right here for leadership, sparkle, inventiveness, the very essence of life in living and moving.

NEGATIVE

Sometimes **1** can be lonely, for he prefers to handle decisions by himself without guidance from authorities. But who are the authorities anyway? Seeking assistance is fine, yet as **1** is a leader it could be better to go it alone. However, listen to other opinions before deciding on the way to go: Personal emotional upheavals could bring distress if others are ignored.

Colour: Red—for energy. Project this to others.
Element: Fire—more energy. Ensure a healthy diet.
Musical Note: C—the self-starter.

DESTINY NUMBER 2

This compassionate number can give great depths to your character. 2 is called the peacemaker and with your leadership ability and gift for thinking on your feet, you could become one of our great politicians. With the entire world at unrest, diplomacy is needed in the 1990s more than ever.

You have the power to concentrate on the smallest detail, although it may take a lot of your energy since you would rather be active. When you encounter obstacles your tendency as an Arian is to move away from them quickly, yet 2 gives you the stability to stick around and try for a better agreement between arguing factions.

You can be a great trouble-shooter, able to resolve tactfully both sides of a problem, partly because of the 2 and partly because your facile mind leaps ahead to solutions.

You can be an intuitive counsellor for you are sensitive to others. You can bring harmony into a chaotic situation even though the ram wants to lock horns in combat and *push* the other person into doing it your way. Just remember that you are the diplomatic 2.

NEGATIVE
Do not expect public rewards, as your part in this scenario is the *keystone* that others want to touch for luck. Do not depreciate your gift of reasoning instead of rushing ahead like other Arians. Your dedication to your cause will bring rich rewards of inner satisfaction for you.

Colour: Orange—for balance and harmony, the vibrant colour of the sun at dawn and sunset.
Element: Water—dealing in and with the emotions; soothing the fevered brow of discontent.
Musical Note: *D*—for harmony and tranquillity.

DESTINY NUMBER 3

This number of communication gives you the creativity of **1** plus the compassion of **2** to send forth your vibrations to others. The combination of the vibrations of **1** and **2** assists you to become more attentive to your job, your family, and your distant or close friends.

This number is connected with the entertainer—one who wants to make people happy. You can express yourself in drama or comedy, projecting images to others and then acting as a catalyst, thereby assisting others to release their hopes and fears and dreams. This ability, projected through the **3** and your Mars energy, can bring others together in harmony—or can send them apart. So be careful with your energy as you pick up the vibrations of those around you.

Both **2** and **3** people can be intuitive counsellors but work from different levels. **2** is the compassionate, patient type and **3** may use a *Gestalt* or Socrates method of arriving at the solution for themselves or others.

As a **3** you can communicate your needs to a lover, giving of yourself joyously. Being an Aries, you are unafraid to tackle the unusual. Use your talent for words.

NEGATIVE
Guard against overacting, as the energy from your birth sign and your ruler (Mars) plus your Fire element can overwhelm people and cause them to withdraw from you. Since you can pick up the rays of others and reflect a personality that is shining, watch that you do not 'take over' the spotlight and invalidate another's talents.

Colour: Yellow—for expression.
Element: Fire—more energy.
Musical Note: *E*—for feeling.

DESTINY NUMBER 4

This is the most practical number for Aries. **4** has a stabilizing effect in your life which will keep you from flying around this planet with no purpose. You can manifest what you want through this number, using your innate ability to begin new projects, and with the **4** you can also organize the project so it can be finished.

An Aries person is usually so full of energy that one project at a time is too boring for him: he starts many enterprises, hoping to keep interested in some of them. The **4** gives Aries the foresight to see just what he is getting into.

Another wonderful aspect of the **4** is that it enhances the healing potential of the hands. You can work on the etheric body if you want to take the responsibility of doing this kind of magnetic healing.

The ruler of Aries, Mars, contributes to your spontaneity. You want to get into action, so don't just sit there—let's go and do something! Mars in Aries, combined with **4** , gives courage and ambition without the rashness inherent in other numbers.

NEGATIVE
The impatience you have with others at times could stem from irritation with people who are not as organized as you are—and you are able to organize so quickly! Many people do not have the energy you have and move a little slower both physically and mentally. You do not have to slow down for them, just realize where they are and the way they perform.

Colour: A beautiful healing green—project this to people from your heart.
Element: Earth—another stabilizing factor, earth-bound, earthy, salt of the earth, etc.
Musical Note: *F*—for construction, building, making things strong.

DESTINY NUMBER 5

You are going to have a good time in 1990 or 1991, this being the travel number, the 'I want to go somewhere' number. It also can mean study, school, travel in your mind, and using your fire to forge ahead in many directions.

A 5 does not stand still to let life happen. He seeks life and is willing to try different approaches to make dreams come true. Admittedly, he does have several dreams! He is the adventurer who travels into places physically or mentally, or even into the spiritual realms, delving into the unknown.

You could profit from these adventures and new experiences if you do not retreat from the new and untried—although you usually go forward with courage anyway. This is the sensual number, relating experiences like feeling, touching and loving to fragrances, colours and other sensual triggers.

This is also the number of Creative Mind, taking the original idea and changing it into something else or something better.

Even though Arians are usually attractive to the opposite sex, the 5 Aries may double this and magnetize the opposite sex.

NEGATIVE
This search for variety can lead you into unhappiness you think that you have to have a thrill every minute. However, if you can handle this you will be all right. Monotony can drive an Arian up the wall, or drive him to drink. Self-indulgence in this way can lead to inelegance and carelessness.

Colour: Turquoise—like a refreshing breeze.
Element: Air—the breath of life.
Musical Note: G—near the middle of the scale, denoting change.

DESTINY NUMBER 6

All people who have **6** as the Destiny Number have the potential of self-realization; they have access to their higher mind through harmony. This harmonious number brings a power of logic so that a person can adjust the problems or challenges in his lifetime. Harmony does not just mean getting yourself in balance, it means projecting this kind, loving attention to others—listening in order to understand just what people are saying to you. This is a great help to you professionally as well as socially.

This number is attuned to the metaphysical mind, and the chaos you could create by being too swift in your judgements can be tempered by just looking at what you are doing. What choices are you making? Is your energy going forth to encompass those around you or are you just forging ahead with no thought for others?

This is the cosmic mother, the one who takes care of people and things. This is the number of home, partner and family—of sharing with your loved ones.

NEGATIVE

If your energy surges ahead too fast to control, this caring can be turned into anxiety and the desire to run everyone else's lives. You are quick on the draw, seeing the solution to the problem before others, literally taking their hands and showing them *how* to run their lives. Perhaps there are others who do not wish to have this close scrutiny. Don't interfere and don't become nasty when you are told, 'I would rather do it myself'.

Colour: Royal blue—for stability. Meditate on this colour.

Element: Earth, our planet, meaning responsibility to yourself and those around you. Getting 'down to earth' with someone.

Musical Note: A—for receptivity. Listen for the harmony or discord in self or others.

DESTINY NUMBER 7

Most Arians live in the here and now, with a look toward the future. With this **7**, you can look at the past and garner wisdom from actions taken long ago. This could take the mystical path, the *thinker* trying to unravel the mysteries of the universe, or this number could take you into analytical approaches toward your goals. Wisdom is the keyword. Seek hidden truths as you contemplate the metaphysical side of life and decide what path to choose to gain the most insight.

You have always wanted to be free, and **7** doubles this desire. This can take on an emotional tone where you struggle to keep yourself to yourself. Yet your realistic outlook tells you that all these experiences are just learning experiences and you want to get on to the next one using your head (the ram) to meet your obstacles and pleasures face-to-face.

Again, your energy drives you forward, giving you the impetus to better yourself with study, bridging from the known to the unknown and the mundane to the esoteric.

Spiritually you can take your Mars fire, your red energy, and use it for healing spiritual gaps in others.

NEGATIVE
Refuse to humiliate others when you are in a downward mood (which doesn't happen often). Your fine and refined approach can make you seem aloof and uncaring when all the time as a **7** you are trying to figure out what is about to happen. The aloofness could keep others away and make it difficult for them to communicate with you.

Colour: Violet—which stands for reverence. This lovely colour can be sent for a distance for healing.
Element: Water—looking at your reflection while crossing the bridge from the known to the unknown and understanding this trip.
Musical Note: B—for reflection.

DESTINY NUMBER 8

This is the number for power. This is where you find yourself in a leadership position, directing other people, handling money and directing the disposition of it, you are working on the positive side of the number and using your Mars-directed energy realistically. If you are flying away in never-never land, full of idealistic fantasies and not putting your good mind and stewardship to practical use, then you are not aware of your full capabilities. Power can be used for good, to bring others to the realization that they *can* handle themselves, their jobs and their families with justice and love—sharing instead of trying to make everything come out 50-50.

On the esoteric level, you have the opportunity in this life-time to open or re-open your third eye. This means many things, including an awareness of other people's energy and how it affects you, so you can handle the flow. You could learn to see auras and assist others to discover where their energies lie.

The main energy of **8** combined with Aries is a practical application of your knowledge. The Mars fire can assist you to know that you can take charge of, for example, large corporations.

NEGATIVE
Here is the schemer; the one who loves glory and fame and attention without really deserving it. If you have put in lots of study, etc., then achieve your rewards; if you have plotted and walked over others to gain money, position, glory and fame, then you really are not entitled to the adulation. Watch your intolerance: Do not become impatient when you are not able to get your own way. As an **8** you can get there because you are the natural leader.

Colour: Rose—the colour of love.
Element: Earth—for achievement on this third dimension, this earth, material gain.
Musical Note: High *C*—for research.

DESTINY NUMBER 9

This is the number that represents the servers of mankind. Your Mars fire reaches out for the universal truths so that you can free yourself from personal restrictions. You can go beyond the self-seeking to expand your horizons, able in time to transcend your bias toward other ideas, races or beliefs.

This is brotherly love, recognizing that all people are in need of strokes of love but are individuals who have unique experiences which compel them to act as they do. This all-encompassing love can spread out to all those you meet and inspire them to act with love for their fellow men (or women).

Your emotional attachments to individuals may be short but intense as you move from one person to another. These intense relationships may bring frustration to others but in time they will realize that you do not want to possess them. You inspire others and then set them free.

Your destiny is to be working in the mainstream of life where you can be an instrument for good, bringing love and desire for a better world to many people.

Awareness and success are keywords to remember. This is the number of completion, getting the job done, finishing tasks, staying with the project.

NEGATIVE
You could rush forward carrying the flag of redemption in your zeal and find no one behind you to carry on your work unless you face facts and operate with practicality. If your zeal is thwarted too often you may become bitter and blame others for not seeing your goals. Discretion is the keyword.

Colour: Yellow-gold—for perfection, or the desire to make everything perfect (in your opinion). At least take time to look at other opinions before you go striding off into the sunset, followed by no one.
Element: Fire—for warmth. People like you, for you inspire them to be more than they think they are.
Musical Note: High *D*—for accomplishment.

DESTINY NUMBER 11

This is the first Master Number after all the single digits from **1** to **9**. All Master Numbers carry a responsibility for they are higher vibrations of the single digit they reduce to. For example: $11 = 1 + 1 = 2$, so **11** should be correctly written **11/2** to show that a person could be vibrating on either or both levels. This holds true for all the other Master Numbers.

This number is for the perfectionist; intuition can develop the mind to a genius level. The search for truth can raise the level of personal intelligence as well as that of others if a desire is present to share what is learned.

Sometimes **11** is reluctant to do this, feeling that if he 'knows about' something then everyone else 'knows about' it too. Aries, take note that you may discover new and exciting ways to examine your way of life, your job, your family or your spouse. Share this knowledge and intuition with whom it may concern if you want to bring a better understanding between you and those who are important to you.

You will receive dreams and flashes of illumination which could light the path for many to follow. Your perceptions can influence those around you and even change the consciousness of humanity for the better.

NEGATIVE
Since you are intuitively brilliant and your goals are inspiring, your fame can overwhelm you if you turn to greed. This is the trap for many a genius who becomes self-superior and fanatical about his mission in life. Some keep their discoveries to themselves, enriching no one.

Colour: Silver—for attraction. You can magnetize other people to your support.

Element: Air—for the idealist who builds fantasies and pictures in the air. Don't knock it, fantasies can become realities.

Musical Note: High *E*—for magnetism.

DESTINY NUMBER 22

This Master Number brings your high-flying energy down to practical application as it is the number of physical mastery over your own body. You have the ability to use the higher vibrations to heal bodies by laying on hands. Search this metaphysical vibration very thoroughly to discover where the healing comes from and how to handle it. There are many theories to evaluate before you decide upon the best for you.

Spiritually you need to harness your Mars fire to learn service on a constructive basis, a much larger scale than the reduction to **4** (the work number).

You can use an international direction, entering into politics, managing large corporations, becoming the nation's foremost diplomat, or in many other directions which coincide with your Mars fire and your Aries energy to sustain your physical stability. You need to have and keep a healthy body to sustain the pressures that seem to be part of the job of positions in high authority.

Your self-mastery can be expanded to show others how discipline can be used to improve conditions in life.

Think of **22** as being a double **11**, the idealism of **11** projected into international realms. If you are not ready for this heady vibration, then operating on a **4** level could bring the manifestation of your desires to fruition. If you think you can do it, you can, with a little effort thrown in.

NEGATIVE
You could feel unfulfilled if you do not attempt to reach farther than your workday world. If you do not follow through with your grandiose plans you will become known as the big talker and not the doer.

Colour: Red-gold—for wisdom. Use things you have
    learned for practical application, not dreams.
Element: Water—for cleansing. Clean out the
    fantasies from your life and see reality.
Musical Note: High *F*—for physical mastery over self.

DESTINY NUMBER 33

This Master Number may be a difficult one for you to handle until you learn how to handle your emotions. When you learn how the emotions work to control your life when you truly can be the emotional master, able to quell groups of people who are fomenting trouble, providing you have the knowledge of how to handle emotional groups. This requires study and lots of patience to understand the power you can wield.

Your Mars fire wants to rant and rave, to yourself personally or to others, over injustices, yet you have the rare opportunity to learn how to count to three before acting (count to six if the situation is almost out of control).

Think of **33** as being the combination of **11** and **22**. **11** is the idealist who wants perfection in all things and **22** is the practical master wo can really put this idealism to use. The combination leads to **33** which would be using feeling to get the job done!

22 knows the plan can be perfect if effort is applied in the right direction (perfection = **11**). Realizing this, a **33** can balance disagreements by using humour in small doses.

Fortunately, our present metaphysical knowledge contains information about the emotions and what to do about negative emotions such as hate, anger, etc.

Use your Mars fire of love as you surge forward (the ram) in your endeavours.

NEGATIVE

You could fall into the trap of trying to control others since you have leadership qualities. Or you could become emotionally impoverished and apathetic. Be particular in your choices of goals for you can sway people through their emotions.

Colour: Deep sky-blue—for intensity. Your feelings are on the surface, your face and actions show this.
Element: Water—for emotional mastery, flowing with or controlling the stream.
Musical Note: High C—for emotional healing.

DESTINY NUMBER 44

If you thought **8** was powerful just look at this number and what it brings. This is double power and is the Master Number of the mental body. The *mind* is a complex structure containing receptors (the way we see and perceive things), reactors (the way we react to different stimuli) and analytical functions. The mental body uses the latter part of the mind (the analytical portion).

You can approach a challenge through the analytical doorway, look at the facts, then use your inherent abilities to forge ahead in your thinking to discover certainties and uncertainties. With these facts, you can then arrive at a conclusion.

33, on the other hand, approaches challenges through *feeling* and reacting emotionally. Think of **44** as being a double **22** with more under your leadership and fire of ambition. Also think of **44** as being a combination of **11** and **33** and you get a little different twist, **11** is the idealist and **33** is the emotional master or the ability to become the master of the emotions.

NEGATIVE
This amount of power would be difficult for some birth signs to handle. Being the leader, and with the fire of Mars, you can handle this much power if you do not become too rigid in your opinions with the attitude 'I am right because I am always right'. Maybe you are, but does this get the job done, or does it cause problems and send others into confusion? The lowest vibration of this Master Number is to try to control people through mental cruelty. Here is the psychotic who controls people by using his mask of righteousness in front of and behind the scenes. Be careful of your camouflage.

Colour: Blue-green—for tranquillity. This colour
    calms the intense fire of ambition and helps put it
    in the right perspective.
Element: Earth—for mental mastery.
Musical Note: High *A*—for mental healing.

DESTINY NUMBER 55

Since most Arians are full of life, it may seem strange that you chose to come into this lifetime with the number of *life energy*. This number brings you the task of bringing light and life to others by looking toward the future so you can excite others about coming events and projects.

At this level you can be a channel, bringing light and knowledge from higher dimensions into the consciousness of those ready to receive this inspiration.

As light from the sun beams down to the earth, breaking through the prism of consciousness to become warmth, intelligence and tranquillity, so does **55** (if willing) act as a prism to bring understanding to us from higher dimensions.

Think of **55** as being a combination of **22** and **33** added together, wherein the practical mastery of things on this plane of existence works with the mastery of emotions to bring a moving life energy force into existence to elevate the consciousness of all those with whom you contact with this energy. Or think of **55** as being a combination of **11** and **44**, wherein the dreamer (**11**) designs a world of his own and is able to make it take form (come true) through the double powerful energy and command of **44**.

NEGATIVE
If you choose this side of the number, Aries, you are karma-burdened with inaction on the right path. Choose to look forward in a positive manner instead of wallowing in self-pity. This is where the victims of life are still walking in darkness, seeing no light or path.

Colour: Red-violet—the abundant life energy.
Element: Air—for spirituality. Discover the way of the masters. Meditate.
Musical Note: Chord of *G*—for spiritual healing.

DESTINY NUMBER 66

This is a powerful number and can be found by the *Research and Discovery* method on page 10. This number radiates love energy; it is a Master Number which carries a great deal of power in love.

This love extends from the self to others, Aries knowing that you cannot love others unless you know and recognize the perfection of your own soul. This is not an ego trip; it is a full realization of outpouring love through the acceptance of karma-free relationship in soul. The inner self receives a vision of perfection and yearns for this love relationship with the soul-mate and the supreme being.

You can seesaw between the Master Number **66** and **3**, which is its reduction, sometimes feeling this love and sometimes just wanting to entertain people with humour and liveliness.

66 is truly the cosmic mother, the double six leading to the nine: i.e., $6 \times 6 = 36$, then $3 + 6 = 9$, brotherly love.

You are here to keep the love flame going and we don't mean sex, although that is a part of it. We are speaking of the joy in the total universe.

NEGATIVE
If your temper gets in the way, you can use this love as a tool to enslave another. Jealousy can rear its ugly head and you can become determined to get even. If this number is used on the negative side you can refuse love through anger, or even become selfish and possessive of your partner, your friends or your things.

Colour: Ultra-rose—meditation on this colour will open the heart chakra more fully.

Element: Fire—for burning away the dross, the contempt, the frustration, the hate, and bringing forth the imprisoned love for self and others.

Musical Note: Any chord struck in harmony that can bring you in balance. Find the particular chord to which you vibrate.

TAURUS

20 April to 21 May   FIXED: EARTH

*The **Bull***   *Ruler: **Venus***

The Taurus person is steady and very patient although he cannot be pushed into something that he does not feel is right for him. If you are working for a Taurus watch him stretch his patience: He can only be challenged for so long—then this nice, kindly, perfectly harmless person turns into a raging bull, crashing through the china shop of your carelessness.

You cannot command the Taurean, although he can be led to think that a 'wonderful idea' you had really comes from something he triggered in you. Then the direction you want to take will be the direction the Taurean wants to take.

Taureans are practical; they admire people who can discipline themselves. They are also fair and recognize talent as well as recognizing the 'games' you could be playing to get what you want. Taureans are so factual and honest in their approach that few of them enter the sales field. However, there are a few customers who prefer the blunt, direct approach and will buy from none other, as the Taurean can be trusted to tell the truth.

When entering a field that is unfamiliar they need the time to adjust. Then their native intelligence will survey the needs of the job, evaluate the problems connected with it and get to work being the most effective employees you ever had as long as you can keep them busy. They like order and make top managers as they will stand for no nonsense once the employee has had a fair chance to learn his job.

The love of beauty is inherent in the Taurean, love of fine fabrics, well-made furniture, a home that is well-planned with coordinated colours and simplicity of design. The art objects he likes are functional as well as tasteful.

Taureans are affectionate: they are passionate in their initial encounters and this develops into a warm, loving relationship. They are ideal for marriage as they are faithful to their committed mate.

PARTNERS

A relationship with a person who has a similar number is best, i.e. a number that radiates confidence, stability, loyalty and devotion, as these are the qualities of a Taurean. Usually Virgos or Capricorns make good mates if their numbers are compatible. Taureans are apt to get confused if their partner wants to command them or is erratic in decisions.

VENUS

This planet, the ruler of Taurus, is love energy. This artistic, refined, courteous and elegant planet of beauty and love rules the stubbornness of the bull. The bull wants to charge ahead, getting his own way, yet the love energy modifies the frontal attack unless Taurus is pushed into a corner.

FIXED

This is a Taurean aspect of force manifesting in matter. This is a power sign, coiled energy ready to manifest as will-power. Interested in ideas and values, ready to put wants into action.

EARTH

The element of Taurus, the virtues we bring with us to assist us in this lifetime, is Earth. This is the practical, patient and loving willingness to build a sign which manifests as all-seeing on the highest level.

NEGATIVE VIBRATIONS

Indifference, indolence, stubbornness, jealousy and greediness, and wanting to possess material things no matter how much force is needed, are the negative vibrations the Taureans should try to control.

NUMBERS

The *number* that is connected to Taurus' birth sign increases or decreases Taurus' energy. Wherever you have Taurus in your chart look at the influence your Destiny Number has on this house in your horoscope.

DESTINY NUMBER 1

This pulsating creative number will release you from that earthbound feeling of moving slowly and deliberately: this number helps you to fly. Your original ideas and innovative methods spiral you out of the *fixed* vibration of manifesting always on a logical plane. This does not mean that you relinquish your analytical attitude toward your life. This number gives you more freedom of expression and confidence in your own creative abilities.

Your quick mind moves faster than the average, leaving your slower-paced friends behind and sometimes in chaos as they cannot follow the different levels of creativity on which you are operating.

You already have a strong personality and are independently oriented, which can be lonely for you. It is difficult for you to manoeuvre others; rather you expect them to go along with you and your novel ideas when you are expressing this creative number **1**.

Remember that authority needs to be delegated and not hovered over if your employees are to do their finest work. Supervision, yes; repression, no. This vibration concerns an employee as well as the boss.

There is constant optimism in communicating with your spouse, lover, etc., for your creative ideas will keep the relationship going. Your partner may end up a little off-balance because of your surprises!

NEGATIVE
Seek assistance once in a while when your creative juices refuse to flow—don't always be a bull-headed 'I'll do it myself' kind of person. How can anyone detract from the firmly-fixed, earthy Taurean who has such splendid imagination?

Colour: Red—for energy. Project this to others.
Element: Fire—more energy. Ensure a healthy diet.
Musical Note: *C*—the self-start

DESTINY NUMBER 2

This is the number of patience which you usually do not need, as you are long-suffering and only explode when the last straw comes floating down to settle on your already burdened back. Then everyone should watch out—the bull paws the ground, snorts, and charges!

This is the number that is responsive to emotional appeal, the sensitive person who can see in others the need to be loved. As a **2**, whenever a person appeals to your sympathies, you are apt to open your arms and embrace them and their woes with an open heart. These people with problems had better be careful with you and not try to trick you or betray you. Your patience is long and you prefer peace, but you can whirl around and face them if you feel they are using you unfairly.

This sensitivity to rhythms gives you the grace to move smoothly through life, using diplomacy and counselling others with rare insight. You would never take them into never-never land as you are too down-to-earth, showing others the sane approach to life.

NEGATIVE
Impatience is the other side of a **2**, wanting to get the job done *now*! Overly sensitive to criticism about your work, your dress, your clothes, or your friends, you *can* turn off your feelings if you feel betrayed and will withdraw into a neutral corner to glower at your enemies. Then you can plan how to get even with a flourish!

Colour: Orange—for balance and harmony, the
vibrant colour of the sun at dawn and sunset.
Element: Water—dealing in and with the emotions;
soothing the fevered brow of discontent.
Musical Note: *D*—for harmony and tranquillity.

DESTINY NUMBER 3

Your humour is warm and earthy, and this number is the one to show others how charming you can be. Play a little and use your Venus ruler to bring yourself love and light. Taureans don't feel that they have to chase after fun and gaiety, it will just gravitate toward them, like moths to a flame, and they are very solid folk, enjoying the antics of others, even as they sit in a corner with little to say.

Many Taureans go into the theatre. Some of Taurus' most famous personalities have taken pathways that lead to fame, like Fred Astaire, Gary Cooper, Margot Fonteyn, William Shakespeare, Harry S. Truman and Orson Welles, to name just a few. Look at the common denominator of these people: They all knew what they wanted, and in one way or another were in the entertainment field—even Mr Truman.

The **1** is the creative factor and it combines with the **2** of compassion to assist you to bring forth your talents so that the world may see them.

3 is expression and communication for you, using your innate honesty and logic for getting your message across to others, whether it be over the footlights or across the table.

Your spouse or lover may never hear flowery poetry from you, but your perseverance in love will sometimes put even Scorpio to shame.

NEGATIVE
There is more chance of becoming conceited with this number if you become negative about yourself. You may dabble in many pursuits without any definite purpose in life. You could also become intolerant of those who do not stay with their life goals. It is good to look at where you are coming from and how to evaluate yourself and others. Are you jealous of them?

Colour: Yellow—for expression.
Element: Fire—for energy.
Musical Note: *E*—for feeling.

DESTINY NUMBER 4

This orderly number agrees with your birth sign and doubles your patience and your endurance. You can go for very long periods of placid acceptance of the way things are as long as there are not chaotic conditions surrounding you. Being devoted to your goal of making money (Taureans usually have this), or planning a home and family, you know where you are going and you also know how to get there.

The ruler of Taurus (Venus) brings devotion as well as love. You may know that you love someone but your intended may be unaware of it until you bring in the plans for 'our house when we get married'. How nice to be wrapped in the warmth of a devoted and loving partner! Who needs sparklers when your partner finally realizes the security of your loyal love.

NEGATIVE
4 brings rigidity to a Taurean if he never lifts his head to see the bright sunny skies. He can become a plodder who is afraid to deviate from the norm and stay in his rut forever. If challenged he becomes argumentative and bull-headed, retiring to home ground or becoming hateful and suppressive. Stay away from negativity!

Colour: Beautiful, healing green—project this colour to people from your heart.
Element: Earth—the stable person.
Musical Note: *F*—for construction, building, making things strong.

DESTINY NUMBER 5

The expanding creative mind vibration of **5** brings change to original ideas that you may have had in the past. With this vibration you could take someone else's inventive ideas and change them slightly to make them better. This is the adventurous number which brings you out of your rut and brings you an exciting life of travel, viewing many new places. The changes can be physical or in your mental viewpoint.

This sensual number brings your Venus ruler into full sway over your emotions. Take hold of the variety that comes your way this lifetime; seize the novel and unusual. Famous Taureans like Salvador Dali, Orson Welles and William R. Hearst were not afraid to try different approaches to their work. Liberace exemplified a **5** Taurus with his sly humour and variety of expressions. This world sophisitication can be yours also as you develop your talents.

This is also the number of the greatest sales people. Use your definite, truthful and logical manner with your customers when explaining the merits of whatever you are selling. Sometimes your inherent brief approach or silence can convince others of your sincerity.

NEGATIVE
Monotony would affect your work or love affairs. Unhappiness comes with too much drudgery as well as too much variety. It would be well to watch your inconsistenty, such as your promises to do something at a certain time only to find that more interesting activities divert your attention.

Colour: Turquoise—like a refreshing breeze.
Element: Air—the breath of life.
Musical Note: G—near the middle of the scale, denoting change.

DESTINY NUMBER 6

Your attention is concerned with home, family and partner during this lifetime. Your family could encompass large groups as well as your immediate, private home life. Your steady, patient manner could assist many to find harmony in their life styles.

You have excellent judgement, and you evaluate situations with logic as long as you are not pushed into making snap decisions. Your sensible soul may take some time to analyse the situation as you deliberate in your careful way to find the best solution. This would make you a brilliant counsellor, as your quiet nature encourages confidences. As a teacher you would demand fair play, protecting the weaker students yet bringing them to an understanding of their own self-worth.

Your home will contain elegant furnishings, not too cluttered, as this number prefers simplicity with quality and serenity.

Your partner or lover will recognize the warmth you bring to the relationship; it may not be as exciting as Aries, but your willingness to take responsibility creates a stable companionship that is long lasting.

NEGATIVE
The nurturing aspect of this number can turn into interference in the lives of your family if you try to govern them with smothering attention. Caring is the understanding and willingness to *share* your love—not overwhelming others with your tedious attention to unimportant details. Use the harmony of music in your meditations to raise yourself to the cosmic mother status.

Colour: Royal blue—for stability. Meditate on this colour.
Element: Earth—our planet, meaning responsibility; getting 'down to earth' with someone.
Musical Note: A—for receptivity, listen for the harmony or discord in yourself or others.

DESTINY NUMBER 7

This bridge from the known to the unknown could carry you through some mystical experiences during your life. Think about yourself, where you have been and where you are going—what do you want to do for the balance of this lifetime?

You could study the ancient mysteries or you could delve into a thorough study of philosophy. Whatever your endeavours, they will concern analysing theories to bring you more of the material things in life or, alternatively, promoting better lifestyles for others.

Wisdom is the keyword, seeking hidden truths as you meditate on the metaphysical issues, deciding which path to take for further enlightenment.

Being a Taurean you will figure out what is best for you even though you want to remain free of mundane occupations. You are not afraid of the hard work involved, but you prefer to investigate before you leap into just any old job. Many scholars have this **7**, and with your tenacity you can travel far in this search for freedom.

You are the gentle lover in this number, wanting affection but sometimes rather undecided how to go about getting it.

NEGATIVE
The intelligent mind of **7** can get confused if pushed too far into concrete decisions. You would rather take as much time as necessary to reach a decision. If pushed too hard you might take the embarrassment route and humiliate people who do not give you air and space.

Colour: Violet—which stands for reverence. This lovely colour can be sent over a distance for healing.
Element: Water—looking at your reflection and wondering what you are 'mirroring'.
Musical Note: *B*—for reflection.

DESTINY NUMBER 8

Here is where your stubbornness pays off. Your need to have things your own way will bring you much material reward, providing you have laid a good foundation on which to build. This takes native shrewdness, education or abilities—or all three—that you brought forward from a former lifetime, plus physical stamina. Conserve your energy for you will be moving forward, building big businesses, corporations, organizations, or your own enterprises.

You radiate power in this number. Learn to operate wisely and make your efforts pay off; expand, capitalize and show a profit in whatever you undertake.

People will be impressed with your ambitions. You will attract many of the opposite sex; just whistle and they will come running. Of course, we are talking about using this tremendous power to build and do things for the greater good with fairness. Don't grind down those who do not have your control and passion to strive ahead.

NEGATIVE

All this sounds great! However, if you become the schemer, the con man who works covertly to undermine his associates, you can fall harder and farther than the 4 who is just trying to get it all together. You are ready for big rewards *and* big pitfalls, so use your slower-going bull-headedness to avoid these pitfalls. Patience is vital to get to where you want to be. Don't play the bigot (others have feelings too) but open your third eye to the beauty around you. Glory, fame, money and/ or psychic enlightenment can be yours if you use that wonderful Venus ruler power of love.

Colour: Rose—the colour of love.
Element: Earth—for achievement on this third dimension, this earth, material gain.
Musical Note: High C—for striving.

DESTINY NUMBER 9

Your love-life and emotional attachments may be intense but brief during this lifetime as you came to serve mankind and free yourself from personal restrictions. This does not mean that you won't have any family life, it's just that your concerns over and above the human family as a whole will attract your attention more and more.

This number is brotherly love for your fellow man or woman, recognizing that everyone needs attention, needs to be listened to so that they can hear themselves complain or brag. Your patience is required in this number if you decide to become the empathetic counsellor, since people do tend to repeat the same mistakes over and over (ad nauseum) hoping for sympathy, not empathy. Your job should be to assist them to heal emotional experiences using the universal love principle.

Awareness and success, keywords to remember for the **9**, providing they do not possess others, combined with the vibrations of the bull, will assist you to continue on this chosen path of Venus' love.

Your chosen profession could be teacher, psychologist, personnel director, or any occupation that requires contact with others.

NEGATIVE
Be sure of the facts before you charge ahead. 'Telling' your clients what to do can attach responsibility to yourself, becoming the guru. If you do not want this role then find out what you really want, and what your clients really want, before exercising your tremendous power for good. Work through your Venus love and the **9** of brotherly love.

Colour: Yellow-gold—for perfection, the desire to make everything, even people, perfect.
Element: Fire—for warmth. People like to be around you, for you inspire others to better themselves.
Musical Note: High *D*—for accomplishment.

DESTINY NUMBER 11

This is the first Master Number after all the single digits from **1** to **9**. All Master Numbers carry a responsibility, for they are higher vibrations of the single digit to which they reduce; for example: $11 = 1 + 1 = 2$. So **11** should be written **11/2** to show that a person could be vibrating on either or both levels. This holds true for all the Master Numbers.

This is the number of the brilliantly intuitive Taurean who wants perfection in all things. You also expect this in others, which may prove to be a little disappointing if you insist on faultless work from employees or those around you.

The impeccable behaviour that you expect in yourself and others should be tempered with compassion. No-one is perfect, yet we can strive for perfection realizing that each person has lived through his own experiences and has been affected by those experiences in one way or another.

This number has a genius quality, so there is a need to relate your mystical flashes of greatness to others as you light their path. This expansion of the creative mind is assisted by staying on the positive side of the number (see 'Levels of the Numbers', pp. 281-285).

NEGATIVE
Your goals are so inspiring that your fame can overwhelm you and turn to greed and self-superiority. On the other hand you may feel that many people know what you know and then refuse to share your knowledge and insights because 'everyone knows that!' A union with a **22** would be perfect if love is there.

Colour: Silver—for attraction. You can magnetize other people to your support.

Element: Air—for the idealists of this world. The fantasies and air pictures you draw can become the realities of tomorrow.

Musical Note: High *E*—for magnetism.

DESTINY NUMBER 22

You already have the practical approach to most things that you do and this Master Number emphasizes this quality. No one can stop you now. This is the number of the Physical Master, the one who can cure his own body of ills and learn healing arts to practise on others. Use your hands to send forth this Venus love and energy. Use massage or some form of touching to relieve traumas of the body.

Rebirth through love brings success by manifesting order and loyalty to your surroundings, to yourself, and to others.

You have an international direction in your work or profession. You can handle big companies, corporations or high government positions—in fact you can use your combined energies of practicality and honesty, your ability to organize and your directness (the bull) anywhere and on anything.

Your independent nature can set the goals, organize the business, get the work started and running more or less smoothly. Then step aside and watch the money roll in. There is definite power here to teach others your expertise and elevate them to positions of authority. Then you can sit back and govern.

NEGATIVE
If this vibration is too heady for you then the reduction to **4** still puts you in a managerial position. If your grandiose plans are just big talk, then you are negative. Get up and get going at your true level of ability.

Colour: Red-gold—for practical wisdom. Use the things you have learned for practical purposes, not dreams.

Element: Water—for cleansing. Clean out the fantasies from your life and see reality.

Musical Note: High *F*—for physical mastery.

DESTINY NUMBER 33

This number brings softness to your personality because it tempers the bull influence with tenderness and concern for others. This is your opportunity to learn how the emotions work, which ones are positive and which are negative.

Emotions are a human trait. We react to situations according to our experiences and here is an opportunity to count to three, take a deep breath and discover just what is making you tick. There is an emotional healing in love when you project it to others, both for them and for yourself.

You can also think of **33** as being the combinations of **11** and **22**—idealism and mystery over the physical body—leading to love and understanding of your fellow humans.

You are the highly emotional lover, or at least have the potential for this. If your partner fails to recognize you as the typical Taurus, deliberate and patient, when you surprise him with fantasies and exuberance, just let it be a mystery.And enjoy it!

NEGATIVE
You can fall into the trap of trying to control others through triggering their negative emotions, finding their buttons to push. A good thing to remember at this point, when all this control is going on, is who is the prisoner? Fortunately our present metaphysical knowledge contains information on what to do about hate, anger, anxiety, and a lot of negative emotions which detract from the loving in life.

Colour: Deep sky-blue—for intensity. Your feelings are on the surface and show in your actions.

Element: Water—for emotional mastery, flowing with or controlling the stream.

Musical Note: High G—for emotional healing.

DESTINY NUMBER 44

You might want to turn to page 37 to review the power structure in **8** (**44** = 4 + 4 = **8**), the other vibration of **44**. All of **8**'s power and vision doubles for **44**. Much material reward this lifetime.

This is the number of mental mastery, which means that you can school your mind to overcome as many obstacles as you want to. Think of **44** as being a double **22**—the practical master—the one who works with physical matter and things like building structures, instituting reforms in government, service, peace, prosperity and many of the fundamental objects and attitudes that affect our daily lives.

Another way to look at **44** is through the eyes of the idealist (**11**) and from this attaining emotional mastery over the self (**33**). Remember that **33** approaches challenges through feeling. This emotional response brings a desired softness to you as a **44**, for who wants to be a machine or a robot?

NEGATIVE
An unbending, inflexible attitude will eventually produce a rigid person or personality. This is one of the traps of **44**. If you feel that you are always right, you could block out the assistance you might need in your job or in your union with your partner. It could also drive away your children. Mental cruelty is as bad as or worse than physical cruelty as it continues long after a bruise would be healed. The scars are deep and hard to heal. Spread the emotion of love and understanding, listen to others: You don't have to take their advice—just listen—they might even be saying something valuable.

Colour: Blue-green—for tranquillity—the magic of speech as well as soft music.
Element: Earth—for mental mastery.
Musical Note: High *A*—for mental healing.

DESTINY NUMBER 55

This is the person who has abundant life, channelling from higher dimensions with ease to bring *life energy* into existence on this level of consciousness. Think of the **55** as being a combination of the **11** and **44**, the idealist connected to mental mastery of the mind. A **55** brings all the ideals through its logical nature and can bring its best visions of a perfect life to a sane and workable conclusion, injecting the spirit of its number (**55**) into all who surround it.

You can also think of **55** as a combination of **22** and **33**, which would define these vibrations as injecting the feeling and caring (**33**) into the life energy (**55**) by way of a practical (**22**) pathway.

55 is the life force that uses energy to move into the light of knowledge. It acts as a prism, bringing the light and breaking it down into seven rainbow colours or rays. Each colour has a different healing power and meaning.

When people come near you they will feel your serenity. You are easier to understand at **55**, as your simplistic nature at this vibration brings all things within easy focus for others to comprehend.

NEGATIVE
Detracting life force from others is something to be avoided. This would mean making others wrong, invalidating others' ideas, trying to be the *only* force in existence who knows anything. This could mean mental cruelty, emotional suppression or scoffing at others' idealism. This is where the victims of life are still walking in darkness.

Colour: Red-violet—for abundant life energy.
Element: Air—for spirituality. Discover the way of the masters. Meditate.
Musical Note: Chord of *G*—for spiritual healing.

DESTINY NUMBER 66

Use the *Research and Discovery* method on page 10 to see if this powerful Master Number is hidden in your birthdate. **66** is love energy, the full realization that one cannot love others until one loves oneself and can outpour this feeling to others.

66 is truly the cosmic mother vibration, the double six leading to the nine: $6 \times 6 = 36$. $3 + 6 = 9$, which is brotherly love for all mankind. We are not talking about sex, although this is an important part of loving, we are referring to the ecstasy that comes over us sometimes in meditation giving us the feeling that we are truly connected with the cosmos and the *Oneness*.

Your logical approach to life may not accept this version until you have thoroughly researched how this came about for you personally. This is not an ego trip; it is the full realization of the out-pouring love through the acceptance of a karma-free relationship in the soul. You may have some more lessons to learn this lifetime about other things, but you have the love vibration to heal the gaps in another's soul at your fingertips.

NEGATIVE
Your logical and down-to-earth vibrations may get in the way of accepting this ecstasy as it may not seem entirely right for you. Why not you? Are you not worthy as a child of the Oneness to use this love vibration to heal others? Do not try to enslave another with your 'love' or in the name of 'love'.

Colour: Ultra-rose—meditation on this colour will open the heart chakra more fully.

Element: Fire—for burning away the dross, the contempt, the frustration, the hate, and bringing forth the imprisoned love for yourself and for others.

Musical Note: Any chord struck in harmony that brings you into balance.

GEMINI

22 May to 20 June   MUTABLE/AIR

The **Twins**   *Ruler:* **Mercury**

The twins, or a dual personality, represent a Gemini person. This does not mean a split personality, just dual forces—material versus the spiritual. You are a mental person, thinking over your goals and purposes very quickly and able to approach them from two sides of your nature. This is the most versatile of all the signs in the zodiac: You can handle more projects in five minutes than most signs can handle in five months. You make decisions quickly, absorb knowledge from several different levels all at one time and handle it all with a sense of humour.

You would make a good writer of technical journals, but don't get yourself in a position where you have to answer a lot of letters because you hate to do this. You are an excellent salesperson too because of your charming way of getting round people: they fall under your spell and often wonder later what happened to make them wait and wait for you or buy the product you are selling (that they really didn't want).

You are the cheerful, dramatic actor who uses a lot of exaggerated expressions, making people believe that you are reacting emotionally while all the time your mind is constantly turning over—perhaps planning a party for next week as you lament how difficult your employees are. A conservative, slow-speaking person could drive you up the wall unless you use this nervous energy to work out something else in your head while they are plodding along. You have already arrived at a solution to whatever they present and are wondering how they can hassle over such trivialities.

Your enthusiasm, eagerness for life, and friendliness attracts many of the opposite sex. Loving a Gemini can be fun for someone, providing they expect lots of changes—even a coldness—if the Gemini wants to hide his feelings. Many Geminis marry more than once and each is faithful in his own way, which may not agree with other people's views of fidelity. You love to broadcast, have fun and experience the wild and unusual.

PARTNERS

Sun sign Aquarius and numbers **3, 5** and **7** would make good partners as these four categories bring life and light into your life. A Sagittarian would bring you spiritual development and wisdom. However, a careful perusal of the signs and number vibrations would be wise.

MERCURY

This planet, the ruler of Gemini, brings you the ability to communicate. Your can develop the awareness of your thinking processes and what effect your actions have on others. You do affect others with your imagination, your verve, your changeability and your dramatic actions.

MUTABLE

This is Gemini's aspect of force manifesting in matter. Flexibility is your great gift, the ability to flow with whatever is taking place—interacting with people, joining causes and clubs. Your flair with entertaining excites those around you.

AIR

The Gemini element, the virtues you bring with you to assist you in this life, is Air. This is the mental plane, the gatherer of knowledge, communication, friendliness and sharing.

NEGATIVE VIBRATIONS

Flippancy, sleeplessness, lack of patience and a changable and unpredictable character, are the negative vibrations the Gemini should try to control.

NUMBERS

The *number* that is connected to Gemini's birth sign increases or decreases Gemini's energy. Wherever you find Gemini in your chart, look at the influence your Destiny Number has on this house in your horoscope.

DESTINY NUMBER 1

'Nothing great was ever achieved without enthusiasm' (Emerson)—a true statement, and especially true for you, as you tell a story with ardour and dramatics so all will listen. Your creativity is at its highest with this number. Your flair for the dramatic enthralls your audience (and you do like an audience).

You can invent, originate, design, visualize and conceive the untried. Or you can take a design and add to it with ingenuity and convince others that *this* is the way to do the job properly.

You may not want to finish all these creations, so delegate someone else to do it while you create more fabulous projects. You can create enough to satisfy several bosses while other people are deliberating over the first idea presented.

You'll also create your own kind of man or woman, as you delight in the language of love. Your attention to the opposite sex will be full of surprises, including faithfulness. A Gemini partner will be ready and willing to move house or area and make the new home a place of beauty.

Find some time for yourself as you reach out in your times of relaxation for these fresh ideas. Your higher mind will assist your awareness and aid you in becoming the searcher for esoteric, metaphysical values.

NEGATIVE
You can become arrogant and boring if you keep reminding others of how good you are. Your innate honesty seldom lets you get to this point, however. A Scorpio may not understand all your flying around but an Aquarius would not feel antagonistic. If suppressed by anyone from expressing yourself you could turn hostile and create ill-will for this person.

Colour: Red—for energy. Project this to others.
Element: Fire—more energy. Ensure a healthy diet.
Musical Note: C—the self-starter.

DESTINY NUMBER 2

You have chosen to come here to learn patience. This calm, tranquillizing number seems foreign to your nature—it subdues the fire of dramatization, giving you the diplomatic capacity to bring people together in peace. As you become sensitive to the world or your family, you are able to see the need for skilled handling of others rather than putting the focus on yourself. You can respond to emotional appeals with love and caring instead of being impatient with them.

Your definite approach to life gives others the hope of a better-planned existence, if only they will listen to you. Your power lies in your enthusiastic certainty of how to make this a better world.

This is the compassionate number, and the one you chose so you could smooth the road to far-reaching goals. Your sensitivity to others helps you to solve problems while making others feel that they found the solution. You are never one to take all the credit—you just put your ideas out there, sharing and caring, and then moving on to the next challenge.

NEGATIVE
You are the keystone that other people touch for luck. You may not receive public rewards for your peaceful endeavours but there is no need for self-depreciation. Self-delusion is the trap: You may begin with high motives and then move into covert hostility if you do not get your own way. After all, you know best how to get the job done—remember that without your minute attention to detail (in this number) there can be no logical decisions.

Colour: Orange—for balance and harmony, the vibrant colour of the sun at dawn and sunset.

Element: Water—dealing in and with the emotions, soothing the fevered brow of discontent.

Musical Note: D—for harmony and tranquillity.

DESTINY NUMBER 3

You move rhythmically through life, your inherent sense of right time and place to entertain, coupled with the right combination of people to make a party enjoyable, bringing few refusals to your invitations. One affair will be a social whirl of lavish entertainment, gourmet food and sparkling conversation; the next will be shoes off and sitting on the rug to discuss philosophy. You are full of surprises, and this makes it so stimulating to attend one of your soirées.

The serious side of your nature can use the 3 for in-depth communicating with your higher self. The information you bring can be used to counsel others, for you can tune into the solutions they need with your intuitive flair for reaching the logical conclusion—just by hearing them talk about themselves.

The combination of the 1 of creativity and the 2 of diplomacy leads to communicating on a very high level of understanding. Learn how to interpret your dreams, elevating yourself from their lessons.

This is the number of social ambition, facility with words and languages, the one whose desire is to succeed in the arts. This is the extrovert, who appreciates the applause from across the footlights as he performs with verve and style. Judy Garland was a typical 3 Gemini.

NEGATIVE

You really love to be in love, no matter how you fight it, and it keeps slipping away as you keep searching for the perfect partner due to your dual nature and your quest for perfection. Also, this perfect companion must not dim your image, as you like centre stage, and this restlessness can change to intolerance and jealousy.

Colour: Yellow—for expression.
Element: Fire—more energy.
Musical Note: E—for feeling.

DESTINY NUMBER 4

This is a balance number for you; it brings you the stability and devotion that you have turned away from in previous lifetimes. This time you can organize your life and stay within the parameters a good deal easier than you could as a **3**. Of course, you cannot go against your true nature of being the Twins, two selves in one body, but you can train both of them to adhere to the principles you elect for this lifetime.

This number is loyalty personified in your sign, ready to adjust to your partners' wishes—yes, partners'—you may have more than one as you live by your rules, being loyal to both (or several).

The **4** is the manifesting number, the four sides of a square encompassing the material world of ideas. Use this power to manifest what you want this lifetime. You are the builder, the most conservative of the Gemini numbers. Do you want to be a scientist, mathematician, engineer or conservationist? These skilled vocations and more are within your grasp.

You have the potential of learning to heal with your hands, using massage, polarity, reflexology or other ways to bring the energy through yourself to another person.

NEGATIVE
This **4** energy, which is conservative, can make you less flexible in handling money and material things in your life. Relax a little, unbend some of your rules and regulations. For most Geminis the **4** energy just calms them a little, rather than making them rigid in their opinions. If conflict arises watch your emotions so that you do not spend too much time trying to get even.

Colour: Beautiful, healing green—project this colour from your heart.
Element: Earth—the stable person.
Musical Note: *F*—for construction, building, making things strong.

DESTINY NUMBER 5

How full of adventure this lifetime is for you! So many exciting things happening, travelling to strange places discovering the true essence of life in experiencing the diversity of cultures. Of course, it takes money and willingness to plan these interesting trips, and you are just the one who can do it. You have above-average intelligence, can handle many different jobs and know how to make money to have all these wonderful expressions of variety in your life.

On the mental level you have the creative mind, which mean that you can create what you want to happen and the means to do it. Your mind gets working and you accomplish your dreams.

Your ability to visualize where you are going and what you want puts your goals on a practical plane. You can aim for them and see them come to fruition.

This is a sensual number, giving you more than one love affair, which you can handle. And your partners will be interesting people, not run-of-the-mill, ordinary folk. Sometimes they will cause you concern and even heartache, yet you will not be able to complain abut their boring personalities. It is change that you will be looking for. Try a Scorpio, a birth sign which will keep you guessing—it all seems very frustrating, since you want to know everything.

NEGATIVE
Self-indulgence in ill-heath may keep you from rewards of the 5 in this life. Look carefully at your life and see, honestly, if you have brought all this anxiety on yourself just to have an exciting game to play.

Colour: Turquoise—like a refreshing breeze.
Element: Air—the breath of life.
Musical Note: G—denoting change.

DESTINY NUMBER 6

Your spouse or lover will appreciate the warmth and love you bring to the relationship. There will also be surprises, for your exceptional talent for making others happy and entertained enters into a close relationship also. Family, friends, employees and employers will all realize that you really wish to take care of their problems.

Your excellent judgement centred in 6 will help to settle disputes. Your courage will keep you willing to be the arbitrator: One side of your nature will see one argument, the other side of your nature will see another argument of the dispute over property, money or in contract negotiations. You would make a fine judge or lawyer.

Your wit and humour will guide you over many rough decisions. Life is a game, sometimes harmonious (as you want it to be with 6) and sometimes we endure. You are good at enduring with this number.

Social work, politics or teaching in many different categories would enhance your growth. You can bring your sparkling mind to professions that tend to become a little stodgy unless invested with the caring ray of the individual.

NEGATIVE
Don't interfere when you are not asked. This is the warning that is useful to all of us but particularly to a 6. They become the cosmic mother (even men) who want to nurture the entire planet, people, plants, rocks and everything that comes under their span of attention. Sometimes this span is short— but volatile while it lasts.

Colour: Royal blue—for stability; meditate on this colour.

Element: Earth—our planet, meaning responsibility to yourself and to others. 'Getting down to earth with someone'.

Musical Note: *A*—for receptivity; listen for the harmonious note or discord in self or others.

DESTINY NUMBER 7

You are the number of refinement, analytical inner wisdom and freedom. You love your freedom and sometimes twist everything around in order to achieve it. This intellectual and spiritual number has the energy to awaken Mercury to greater intensity.

This means use your head, your mental prowess to analyse whatever situation you are in, and solve it by obtaining the facts instead of getting emotionally upset and dramatizing.

You can be the mystic who sees farther than any other number; working alone, taking apart anything from philosophical discussions to clocks to find out how something works. You are efficient, exacting and use your wisdom to define the knowledge you receive from higher planes.

'Thinkers' like you are much needed. 'He most lives who thinks most—feels the noblest—acts the best' (P. Bailey). Give love and joy with a careful heart. Love begets love and your inner wisdom knows when true love comes.

7s are the bridge from the mundane to the esoteric, from the known to the unknown. And sometimes they even have to build their own bridge.

NEGATIVE
If you become confused because too much knowledge is coming in at one time, you may want to hide from others, or even boast and brag about your prowess. Remaining aloof from the madding crowd gives you space to get your act together although it is difficult for others to communicate with you at that time. The worst that can happen is that you want to suppress knowledge or suppress people and keep them from succeeding in their vocations.

Colour: Violet—for reverence.
Element: Water—for reflection, mirroring your attitudes.
Musical Note: *B*—for reflection.

DESTINY NUMBER 8

How pleasant it is to have money; though it may not be the answer to everything, it certainly is handy to have around. **8** is the money and power number—their acquisition, spending and handling. They can bring happiness and they can bring harm; it depends entirely on how they are used.

Finance, business, industry and government are the best outlets for this ambitious number. Large corporations have always needed **8**s to organize and delegate positions of authority to others to keep the wheels of commerce moving.

Cultivate a broad outlook, postulate the future so that your plans have meaning and purpose as you move forward in your chosen work. An overall plan is best for you in this powerful number, for you can handle the many facets needed by commanders to achieve the best for the most people.

You attract the opposite sex with your virility and confident attitude. Your powers of persuasion are potent. Material gain in love, glory, possessions and fame could be yours.

Another aspect is the opening of your third eye, the revelation of your spiritual nature to gain power over yourself so you can pass on this love and vitality of soul to others.

NEGATIVE
If you fall into the trap of scheming to get what and where you want, the power of **8** will be much abused. Sometimes people who discover they can sway others let the ego get away from them and they create injustices instead of justice. They blame others for their failures, and can even become cruel to those around them. Con-artists are traditionally supposed to have a heart of gold (hard and metallic perhaps?); wouldn't it be better to have a warm, caring and empathetic heart?

Colour: Rose—the colour of love.
Element: Earth—for achievement in this third dimension, material gain.
Musical Note: High C—for striving.

DESTINY NUMBER 9

This number is brotherly love: You choose to serve mankind and free yourself from personal restrictions. This is the number of the true humanitarian.

Whatever profession you follow, it will be an expression of benevolence toward your fellow man. Your destiny is to deal with people, help them, counsel them, encourage them, using your gifts of communication to bring compassion and love. You can receive information from higher beings to assist you in your work. Meditate, seek universal knowledge to bring to your contemporaries.

You will need to watch that you do not become emotionally drained. Get some good feedback yourself by being around friends who can contribute to your well-being with good music and conversation. People will seek your advice and sometimes this becomes a drain on your physical resources, so find a quiet time to recharge your batteries.

Success and achievement are inherent in this number also. Finish your cycles of work and you will find yourself with more energy.

NEGATIVE
Too much strain on your resources could make you inconsiderate of others. When dealing with those in trouble you can become the 'do gooder' who looks with scorn at those who seem to be unable to handle their own lives. Your natural good humour protects you from selfishness (though this is a trap for **9**s). Immorality is the lowest expression of this number, as is bitterness.

Colour: Yellow-gold—for perfection, the desire to make everything, even people, perfect.
Element: Fire—for warmth. People like to be around you, for you inspire others to be more than they think they can be.
Musical Note: High *D*—for accomplishment.

DESTINY NUMBER 11

This is the first Master Number after all the single digits from **1** to **9**. All Master Numbers carry a responsibility, for they are higher vibrations of the single digit they reduce to: **11** = 1 + 2 = **2**. So **11** should be correctly written **11/2** to show that a person could be vibrating on either or both levels. This holds true for all the other Master Numbers.

This idealistic number taps the subconscious dreaming of perfection that was and will be. Between the idea and the reality falls the shadow of doubt. Your native confidence in yourself fires your imagination with concepts foreign to many who function on a limited plane, then your doubting turns to positive conclusions. You have Mercury to give you the impetus to forge ahead with your idealistic plans. Your flashes of intuition could light others' decisions.

You try to find the ideal partner or lover, this being difficult as perfection is seldom in the physical. We all have our little habits that are left from former lifetimes. Use your ability to see both sides (the twins) of a personality so you can understand where others are coming from and how this can change—or how *you* can change, the latter being more difficult for you.

NEGATIVE
Looking for perfection in all things is inspiring to your spiritual side and also disappointing if you insist on perfection. Your goals are inspiring but could turn you into a fanatic if you fail to see both sides or the true side of your ambition.

Colour: Silver—for attraction.
Element: Air—for the idealist.
Musical Note: High *E*—for magnetism.

DESTINY NUMBER 22

This is the number of physical mastery, here and now: Power over your own body to heal it and over your physical surroundings.

You can move in international directions in your work, being able to deal with diplomats and heads of other nations as well as your own. Your cultural level will determine your expertise in handling important matters of State.

On another level you can handle and manage large corporations, your own business or be an advisor to those who do this. Your Air sign snatches ideas out of the imaginative portion of your mind, the right side of your brain.

22 reduces to 4 for those not ready for this heady vibration, yet 4 is the manifesting number, getting what you want. 4 is also known as the work number, and you usually love to work. Work is play for you, putting your ideas into motion, moving the pieces on the chessboard of life.

You may try to exert this mastery over your partner, so watch out. If you want a submissive lover (though this is not commensurate with your birth sign) then go ahead and rule. It would be better to use your humour and wit to endear yourself to your selected partner.

NEGATIVE
If you do not reach farther than your fellow man you could become frustrated. Follow through with your grandiose plans instead of being just the big talker.

Colour: Red-gold—for practical wisdom, using the things you have learned for practical application.
Element: Water—for cleansing. Clean out the fantasies from your life and see reality.
Musical Note: High *F*—for physical mastery.

DESTINY NUMBER 33

It would be wonderful if we could understand all about emotions and how to push certain buttons to get what we desire out of others. It sounds fantastic, but we must not forget that other people have desires too.

Used correctly, **33** signifies great ability to quell riots, subdue quarrelling groups and bring a balance to disagreements by using your wit and humour. Here is where your dramatization takes wings to offer mental pictures of riotous or peaceful outcomes to those conflicts of emotions. Let your associates or family see the futility of a Pyrrhic victory—winning the battle and losing the war. Paint these vivid pictures in live action and use them for therapy.

Enthusiasm for your work, your loves, your family or your private life can fire others with optimism.

33 includes the **11** for idealism and **22** for the practical application of ideals which lead to action—getting the job done, but with spirit and fun too.

NEGATIVE
If you try to control others with your whip of emotions you can fall into the trap of fomenting hidden fears, which could erupt at the moment when you least expect a rebuttal. You may have thought your partner was here to do your bidding: A soft answer turneth away wrath. Or you could say, 'I do that sometimes', when accused of leaving dirty dishes in the sink. A truthful answer leaves your accuser speechless!

Colour: Deep sky-blue—for intensity. Your feelings are on the surface and show in your actions.

Element: Water—for emotional mastery, flowing with or controlling the stream.

Musical Note: High *G*—for emotional healing. Heal emotions, don't excite them into performing evil. When we are triggered into our negative emotions by fear, anxiety or grief we are open to suggestion. Suggest the positive solutions to problems.

DESTINY NUMBER 44

Logic is a product of our mental processes. There is two-valued logic ('right and wrong'), three-valued logic ('right, wrong and maybe'), then there is simply 'your side, my side and the correct side'. If we take a quantum leap we get to infinite-valued logic, 'righter' or 'wronger' at one time than another—i.e. there is always scope to be better or worse.

You have the ability to use any of these processes, since your mind works on several different levels at one time. You become the mental master with a Destiny Number **44**, the universal builder; power on a high government level that can institute world-wide reforms for the good of mankind. It is easy for you to do this because you do your homework in advance, laying out your charts and proposals in an organized fashion, then using your charm and quick mind to push the right buttons to accomplish your desires.

44 is a combination of **11** (idealism) and **33** (emotional mastery). **44** is also a double **22**, the physical mastery number (power over self). **44** can stand alone as the powerful manifesting number on the material side. How about going into law, medicine or some healing science?

NEGATIVE
Sometimes you need assistance or advice from someone more knowledgeable than ourselves. If rigidity in your personality sets in—'this is right because I know it is right'—and we brook no interference (when really you are slightly off-course), then you incur the wrath of those in power—or even those not in power. You also have moments of discernment: The lowest vibration uses the mask of righteousness to camouflage the real action behind-the-scenes.

Colour: Blue-green—for tranquillity, the magic of speech as well as soft music.
Element: Earth—for mental mastery. Speak softly to your love, not with numbers and charts.
Musical Note: High *A*—for mental healing.

DESTINY NUMBER 55

This number gives you the essence of life in abundance. All the good things you read about Destiny Number **1** (page 47) apply to **55** many times over. The creative principle is at work to bring you ample life force, physical stamina, a healthy creative mind and a receptive spirit.

You can assist others by helping them to gain, regain and reinforce their actual sparkle, by being in the room with them, listening to them and counselling them. Counselling energy requires knowledge, education and a certain talent for magnetizing the actual problem so it can issue forth for examination and solution. You can help dramatize situations by having people play a role and act out fears and anxieties.

55s have the combination of **11** and **44** to express their lives; idealism (**11**) plus mental mastery (**44**) leading to the explosion of life. **55** also has the **11** plus double **22**, idealism expressed in physical mastery blessed twice over. Separating **55** into **22** and **33** gives you physical mastery over yourself with emotional mastery over yourself and others. You know when to push the correct button to bring into existence the things that you know to be good for mankind.

NEGATIVE
All Master Numbers have a stepped-up vibration that some people are unwilling to handle: You can operate as the **1** if you think that this could be true for you. Meditate and contact your guides, angels, or whatever can assist you. Do not drain anyone else's life force or become a karma-burdened victim of life, walking in darkness.

Colour: Red-violet—the abundant life energy.
Element: Air—for spirituality. Meditate.
Musical Note: Chord of *G*—for spiritual healing.

DESTINY NUMBER 66

Use the *Research and Discovery* method on page 10 to see if this powerful Master Number is hidden in your birthdate. **66** is love energy, the full realization that one cannot love others until one loves oneself and can outpour this feeling to others.

66 is truly the cosmic mother vibration, the double six leading to the nine: $6 \times 6 = 36$. $3 + 6 = $ **9**. This is brotherly love for all mankind. We are not talking about sex, although it is an important part of loving, but are referring to the ecstasy that comes over us sometimes in meditation, giving us the feeling that we are truly connected with the cosmos, and the *Oneness*.

Your exuberance for life brings a unique energy to a roomful of people; you can sway them to your way of thinking or acting. This is a powerful number for you to handle and it should be done with love and care. You state your opinions and are unafraid to march with the Martin Luther Kings of this world who want to bring equality to everyone. As keeper of the love flame, share this with many others and teach them how to accomplish the circle of love around the world.

NEGATIVE

A negative **66** would gather many people into his camp by selling them on the idea that 'this is the only way to salvation'. He would use the love energy to enslave others, make them do things 'in the name of love' that go against their moral codes. Another negative vibration is repressing love for oneself and for others, keeping family and friends chained with 'you don't really love me'.

Colour: Ultra-rose—the fullest expression of love on this planet. Meditate on this colour, it will fully open your heart chakra if all the other laws are followed which have led you to this initiation.
Element: Fire—for burning away the dross.
Musical Note: Any chord struck in harmony.

CANCER

21 June to 22 July   CARDINAL/WATER

The **Crab**   *Ruler:* **Moon**

The crab symbolizes the physical and emotional planes. Since we think of the physical as being connected with the Earth, and the emotional as being connected with Water, both environments are familiar to the crab.

This sensitivity is shown in Cancer people who are at the mercy of their moods. Or perhaps these are not moods as most of us understand them but an ESP connection to the world around them. Cancer people feel deeply, are easily hurt, then withdraw into their shell (their home), and until they are back there, they never feel secure.

You need to be told that you are loved. You need to be soothed and fussed over. Beneath this sensitive spirit lies the sentimental lover, the Moon child, who brings you posies and sonnets. Just as you are getting used to being this part of Cancer, he will quote limericks. Don't despair, for he is a faithful and tenacious lover who hangs on to what he is promised. He'll camp on your doorstep if there is a chance you will capitulate. Here is an excellent parent.

You like the sound of money, and can figure out how to hang onto it. Money does not represent status for you, but it is nice to have it around. Your economies may seem weird to others, since you figure your profits and losses far into the future by buying quality which will last for more years than the cheap article that breaks or disintegrates.

Family is important to you, especially your mother, and if your partner cannot make peace with this angel your romance is a lost cause. You can be a tower of strength to your partner and family because you appreciate the value of things.

A person might feel that he can play it straight to Cancer

because of the latter's wit and humour, but don't be fooled; he is hard-working and probably unconscious of his almost perfect wit and irony.

PARTNERS
Capricorn and numbers **2, 4, 6** and **9** would make good partners, as these categories bring patience, loyalty, home, family and love into your life. Other numbers and Sun signs could bring you more sparkle, however, as well as numbers **3** and **5**.

MOON
Rules the subconscious and the emotions bringing you insight and awareness, tearing away the veil of misunderstanding. You can use this ESP to assist others as well as to help yourself understand your mood swings, if you desire.

WATER
Water is many things to you, Cancer. It can be a cold drink to a thirsty soul; a river, flowing in your stream of consciousness to dig deeper channels of understanding; ice, for withdrawal to safer places; and steam for explosion and elevation of your spirit. These are the virtues you brought with you.

CARDINAL
This is the fire that turns the water to steam, heightens your activities, drives you forward, creating and expressing itself. It is your aspect of force manifesting in matter.

NEGATIVE VIBRATIONS
Instability, worrying, moodiness and over-sensitivity are the negative vibrations the Cancer should try to avoid.

NUMBERS
The *number* that is connected to Cancer's birth sign increases or decreases Cancer's energy. Wherever you find Cancer in your chart look at the influence your Destiny Number has on this house in your horoscope.

DESTINY NUMBER 1

How fortunate if you are a **1**—this brings you the creative vibration and vision to expand your intuitive awareness. You will need to develop a strong personality so that others cannot push you around. If you are a woman, men will want to govern you and make your decisions for you; if a man, then women will want to take over your life. Some Cancers like this total attention from the opposite sex but **1** is very independent and wants to stand on his own two feet—not be bowled over by the windstorm of your partner's opinion.

Create, invent, forge and visualize the untried viewpoints in material and esoteric form. Your imagination will soar, guided by your intuitive abilities to devise new pathways to accomplish your goals. And you can think of more goals in five minutes than most can in five years. Find some time to recharge your batteries and get yourself back together after a long session of creativity though.

Of course, all this creativity can mean money and success if you do not sidle away like the crab, refusing to face your abilities. Ringo Starr and Ernest Hemingway faced their talents and you can remember how far they got as Cancers.

Your cautious nature may cause you to retire within your shell, making all your own decisions, being lonely or at least feeling lonely. Never fear, you are a leader; everything you do will have your integrity. Hang on to that when the going gets tough.

NEGATIVE
You can abuse this intuitive power by anticipating others' stories and stepping on their punch-lines. Flow with your Water sign instead of damming the creativeness of others. Worry and anxiety can make you ill, for you fear insecurity.

Colour: Red—for energy. Project this to others.
Element: Fire—more energy. Ensure a healthy diet.
Musical Note: C—the self-starter.

DESTINY NUMBER 2

Wonderful, gentle, compassionate Cancer is at home with Destiny Number 2. You have many moods, but you do love the smooth road rather than all that bumping up and down on bad feelings. This compassion exemplifies the intuitive counsellor, the one who is needed to understand the reasons for great 'causes'. Your tact moves in rhythmic waves to calm the hot heads of leaders who strive forth to fight many battles.

No business with more than five employees does very well without a 2 to keep the company going in all its minute detail. Your Water sign brings a continuous flow of personnel problems to the management. Your peacemaking objectives heal many a sore wounded pride.

As an intuitive counsellor, you reach out with your heart in empathy, securing the client's trust. You can concentrate on the smallest detail that would drive a Gemini 2 up the wall.

'A penny saved is a penny earned' is a saying from Ben Franklin's *Almanac* that records your feelings towards money. 'Stop that leak', 'invest wisely', 'plan for the future', 'insure for protection', 'don't rock the boat' and many more expressions of safety are your bywords.

Here is the patient lover taking extreme care in the court-ship ritual for he knows that when he finds the 'one and only' it will be difficult to give up the conquest. Cancer does not want to give up possessions and will hang in there almost forever.

NEGATIVE

It won't bother you to let the others receive the credit for their work or expertise, for you know who helped them to get there, don't you? You are the power behind the throne in many little ways that could be a stumbling block to a lesser person.

Colour: Orange—for balance and harmony.
Element: Water—dealing with the emotions.
Musical Note: *D*—for harmony and tranquillity.

DESTINY NUMBER 3

Since you respond to life with your feelings, come out of that shell and enjoy it. This is the entertainment number, the joy of living, the giving and sharing of yourself so that you can move up to being the intuitive counsellor.

You truly care and love to be loved but you will sit back and wait for someone to make the first move in most of the numbers. 3 releases you to bring those positive enthusiastic vibrations to the foreground. This number is social ambition, a facility with words and languages. If you are an artist you can make your paintings express the real feelings that you are projecting.

Cancer 3s have a contagious laugh and see humour in other people. If there is a stage handy, Cancers can act and spread their charisma at will if they are in the mood. Cancer children love to strut about and dress up and preen themselves—of course, this applies not only to children... Dressing up can come from their love of history, the drama, the costumes and the flair that other generations had.

NEGATIVE

Your mood changes as rapidly as the moon. This can be good when changing from being miserable to cheerful, but can be a hardship when your mood is going downhill faster than a skier. Successes in entertainment could make you conceited unless you face yourself honestly. This mirroring of the adulation of your successes on stage (or on camera) is enthusiasm for the moment—even success in business. Enjoy and evaluate and next time do even better. As a 3 you have the intuition to be aware of your audience.

Colour: Yellow—for expression.
Element: Fire—for energy.
Musical Note: *E*—for feeling.

DESTINY NUMBER 4

You have a practical nature that knows how to make money and hang on to it, for this number gives you additional organizational ability to fulfil your goals. **4** is known as the 'work' number, something that does not bother you, for you take your work seriously. You would be successful in management, in teaching, in accounting or as a loan officer— all professions which require attention to detail.

Teaching requires insight into the students' minds, and with your sensitivity you would be able to reach your students by that route. Also the time it takes to explain different subjects would not trouble you too much, for you want your students to learn the subject in depth.

Your humour does not encompass practical jokes, especially if you are the boss. Jokes are fine, just leave them behind when you come to work. Work is serious business to a **4**.

You would be loyal and faithful to the one you chose, and would expect your partner to be the same. If your spouse does or says something that is not within your code of honour it would be very difficult for you to forgive. One of the reasons is your excellent memory for every detail.

NEGATIVE
There is always the chance that in spite of your sensitivity to others you might become rigid in your belief systems— unyielding and argumentative when in one of your dark moods. If the mood continues for too long, you might want to get even with the person who hurt you. Usually you just sulk or withdraw to your corner to brood.

Colour: Beautiful, healing green—project this colour from your heart.
Element: Earth—the stable person.
Musical Note: *F*—for construction, building, making things strong and lasting.

DESTINY NUMBER 5

It would be better for you to concentrate on the *now* instead of the past or worry about the future when you have Destiny **5** which seeks adventure and variety. What is done today or thought of for tomorrow becomes the future.

This number can bring you all sorts of interesting occupations, travel, personal freedom and opportunities to learn about life. You like to have things planned well ahead and yet many of the plans could take a different turn which really could be beneficial. Haven't you perceived practical future projects only to have them collapse in the middle because of unforeseen events? As a **5** you can flow with this and change in midstream to align yourself and your goals in an even better direction.

This is a sensual number. Art, sports, science and just about everything interests you—for a time. You can be at home in any country or any gathering, for your sensitivity tunes in to the best way to achieve communication with strangers.

Your moods can vary a great deal with this number, but this is not necessarily a bad thing. You need to fluctuate with the temper of the group to which you become temporarily attached. You are sensually attracted to the opposite sex, yet faithful in your own devoted way.

NEGATIVE
This number can turn from the positive seeking of more knowledge and friendships to a selfish attitude, oblivious to all desires but your own. Sliding downhill through indulgence in the desires of the flesh could increase carelessness in your dress and communication with people.

Colour: Turquoise—like a refreshing breeze.
Element: Air—the breath of life.
Musical Note: *G*—denoting change.

DESTINY NUMBER 6

You can share your world in a very private way with people whom you trust. There must first be that link of faith made between the two parties, however, whether it be family or friends. Once the link is forged you will not be the one to break it. This possessive attitude remains even if the link of trust is broken. You really want to keep love in your heart for your family and friends.

This also is true of your affection for your partner. Don't betray a Cancer or even a person with Cancer rising as they will remember the injustice for infinity.

There is good judgement in a **6**, the ability to evaluate business or personal relationships. Your Water sign cools the arguments that occur in your presence as you temper each side with the disclosure of facts and what to do about them.

In this number you seek harmony and balance, becoming the cosmic mother who nurtures and protects those around her (or him). A **6** is probably an ideal parent, taking care of children and deriving much pleasure from them. Sometimes Cancers become overindulgent and overprotective in this number.

NEGATIVE
Overprotectiveness could lead to interference in your children's lives. They need to grow, too. The anxiety over friends' problems may cause you to get too nosy and bossy with them, giving advice when it is not wanted.

Colour: Royal blue—for stability. Meditate on this colour.
Element: Earth—our planet, meaning responsibility to yourself and others. Getting down-to-earth with someone.
Musical Note: *A*—for receptivity, listening for the harmonious note or discord in yourself or others.

DESTINY NUMBER 7

5 gives you the freedom to unstick yourself from whatever past life or trauma triggers upsetting emotions. **7** is called the 'Eye of the Needle', where you pass from the known to the unknown, from the mundane to the esoteric.

In this position your inner wisdom can form a bridge to your goals, to the desires of your heart. Your sensitivity to the colours in the rainbow can turn on the healing power that is hidden in this number. Violet, the colour of the crown chakra, can radiate through your body to heal itself and outward to heal others.

Use your analytical powers; refine and focus them on the challenge you wish to conquer. It could be about family, business, the arts, sports or in whatever field of endeavour you choose. You are seldom bored in this number as you are always watching people and what is going on. There are many subjects that you could study—metaphysics would be a good one as it delves into the mysteries. Mysteries are fun to unravel, and with your intuitive approach, you could become interested in the games that people play on each other.

NEGATIVE
Confusion could follow you if you delve into too many subjects at one time. Listening to negative people could turn you into a sceptic who finds fault with every positive idea. There is a lot of emotional content in **7**. If you are trapped into making a decision for which you are not ready, you could become malicious and humiliate that person to get even.

Colour: Violet—for reverence. Appreciate the healing gifts that you have been given.

Element: Water—for reflection, a mirroring of your attitudes.

Musical Note: *B*—for reflection.

DESTINY NUMBER 8

We are finding more **8**s in Cancer than we did in past years, probably because Cancer will be elevated to a higher position in the New Age. You will then become stronger-willed and persistent in your endeavours. Now this **8** brings power to complete your ideas and ideals. Your masterful approach to life accompanies an active quest for success.

You have always been interested in making and holding on to money and power in a sort of quiet way, and now knowing that you do have this primal energy to forge ahead, you can surge towards your goals.

You usually operate in present time in this number, taking care of your daily tasks with full attention centred on the project, whether it be making money, plans or bread. You live more in the now with an **8** than with most numbers.

On the esoteric level, you have the opportunity to reopen your third eye, receiving at the level of intuition the healing rays and the knowledge that you had in the past. Meditation will assist you to bring this forward.

Shine your love from those expressive eyes with the one you adore and bring your partner closer to you in spirit. Your spouse or lover will recognize the power you have and respond to it with love.

NEGATIVE

If you go undercover and scheme to get ahead because you recognize your powerful commanding rays, you could become abusive and intolerant of others. In time this will cancel your influence. You are a leader already, so why oppress others just to get to the very top of the heap? *Playing* the game is the fun, and once you reach the top you will not have a game left to play.

Colour: Rose—the colour of love.
Element: Earth—for achievement on this third dimension, material gain.
Musical Note: High C—for striving.

DESTINY NUMBER 9

The love of the arts, your fellow man, animals and inanimate objects is your vibration for **9**. Music is one of the important objects of your affections. This compassionate number fits your Cancerian nature by contributing empathy for mankind's troubles. You see, you feel and then get yourself into action, trying to change this inhumanity to man. **9**s are the servers of mankind; they express this benevolence toward their comrades with gifts of love and a cherishing attitude that brings out the best in most people.

With your intuitive out-pouring of love you could become emotionally drained if you do not get some affection for yourself. Giving has to include some taking although it is better to share your feelings. Let your friends assist you part of the time. They also need to share energy in this caring way.

This is also the achievement number, providing you can find time to finish all those projects you started. Finishing your cycles will bring your energy level up to *now!*

Align yourself with a spouse or lover who understands that you will tear out of the house at any hour of the day or night to help a friend in need. Aquarians understand this compulsion.

NEGATIVE
If too many people drain you of your empathetic energies, you may become selfish and unkind. This is just a way to get time for yourself. The opposite of being charitable is being mean: the opposite of being merciful is being unforgiving; the opposite of trust is being indiscreet. Consider these vibrations.

Colour: Yellow-gold—for perfection and the desire to make everything, even people, perfect.
Element: Fire—for warmth, cuddling up to.
Musical Note: High *D*—for accomplishment.

DESTINY NUMBER 11

This is the number that desires perfection in all areas— people, animals, plants, houses, children and inanimate objects. In the healing professions, if you can visualize the perfect body and project this vibration, healing occurs if the person desires to be healed. You can perfect this as you have an intuitive feeling about people.

This is the first Master Number after all the single digits from **1** to **9**. All Master Numbers carry a responsibility for they are higher vibrations of the single digit to which they reduce: **11** = 1 + 1 = **2**. So **11** should be written **11/2** to show that a person could be vibrating on either or both levels. This holds true for all the other master numbers.

You are able to do two tasks at once, getting your ideas across in both a practical and idealistic manner. Your psychic ability knows what is going on at both levels. This is called ESP by many, the joining of two minds so that they come up with the same invention at the same time.

You have clairvoyant ability or can develop this capacity by studying and by meditation. Seeing into your partner's mind may not be the nicest thing in the world—yet, it just might avoid some problems.

NEGATIVE
Your goals are inspiring but could turn you into a fanatic if you fail to see both sides of your ambition or the true side. This demand for perfection could make you feel superior to others and turn you into a cynic. Haven't we been saying that this is the number of the genius? When you rise high you can also fall further into disrepute. The lowest vibration of **11** is dishonesty and insolence.

Colour: Silver—for attraction.
Element: Air—for the idealist.
Musical Note: High *E*—for magnetism.

DESTINY NUMBER 22

This is the number of the master organizer and *doer*, the one who gets things done by practical means. You can be a builder of strange and wonderful edifices, a statesman, a famous stage and screen personality or whatever you wish.

Remember that with the advent of the Aquarian Age you are moving away from your super-sensitive nature into being the strong person with super-powers of observation and intuition.

In other numbers Cancers give the impression of needing lots of attention; in this number you can stand on merits alone, doing the projects that you have longed to do for many lifetimes.

Most **22**s are very healthy people because they have little time to spend being sorry for themselves. They seem to be removed from emotional stress or have learned to handle it with ease. Of course, we are talking about the positive **22**.

Your love life yields to romance, dinner at the finest restaurants, theatre tickets to the latest shows, expensive (but practical) gifts to your lover and concern for your spouse. How lucky it must be to have you as a partner!

You can be trusted with state secrets or the confidences heard in the privacy of your office or home because you cannot be bothered with manoeuvring people to obtain your goals. You know that you can achieve them on your own.

NEGATIVE
This positive power carries a great responsibility and if turned to the negative or repressive side, it can emit a destructive force. This can also be the big talker and little doer who tries to sway his audience like a big bag of wind.

Colour: Red-gold—for practical wisdom, using the things you have learned for practical application.
Element: Water—for cleansing: Clean out the fantasies from your life and see reality.
Musical Note: High *F*—for physical mastery.

DESTINY NUMBER 33

This is the highest number of exploring intuitive processes, **33** being the emotional master who understands or can learn about the scale of emotions. On a scale of 1 to 10 you can divide the emotions into negative and positive with 'death' at the bottom and 'life' at the top—a gradient scale leading upward into life and abundance.

Think of **33** as being a combination of **11** (idealism) and **22** (practical mastery or physical mastery of the self). This idealism and practical application of ideals leads to action, getting the job done with visionary control. You see what needs to be done, yet use your cautious nature to proceed at a slower pace than other numbers or signs of the zodiac.

This being an emotional number, you will of course fall in love many times: You need to love and be loved. You also need an audience, someone to listen to *your* problems, to your interpretations of what is going on. This leads to communication—but are you withholding? Do you withdraw from the conversation because your intuitive sense tells you to work out exactly what you are going to say before you speak—then someone else jumps in to explain *you*? Just stopping and crawling back in your shell like the crab, however, will not solve the problem.

NEGATIVE

Withdrawal from whatever you think is or could be a problem is not a solution. This only helps to build your shell thicker and tougher. You'll return to fight another day.

> **Colour:** Deep sky-blue—for intensity. Your feelings are on the surface and show in your actions.
> **Element:** Water—for emotional mastery, flowing with or controlling the stream.
> **Musical Note:** High *G*—for emotional healing. Heal emotions, don't trigger them into performing evil. When we are triggered into our negative emotions by fear we are open to suggestion. Be positive.

DESTINY NUMBER 44

Your mental prowess is at its highest level in this number. In our mental processes we use logic to weigh one idea against another. There is two-valued logic ('right or wrong'), three-valued logic ('right, wrong or maybe') and there is simply 'your side, my side and the correct side'.

If we take a quantum leap we get to infinite-valued logic, 'righter' or 'wronger' at one time than another—i.e. there is always scope to be better or worse.

You have the ability to select one of these processes since your mind works on a couple of different levels at once. One level is considering the possibility of doing one thing, and pushing the idea to its conclusion, the other level is considering how it will affect a person, a business or tools that need to be handled.

This is the number of the universal builder, power in high government circles, instituting world-wide reforms for the good of mankind.

44 is a combination of **11** (idealism) and **33** (emotional mastery). **44** is also double **22**, the physical mastery number, power over oneself. **44** can stand alone as the powerful manifesting number on the material side. Medicine, law, social services or some healing science would actively put your sensitivity to work in this number.

NEGATIVE

When you know that something is right it is a little difficult for you to let go (the crab) and accept other people's authority. Bide your time—you are good at this, and the truth will out. Since you have this strong intuition you *could* get your own way by twisting the facts—but don't be tempted!

Colour: Blue-green—for tranquillity, the magic of speech as well as soft music.
Element: Earth—for mental mastery. Speak softly to your love, not with numbers and charts.
Musical Note: High *A*—for mental healing.

DESTINY NUMBER 55

This number gives you the essence of life in abundance. All the good things you have read in Destiny Number **1** (page 64) apply to **55** many times over. The creative principle is at work here to bring you abundant *life force*—that's physical stamina, a healthy creative mind and a receptive spirit.

You can assist others by helping them to gain, regain and reinforce their actual being by using your intuitive capabilities to counsel them. Your insights will provide part of the background you need, the balance being your studies in human nature and the humanities. You have a talent for listening before you speak or come to conclusions.

Perhaps you came here to help people understand themselves or to teach them philosophy. You can no longer play the game of being hurt or criticized, for the sign of Cancer has moved upward from the search for his own self to being transformed into the life bringer.

Think of the **55** as being the combination of **11** (idealism) and **44** (mental mastery) leading to the explosion of life (**55**). Separating **55** into **22** and **33** gives you physical mastery over yourself with emotional mastery over both yourself and others.

NEGATIVE
All Master Numbers have a stepped-up vibration that some are not willing to handle. If so, you can operate as the creative **1**. Meditate and contact guides, angels or higher beings to assist you. Do not take anyone else's life force or you will become a victim of life.

Colour: Red-violet—for abundant life energy.
Element: Air—for spirituality. Meditate.
Musical Note: Chord of G—for spiritual healing.

DESTINY NUMBER 66

Use the *Research and Discovery* method from page 10 to see if this powerful Master Number is hidden in your birthdate. **66** is love energy, the full realization that one cannot love others until one loves oneself and can outpour this feeling to others.

66 is truly the cosmic mother vibration, the double six leading to the nine: $6 \times 6 = 36$, $3 + 6 = \mathbf{9}$, which is brotherly love for all mankind. We are not talking about sex, although that is an important part of loving; we are referring to the ecstasy that comes over us sometimes in meditation, giving us the feeling that we are truly connected with the cosmos and the *Oneness*.

Your sensitive, psychic ability to see beyond the façade most people present to the world can heal the wounds of others through your love. This eagerness to help others is not an ego trip, it is an awareness of the needs of others. As keeper of the love flame, share this with many others and teach them to accomplish the circle of love around the world.

NEGATIVE

A negative **66** would gather many people into his camp by selling them on the idea that 'this is the only way to salvation'. He would use the love energy to enslave others, make them do things 'in the name of love' that go against their moral codes. Remember sex is great but lust is evil. Another negative vibration is repressing love for the self and for others, keeping family and friends chained to you with 'you don't really love me'.

Colour: Ultra-rose—the fullest expression of love on this planet. Meditate on this colour, it will fully open your heart chakra if all the other laws are followed which have led you to this initiation.

Element: Fire—for burning away the dross.

Musical Note: Any chord struck in harmony.

LEO

23 July to 22 August   FIXED/FIRE

The **Lion**   *Ruler:* **Sun**

The lion symbolizes the King, the ruler by divine right (or so he thinks). The lion, who belongs to the cat family, can be soft and cuddly, purring away on your lap as he gently digs his claws into your thighs, but soon tires of it and jumps down to pursue game he can stalk.

Leo is like the cat, independent, full of pride, roaring when he doesn't get his own way, then purring and smiling and petting you until he wins his objective.

Leo has a commanding air, carries himself with pride and is not easy to ignore in a crowd—maybe it is better you do not ignore him for you will be detracting from his outgoing radiance. This regal manner of Leo brings up the tone of a crowd. We all stand straighter when faced with a Leo, for we instinctively recognize authority in him.

The *will*, individualized by Leo, is the spirit of power and vitality directed toward bringing light and energy to others. He is faithful to those he loves and does not change his affections easily.

He is loyal to his associates: Don't betray a Leo or he will roar and destroy your ego. He can't understand why you should not follow his direction when he is so good to you, supplying you with money (that you earn), food, superb wines, excellent entertainment and encompassing love to shelter you from all ill-will.

Here is the organizer of splendid projects, the fun-loving, generous and courageous person whom most people love to follow, for he is the king of the beasts, unafraid to charge ahead into the unknown, bringing success to his followers as well.

PARTNERS

There is no particular birth sign that can easily be ruled by Leo. One would think that the feminine signs of Taurus, Cancer, Virgo, Scorpio, Capricorn and Pisces would be compatible with this male energy but each of these has its own peculiarity by which it rules its own nature. Cancer and Pisces, being sensitive compassionate signs, would understand a Leo better if they were not totally inundated by Leo's powerful influence: they *could* tame him with soft love and flattery. Leos love to have people appreciate their reliability.

SUN

Rules the self-consciousness, the self-respect that is inherent in Leo. He has the courage and integrity to move into areas where angels fear to tread. In doing so he breaks established barriers so that others can follow and reap the benefits. He is as honest and direct as the Sun, shining on everyone who comes within range. His space reaches as far as he can see, hear or imagine.

FIXED

This is Leo's aspect of force manifesting in matter. It is active power, visible and unswervingly stubborn when he decides on the path he wants to take to achieve his goals.

FIRE

These are the virtues you brought with you from former lifetimes. This fire of the inner heart surges forth to bring success and love to everyone if the Leo is on his way to being evolved. The Leo destiny is a high one, reaching to the Sun, being leader and servant at the same time. He is vital and warm.

NEGATIVE VIBRATIONS

Brusqueness, dominion over others, arrogance, vanity, egotism and carelessness are the negative vibrations the Leo should try to avoid.

NUMBERS

The *number* that is connected to Leo's birth sign increases or decreases Leo's energy. Wherever you find Leo in your chart look at the influence your Destiny Number has on this house.

DESTINY NUMBER 1

Destiny Number **1** gives you even more impetus to create your own world or kingdom. This creative force helps you to charge ahead with innovative projects and original ideas.

The fire of ambition erupts into a moving force that assists others to inaugurate ideas beyond their original concept. You help others turn on a creative ability they may not be aware of. This is why Leos make good teachers—they inspire students to better performances.

You would do well in the entertainment world as a director of plays, films and TV documentaries. Once an idea has taken hold for expression on film or in live performances it will be hard to dislodge you from your viewpoint. 'Live performances' could also mean action in your own family. You want to go to the theatre and your family wants to go to the beach: you *know* that the theatre will give your family more ideas than playing in the sand. Take a good look at what you are insisting on and evaluate it; is the play at the theatre instructive or would playing in the sand give your family time for restful reflection?

1 brings success because of your optimistic outlook. Yves Saint-Laurent, the designer, knew that given an opportunity, he could become a world-famous designer—and he did. Confidence in your own creative ideas will bring the same, or similar, success.

NEGATIVE

You could be forcing your will onto others without their permission. Also, it is not easy for a **1** Leo to accept ideas from others. Could this be a lack of courage? The quavering inside, the arrogance showing outside?

Colour: Red—for energy. Project this to others.
Element: Fire—more energy. Ensure a healthy diet.
Musical Note: C—the self-starter.

DESTINY NUMBER 2

This is not the easiest Destiny Number for you as it requires all your patience to pursue your goals. It means using diplomacy to get your desires, listening and not reacting immediately when presented with ideas contrary to your own. Though you chose to come into this lifetime to be the ruler, you cannot rule by force under this vibration. Get the co-operation of your associates by using your leonine charm and wit. Your sex appeal (whether male or female) will garner your wishes faster than pounding your fist on the table.

The intuitive aspect of this number can be used to counsel others by sending your intense vibrations (positive, hopefully) across whatever distance to another person or group. Others will feel your energy and will react in similar manner. This means if you send positive creative ideas to people, they will react with positive ideas—unless the person receiving the energy is wallowing in his own self-pity so much it would take several therapy sessions to raise him to the level of listening to what is being sent or said.

When speaking to groups or your family, smile a lot. Treat your friends and associates as you like to be treated and complimented. There lies your secret of success in this number.

NEGATIVE
Your impatience does get the better of you. Scream and rant by yourself, throw rocks, run or swim or do some exercise that will extinguish these negative vibrations. You do have the power to get what and where you want if you exercise a little caution in this diplomatic vibration.

Colour: Orange—for balance and harmony.
Element: Water—dealing with emotions.
Musical Note: *D*—for harmony and tranquillity.

DESTINY NUMBER 3

Leos love to have centre stage and be the object of everyone's attention. In this life you can exercise this feeling of being the entertainer, the one who provides laughs and good humour in any gathering. Relax—3 is the joy of living; perhaps you are here on earth this lifetime for a vacation!

If you are working harder than you think necessary, perhaps you are vibrating on the 'strength' of the 3. 3 contains the creativity (1) and the diplomacy (2) which leads to outpouring activity. The creating you are doing, whether it is on the positive or negative side, takes energy (3). Energy is also involved in playing the diplomatic role. You can take ideas suggested to you (if you are in a listening mood) and carry them to fruition with your usual action-oriented energy.

Communication is the keyword for this Destiny Number. Talking, listening, exchanging ideas, entertaining your clients, your boss and any other road or avenue you can think of will bring results in the near future. Advertise your skills and your worth to your family. Use your talent for words and learn another language. Pursue knowledge as a lion pursues his game.

Esoterically you can remember your dreams and establish contact with higher beings if you desire.

NEGATIVE

Since you love to be the centre of attention, it is hard to guard against overacting. Your excessive energy can wear people down. The opposite of this would be a lack of energy to carry through your purposes. If this is true, check carefully and see what is causing this, for a 'not caring' attitude is not natural for you as a 3. Even problems shouldn't affect you for long. If you do find yourself just dabbling in life, is it because you are playing the cowardly lion?

Colour: Yellow—for expression.
Element: Fire—for energy.
Musical Note: *E*—for feeling.

DESTINY NUMBER 4

There must be a product, something you can touch, see, feel or handle to make the best use of this **4** Destiny Number. There is an esoteric side for manifesting what you want, yet these manifestations are usually on the practical side. You are already someone whom people look to for guidance, for your clear thinking mind sees solutions (on the practical side again) and remedies for many problems and challenges.

Since you are orderly and devoted to duty, your patience may be a little short with those who are careless and inconsistent in their work. You won't waste time with these types of people for you value your time and your talents to such a degree that using your energy to straighten out the problems of careless people is a waste of your valuable time and space.

You will endure hardships because you can see the rewards for when the task is complete. Then you can bask in the sunshine of adulation for a job well done.

Though you have a good sense of timing and humour, you are not amenable to practical jokes, especially about yourself. The lion roars when upset but purrs when stroked.

Your love interests are clearly defined in this number. You always enjoy ruling and in a **4** you are not interested in being ruled. Your spouse or lover can enjoy the adoration you give them as long as you come first.

NEGATIVE
Your thoroughness, exactness and self-discipline can become directed toward others to your detriment, as they will see only rigidity to your purposes and goals. Too much rigidity makes you stiff and clumsy in your approach to others.

Colour: Beautiful, healing green—project this colour to people from your heart.
Element: Earth—the stable person.
Musical Note: *F*—for construction, building and making things strong and lasting.

DESTINY NUMBER 5

Destiny Number **5** is a type of freedom. You are unstuck from the average humdrum life and can move freely in many directions if you take advantage of the adventurous vibrations this number has. **5** means travel, either physically by boat, train or plane or in your mind or spirit. There are opportunities for you in many strange places. You do not have to seek adventure—it will come to you, changing your stated plans, bringing excitement into your life that was totally unexpected.

Many of the changes in your life may seem difficult since they involve friends and family. You will be seeing people differently as you absorb new ideas through studies in which you become involved.

You can be the world's best salesperson with the ability to sell the beautiful, quality items. Use the sensual approach in promoting your products.

Although you are an inherently faithful partner, you have a roving eye with this Destiny Number. Since variety is the spice of life you may find yourself delving into the mysteries of several intriguing affairs with the opposite sex before you 'settle down' and become devoted to one person.

NEGATIVE
Selfishness rears its ugly head when the negative vibrations take action. Since you want so much diversification you might indulge in drink, over-eating, drugs or some such stimulant. This will only bring in false pictures and thought forms which will lead you away from your goals.

Colour: Turquoise—like a refreshing breeze.
Element: Air—the breath of life.
Musical Note: G—denoting change.

DESTINY NUMBER 6

As a **6** you make a wonderful loving parent. Your children may come under a strict disciplinary régime with you, which is no deterrent to love. We all need a modicum of discipline to learn and understand where our parameters are, how far we can go in a certain circumstance without incurring the wrath of the gods. If children do not know the rules of kindness, courtesy and love, how can they grow up to be kind loving adults?

This love moves on to include your partner, your friends, your associates and the world. This is the number of the cosmic mother who embraces all levels of consciousness and nurtures on all levels. If you go into socially-conscious professions you will be the one to carry the flag, lead strikes for better working conditions, and be in the front in the demonstrations for equality.

As a Leo you have the strength of the lion to help you stride ahead in your chosen profession. You have the will to succeed in creating harmony in this **6**. Sometimes justice or judgement does not seem harmonious yet true justice means being fair and judging by using well-founded reason.

NEGATIVE
The mental approach to reaching a fair decision when faced with disciplinary action is better than letting your feeling of superiority goad you into making a rash judgement. Think it through before acting; you could be interfering in others' lives. The anxiety you feel about your family could make you bossy and nosy and a general nuisance.

Colour: Royal blue—for stability. Meditate on this colour.
Element: Earth—responsibility to self and others.
Musical Note: *A*—for receptivity, harmony.

DESTINY NUMBER 7

Your ruler, the Sun—or radiance as we prefer to call it—is the fire of wisdom that you use from past experience to project into the future. This analytical number gives you the opportunity to search for your successes and mistakes in the past. As you search for past successes to use as a foundation on which to secure a better future, you also encounter the mistakes. But remember, what is done is done—analyse the mistakes and turn them to your advantage.

On the esoteric level 7s are the mystics who can heal spiritual gaps in a person's aura. Remember that permission must be asked of the person *you* feel needs healing. You are apt to go around *telling* others of your power which, of course, reduces the energy. Let this healing power come through you as you project this beautiful violet colour to those who ask.

This perfect occult number is the bridge from the mundane to the esoteric, from the known to the unknown, from knowledge to performance.

You spouse or lover needs patience to understand your 'indepth' contemplation. This need to be quiet and contemplative is not compatible with responsibility to family. As a Leo you have enough stability of character to overcome this 'priestly attitude' than some of the other signs, and can better adjust to functioning on this 7 level of consciousness (third dimensional) as well as on furthering your studies in the metaphysical world.

NEGATIVE
You could become sceptical about the information you receive from higher dimensions and try to ignore this knowledge. Or you could remain aloof and uncaring and be difficult to communicate with.

Colour: Violet—which stands for reverence.
Element: Water—flowing with your knowledge.
Musical Note: *B*—for reflection on the past.

DESTINY NUMBER 8

8 symbolizes money, power and glory, and all this can be yours if your foundation has been laid with care, study and honesty. If you climb over or step on the 'little people' to get to the top, your underpinnings will become very shaky: We all get what we deserve.

Handling this power, this primal energy, becomes a study in the correct posture to hold the reins of those wild horses of success. The fire of your ambition and the courage of the lion will carry you far in your endeavours.

You operate in the present in this number, taking care of your daily decisions with full attention centred on the immediate project. You live in the *now* with **8**, planning for the future but using most of your energy to make your plans work in the present. On the esoteric level you have the opportunity to open or reopen your third eye during this lifetime if you wish to follow the metaphysical teachings.

In this world, finance, government and industry are the best outlets for your energy. Large corporations need Leos who are willing to charge ahead with confidence to organize and use the potential of those employed by the company. If you choose the arts you can become famous as a dancer, painter or sculptor, or in any field you choose. Lucille Ball became famous by using this **8** Leo energy, this urge to succeed.

You will attract many of the opposite sex to you, for your shining success is like a beacon of light and energy for others.

NEGATIVE
If you scheme to get ahead with negative thoughts you will attract vibrations that will come and sit on your doorstep later to haunt you. Be careful in your dealings with your colleagues. Your ego could get away from you if you become greedy and abuse those 'beneath' you.

Colour: Rose—for love.
Element: Earth—for achievement, material gain.
Musical Note: High *C*—for striving.

DESTINY NUMBER 9

This is an achievement and success number for you. **9** means completion, finishing your job, your programme of work, your cycles of thinking and planning. Projects started some time ago are awaiting your attention, and when they are finished you will feel a surge of energy which can be used on many other projects. When things are unfinished the energy they contain hangs over us like a heavy cloud.

9 also means brotherly love, the concern for mankind in general. **9**s go beyond the self to expand horizons, able eventually to transcend bias or prejudice against other races or belief systems. When you reach the positive side of this number it will touch a responsive chord of recognition in vast numbers of people.

The destiny of the **9** is working in the mainstream of life where you can be an instrument for good. You would do well as a civic worker, reformer, composer of uplifting music or writer of philosophical treatises. You would also make a wonderful teacher.

Align yourself with a companion who undertands that you are on call to help with your friends in need, no matter when.

NEGATIVE
Since many people will come to you for advice and counselling, keep your vitamin pills handy so your energy is not depleted. The opposite of charitable attention is being unforgiving and the opposite of trust is being indiscreet. Consider these negative vibrations.

Colour: Yellow-gold—for perfection, the desire to make everything perfect, even people.
Element: Fire—for warmth, cuddling up to. People gravitate to where you are as they feel the warmth and the caring that you have.
Musical Note: High *D*—for accomplishment.

DESTINY NUMBER 11

You are the intelligent idealist who governs yourself so well that you are seldom cornered into action against your principles.

Your sign is the one that can assist you to put your dreams into action. Your inner self is constantly urging you to create a better world, better inventions and better understanding between nations: The latter starts with understanding between individuals, spreading to groups and thence to mankind.

This striving for perfection in yourself and your ideals assists you to project your radiance to others. They can see the wisdom in the goals that you propose, and though they may fight against this idealistic aim they are only doing so because of the seeming threat to their survival.

In our industrial society, workers were able to have more goods and higher wages until the whole system became greedy. With greediness the system collapses in on itself. You can bring back quality to industry by leading the people back to sanity of purpose.

Your magnetic personality draws people to you, including the opposite sex. A **1, 3,** or **5** Destiny Number would provide impetus and expansion to your doubly creative essence.

NEGATIVE
Leo, the lion, with fixed ideas on how to change the world, charging ahead with banners flying, could turn into the fanatic, the one who *makes* people do what he wants them to do. The other negative vibration is holding onto all these ideals and refusing to share knowledge. This demand for perfection could make a Leo feel superior to the little people and turn him into a cynic.

Colour: Silver—for attraction.
Element: Air—for the idealist.
Musical Note: High *E*—for magnetism.

DESTINY NUMBER 22

This is another good number for you, as it expresses your practicality and your mastery of the physical in yourself and in your surroundings.

You can put into practice the idealism of the **11** as it is contained in the **22** (**11** + **11** = **22**). This need for perfection is carried into action on your projects, whether they be ideas or concrete buildings. There is no carelessness or sloppiness allowed if you are in charge of the job; You have already learned that it is easier to do it right first time, rather than go back and do it over again.

There is diplomacy built into this number also. The double **2** gives you added strength to put your ideas across with proper words and gestures: You are dramatic.

You could head toward an international direction in government or politics, direct large corporations or succeed in some form of communications work.

As a lover you would be dynamic, as you have control of your physical self. Team up with an **11** Capricorn and see sparks fly!

Spiritually you can be a strong force to build and support a belief system that is based on logic. Your magnificent dream of peace and prosperity for everyone is inherent in this belief.

NEGATIVE

Your base of operations may be limited if you are working on the negative side of this number with fixed ideas of how things should be done. Sometimes we need to compromise a little. If you do not follow through with your grandiose plans you become the big talker and not the doer.

Colour: Red-gold—for practical wisdom, using the things you have learned for practical application.
Element: Water—for cleansing: Clean out the fantasies from your life, see reality.
Musical Note: High *F*—for physical mastery.

DESTINY NUMBER 33

People are swayed by a good orator like you. You love to be in front, guiding others, being dramatic and holding your audience in the palm of your hand, tightly closed around your ideas. This flair for drama can sway many people, so watch your emotional control over them. You don't want more karma.

You can learn to experience many emotions and then share the knowledge of how to move vertically up the emotional ladder through hate, anxiety and anger, the minus factors, to the plus emotions of love and enthusiasm.

You would do well governing a large corporation with many employees to oversee. Being a minister, leader of awareness groups, a lecturer or an actor would put your dramatics to good use.

This is an intense vibration to handle, but with your leadership abilities there should be no problem. This range of feeling should give you a wide choice in the selection of a spouse or lover. You can be the soft, attentive lover or the firm, passionate, exciting lover—depending on your mood.

33 is a combination of the idealistic **11** and the practical **22**. This means that your concepts would be hard to challenge because you have worked your ideas out in a very practical way to appeal to most people.

NEGATIVE

The most serious negative vibration would be to try to control others through your negative emotions. On another tack you could become cold and uncaring about others. Important decisions need a clear and logical approach; you cannot shirk your duty, becoming uncaring and erratic.

Colour: Deep sky-blue—for intensity.
Element: Water—for emotional mastery, flowing with or controlling the stream.
Musical Note: High *G*—for emotional healing: Help people to heal their negative emotions.

DESTINY NUMBER 44

This is the number of the universal builder, power in high government circles, instituting world-wide reforms for the good of mankind.

Your mental prowess is highest in this number. In our mental processes we use logic to weigh one idea against another. There is two-valued logic ('right or wrong'), three-valued logic ('right, wrong or maybe') and simply 'your side, my side and the correct side'. If we take a quantum leap we get to infinite-value logic, 'righter' or 'wronger' at one time than another—i.e. there is always scope to be better or worse.

You have the ability to use one of these processes, or to change in the middle to use another process as you judge your opponent. Your quick mind and confidence can rule over the slower thinkers and deciders.

Your spouse or lover would need to be someone who can at least be only one step behind you in intelligence. Someone who is one step ahead of you would be a real challenge!

44 is a combination of the idealistic 11 and the 33 which is emotional mastery. This means that the creative, idealistic ideas you have are put forth with emotion (which you control) and feeling to accomplish your goals (44).

44 is also the combination of two 22s, the physical mastery over self. 44 can stand alone as the powerful manifesting number of material goods. Medicine, law, social service or some healing science would put your energies to good use.

NEGATIVE

If things do not go your way, you can roar like a lion, scaring everyone. You fix on one idea and want to carry it through to its completion, which is positive unless your idea was incorrect—a viewpoint that you find hard to accept.

Colour: Blue-green—for tranquillity, the magic of speech as well as soft music.
Element: Earth—for mental mastery.
Musical Note: High *A*—for mental healing.

DESTINY NUMBER 55

The divine fire, the eternal flame that is Leo, creates the vortex of energy from which life flows. Leo's fire does not stop burning, but the fuel he uses determines the quality of the fire. The unevolved Leo feeds on his own ego. This 'ego' fuel could create a very conceited person; if Leo's fire is fed from vibrations of divine inspiration then he becomes a flame with spiritual zeal.

At this level you can become a channel, bringing light and knowledge from higher dimensions into the consciousness of those ready to receive this inspiration.

Think of **55** as being a combination of **22**, the physical and practical master, and **33** the master of emotions. **55** brings these together with the life essence which means that you can learn to understand how to control emotions in a practical way; looking at just where you are and where other people are when they react with exposed emotions to events that transpire on this level of existence—the third dimension. This life energy can elevate the consciousness of all those you contact since this fire of leadership is inherent in your sign.

Or you can think of **55** as being the combination of **11**, the idealist, and **44**, the spiritual master. The idealist provides the creative inspiration that the spiritual master sets into viable form, then the **55** gives life to the project. So you can be creative and practical as you put your project into action.

NEGATIVE
This is the victim, working to decrease knowledge, burning books, repressing the ideas of others, refusing promotions to deserving employees, suppressing action toward expansion, invalidating others as well as himself.

Colour: Red-violet—the abundant life energy.
Element: Air—for spirituality. Discover the way of the masters. Meditate on your colour.
Musical Note: Chord of *G*—for spiritual healing.

DESTINY NUMBER 66

Use the *Research and Discovery* method on page 10 to see if this powerful Master Number is hidden in your birthdate. **66** is love energy, the full realization that you cannot love others until you love yourself and can outpour this feeling to others.

66 is truly the cosmic mother vibration, the double six leading to the nine: $6 \times 6 = 36$; $3 + 6 = $ **9**, which is brotherly love for all mankind. We are not talking about sex, although that is an important part of loving; we are referring to the ecstasy that comes over us sometimes in meditation, giving us the feeling that we are truly connected with the cosmos, the *Oneness*.

Your eagerness to be up front, leading the battle for justice, is not an ego trip in **66**; it is an awareness of the needs of others. You can lead and others will follow your banner.

NEGATIVE

A negative **66** would gather many people into his camp by selling them on the idea that 'this is the only way to salvation'. This **66** would use the energy to enslave others, make them do things 'in the name of love' that go against their moral codes. Another negative vibration is repressing love for self and for others, keeping family and friends chained to you with 'you don't really love me!'

Colour: Ultra-rose—the fullest expression of love on this planet. Meditate on this colour, it will fully open your heart chakra if all the other laws are followed which have led you to this initiation.

Element: Fire—for burning away the dross, getting rid of the unwanted attitudes and habits that keep us from progressing, indulgences that cloud our aura.

Musical Note: Any chord struck in harmony.

VIRGO

23 August to 21 September   MUTABLE/EARTH

*The **Virgin***   *Ruler:* **Mercury**

The virgin holding a sheaf of wheat symbolizes harvest time. Leo has ruled over the land with the heat of summer when the crops ripened and man more or less rested as the growing process took place. The Mutable/Earth sign means that the earth is ready to give up its bounty, its creations that began with Aries (spring).

Virgo is the nurturing sign, the gatherer, the harvester; she gives us our just rewards provided we have done the spade work and the planting of ideas.

On the positive side, Virgo is fastidious, wanting everything in order, categorized and catalogued. Virgo is usually willing to take care of endless details, and makes an excellent Person Friday for the office. He will know where everything is and produce it on demand as Virgo is willing to serve by anticipating the needs of boss or family.

This may stem from a feeling of inferiority, being sandwiched between the power of Leo and the Libran balancing power, both male signs. Virgo has exceptional power which may be neglected when he is involved in petty details, not looking at the entire plan or picture of the goal.

This last of the personal or involving signs has to do with the personality of man. From now on we will be exploring how the soul of man is developed.

Most (but not all) Virgo types are quiet and retiring. Don't expect a 'good time Charlie' from Virgo—life is too serious a business to be spending it at parties when there is work to catch up on at the office or at home. You'll find him right at your elbow to help if the job needs someone to make order out of chaos, but he can also criticize your methods or get into minute details of arguments that drive others crazy!

PARTNERS

Virgo is a very devoted family person, dispensing discipline, orderliness and good manners with a lavish hand. Virgo is not particularly interested in romance, mushy poetry and gushy lovers but prefers quality, the self-made man or the independent woman. Generally you are faithful, yet if 'true love' comes along you will leave the comfortable hearthside because this is 'right'. You are thrifty, meticulous about your home (on the positive side) and honest, for you like to keep your accounts in the black.

MERCURY

Mercury, ruling intelligence, reason and perceptiveness, is the messenger, bringing the good news (accurately so in solutions to problems, sometimes verbose, telling you more than you desire to know about a subject. On the negative side you can be restless and indecisive.

MUTABLE

This is Virgo's aspect of force manifesting in matter. It is flexibility, adapting to changing forces.

EARTH

These are the virtues brought forth from former lifetimes. It is discrimination, the power to choose between right and wrong. Virgos make good judges and lawyers.

NEGATIVE VIBRATIONS

The practical and stolid Virgo can become rigid about opinions, never confessing any wrong—changeable, sloppy, unable to make decisions, incoherent. As a general rule Virgo looks at both sides of a problem before arriving at a decision. The negative side would be taking forever to decide. You are truthful, no matter whom it hurts.

NEGATIVE

The *number* that is connected to Virgo's birth sign increases or decreases Virgo's energy. Wherever you find Virgo in your chart, look at the influence your Destiny Number has on this house in your horoscope.

DESTINY NUMBER 1

This creative influence of the **1** Destiny Number is a good vibration for you. It gives you the impetus to 'go for it', using your imagination and your expertise to get that better job, the man or woman you desire and the children you want.

Your originations will be more behind-the-scenes and it will take the courage of **1** to bring them into the open where people can appreciate your love of beauty, your accuracy with figures or wherever your talents lie.

As a floor manager in a television studio you could keep everything straight, for it is one of the most demanding jobs in the entertainment field. The same influence is felt in any job situation, including home management, for the home manager handles the most complex occupation in the job market: The housewife (or husband) is nurse, taxi-driver, doctor, cleaner, psychologist, cook and handler of a dozen other duties—and still manages to greet their companion after 'work' with a smile and a hug.

There is a future for you in scientific or research work; it is demanding and requires close attention to detail, at which you are particularly good. The creativity would be in your searching mind, your inquiring spirit, and would lead to accurate reporting of your discoveries.

NEGATIVE
You could be forcing your rigorous demands on your family and your co-workers. It's a little lonely up there in the creative world, especially for those who prefer to handle their decisions by themselves. Emotional upheavals (Mercury) reflect on the ego like an invalidation of your worth.

Colour: Red—for energy. Take some, give some.
Element: Fire—more energy. Ensure a healthy diet.
Musical Note: C—the self-starter, the innovator, the
   originator. The one who puts things into motion.

DESTINY NUMBER 2

Patience and attention to the details of life and work are right up your street. You may not be going seventy miles an hour, but your progress is steady and sure. Businesses, whether big or small, cannot survive very well without a **2**, and a Virgo **2** is the best possible person to keep systematic control of a business, family or government. Your work behind-the-scenes guarantees a fast track for the **1** creative people, the **5** adventurous people and several other forward-moving numbers.

Your Mercury energy is cooled by the **2** water element, meaning you approach problems with zeal (Mercury) yet use common sense and a cool head to unravel the problems of the day. Once you analyse a challenge you can figure out a way to get it done, and arrange it in such a way that others can also understand how to continue the process.

The earth quality directs your logical mind to bring problems down to earth where they can be dissected into smaller and smaller workable sections. Most people can understand a small portion of a puzzle, the difficult thing is to see the puzzle as a whole and then be able to put all the pieces in their proper places. As a **2** you can do this because of your patience and perception.

Don't expect the grand awards that happen to those who are 'up front'. You know that without your attention to detail they would never get that far. Your reward will be personal satisfaction knowing that you did an excellent job.

NEGATIVE
You could become too set in your ways and refuse to listen to other people's viewpoints. The impatience you feel at seeming injustices is turned in on yourself to your health's detriment. Ease a little with those subjects over which you have no control or you will make yourself ill.

Colour: Orange—for balance and harmony.
Element: Water—dealing with the emotions.
Musical Note: *D*—for harmony and tranquillity.

DESTINY NUMBER 3

This is the number of communication; you can meet and greet strangers and friends alike with great charm. You love entertaining and are happiest at this when everything is correct—the silver gleaming, the flowers perfectly arranged, the guests properly seated and the food superbly cooked. **3** is the joy of living well (perhaps you came to this life on a vacation!).

Communication is the keyword for this Destiny Number; talking, listening, exchanging ideas, entertaining your clients, your family, your boss or any other group that you feel will enhance your financial security. You always have a careful eye observing the monetary value of your service to others, though at times you give very freely of your self and your time.

You dislike accepting favours—it might incur obligations to that person and you prefer to keep the slate balanced—no debts, no favours.

With your keen perception of values you could be a well-intentioned counsellor in money matters. Your intuitive reasoning could inspire others to acquire knowledge and become better educated.

Your lover or spouse must meet certain standards; no vulgarity in his speech, no loud overacting in public, and neatness in dress. You have the ability to put these ideas across without hurting your loved one's pride.

NEGATIVE
As a Virgo it is difficult to be out front, the star of the show. Supporting numbers in your chart could be the way out. Intolerance rears its ugly head when things do not go (exactly) the way you have planned.

Colour: Yellow—for intelligence and expression.
Element: Fire—for energy.
Musical Note: *E*—for feeling.

DESTINY NUMBER 4

This organizational number equates with your birth sign, for you belong to a group who pays minute attention to detail, catalogues the results, and tackles more jobs than is reasonable for your highly-tuned mechanism. You need to evaluate the priorities in your life. Your need to have everything orderly and neat and a calm atmosphere in which to work is vital to you. If things get chaotic your delicate nature could blow a few circuits.

As a **4** you could be valuable in any profession where attention to detail is important, such as a surgeon, a doctor, an economist or an accountant: There are many more fields—these are only examples.

Your self-discipline and mental energy is reflected in your perseverance toward your goals and you express your personality best through material mediums, working with your hands, constructing things or fixing things—even people.

Your ruler (Mercury) gives you some release for fun in this number. Keep it light and take time to play hard too. Not everything fits into a systematic approach, especially partners. Attract a **4** or **8** spouse, for example, who can appreciate your passion for order and compassion for people.

NEGATIVE

Your self-discipline can become directed toward others to your detriment if you insist on exactitude in all matters. They will fail to see your loyalty and will only see the rigidity which can detract from your natural graceful manner. Since your positive side can change structure, let this humanizing part of you shine through. Don't try to fit everyone into your mould—it might become a little mouldy!

Colour: Beautiful, healing green—project this colour from your heart.
Element: Earth—the stable person.
Musical Note: *F*—for construction, building and strengthening things.

DESTINY NUMBER 5

This is the number than can unsettle you with experiences from a former lifetime that trigger you into emotional upsets. 5 gives you the freedom to travel, to see new sights and live it up a little. With 5 you could adapt to new situations in minutes, and step out of the shy character most people feel that Virgos embody. In your travels you'll probably take precautions and carry all those little pills for minor aches and pains that could possibly happen. You don't have to worry too much about your health for you always take very good care of yourself.

This is a sensual number. Rather than relating to one person for a lifetime of love, you may find that two or three are more exciting. You can take advantage of the variety these affairs bring if you keep yourself free of heavy responsibilities.

Cultivate many different kinds of people. A typical 5 Virgo is a splendid entertainer, a good host with a quick wit and good sense of fun. Virgos have a subtle humour that only quick-witted and intelligent people can understand. Many people think Virgo is a prim and exact personality for they are exasperated at slower-thinking people—maybe the slower thinkers ought to speed up a bit. You could be a good salesperson with Destiny Number 5.

NEGATIVE
If you are afraid of change, or moving to different places and experiencing new people, you will not be taking advantage of the freedom of 5. Profit from the new and exciting.

Colour: Turquoise—for a refreshing breeze.
Element: Air—the breath of life.
Musical Note: G—for changeability.

DESTINY NUMBER 6

You came here to create harmony among your family, friends and associates. Your intention to keep the rhythm of life flowing is paramount in this **6** vibration. You want it to be right and in accord with the correct way to accomplish this ideal.

You have a strong appeal to the opposite sex; this may be because of the delicate, virginal look that emanates from your eyes. Your love for all people and plants and animals radiates from your aura. You are called the cosmic mother, the nurturer, as you want to take care of things.

Artistic talent could show up in this number as you have the delicate touch of the artist, the subtle humour of the comedian who uses the *low energy* approach, 'low' meaning gentle and soft.

Marriage is an attraction for you, as is business. It would be difficult for you to handle both at the same time because of your need for perfection in all that you do. This could be very wearing on your nerves. Other numbers in your complete chart could give you the strength to carry this double burden.

Many **6** Virgos are psychic and receptive to the vibrations of their guides. Some can tune in to these powerful vibrations and bring harmony and peace to those around them.

NEGATIVE
Creating harmony does not mean interfering in other people's lives and telling them what to do. Your Mercury energy gives you the zeal to push ahead with your 'fixed' ideas, which may not agree with the ideas of others—therefore a peaceful settlement cannot be reached if you press your point. Another side to the negative vibration is a sense of pride which tells you that you are always right, and if this pride suffers a fall then you could become cynical.

Colour: Royal blue—for stability. Meditate on this colour.
Element: Earth—responsibility to self and others.
Musical Note: *A*—for receptivity, harmony.

DESTINY NUMBER 7

This perfect occult number is the *eye of the needle* when we stand at the crossroads of mundane and esoteric knowledge. Using the power of this vibration will move you from the known to the unknown. You can also build your own bridge using any kind of planks of inspiration you wish to select.

This number also gives you the opportunity to analyse your past successes and mistakes so that you can build a more secure future. Reverse the mistakes and make them the building blocks for a secure foundation or abutment for your bridge. It's no good crying over wasted cement (the rigid ideas you had felt so *right*); what was done was done, now you can analyse a situation to make it profitable.

On the esoteric level, the **7**s are the mystics who can heal spiritual gaps in a person's aura. Remember that permission must be asked of the person *you* feel needs healing. You are apt to go around *telling* others what they need, rather than letting them tell you what they want.

Your partner needs patience to understand your 'in-depth' contemplation or mood. This requirement to be quiet and contemplative is not compatible with responsibility to family unless you have such numbers in your chart.

NEGATIVE
Remaining aloof from the problems of the people will not get you across your 'bridge'. In a way this is protecting your space and your time, yet in this number you have the opportunity to *do* something which will benefit those around you. Since you can heal spiritual gaps, *playing* the game of the mystic will not further your ambitions or your fruition.

Colour: Violet—which stands for reverence.
Element: Water—flowing with your knowledge.
Musical Note: *B*—for reflection on the past.

DESTINY NUMBER 8

'Oh! It is excellent to have a giant's strength, but it is tyrannous to use it like a giant' (Shakespeare). **8** is power on the material level.

Your dependability and primal energy can be directed towards attaining your purposes during this lifetime. There are a variety of occupations which would interest you and that would reach into the higher positions in government or entertainment. Lyndon Johnson became the President of the United States and Darryl Zanuck became the giant of the film industry. George Wallace, another **8** Virgo, overcame immense obstacles to reach and keep his high position.

Think big. Reach for the opportunities which can advance your position. Choose people who are positive in their outlook to assist your career.

On the esoteric level you can reopen your third eye, turn on your psychic ability to discriminate between fact and fancy. Use the love vibration of your colour, rose, to further your studies in esoteric avenues.

If you choose the arts you can become famous as an artist, a dancer, a sculptor or any field that you choose because you set your goals and have the determination that such endeavours require. Sport could also attract your dedication.

Don't worry about the opposite sex; they will be attracted to your successess and your energies.

NEGATIVE
Be very careful of your selection of co-workers. Successful people need some form of reward; negative people will be jealous of you, positive people will share in your success.

Colour: Rose—for love.
Element: Earth—for achievement, material gain. Your earth sign and Mercury ruler are compatible with this number.
Musical Note: High C—for achievement.

DESTINY NUMBER 9

This **9** is the easiest vibration for you to live with. It means brotherly love for all mankind, and with your compassionate nature you will be able to transcend all bias and prejudice against other races or belief systems.

Your sincere desire to help those less fortunate than yourself goes beyond your personal desire to serve yourself. When you use the positive side of this number you touch a responsive chord of recognition in vast numbers of people.

This is also the number of the one who finishes his projects, his cycles of work, his cycles of thinking and planning. When these cycles are complete there comes a surge of energy to lift your physical and emotional spirit.

Align yourself with a lover who understands that you are 'on call' for service to your friends, no matter what the hour. You have come to teach the law of love—and also know that you must love in order to be loved.

9 is a compilation of all the numbers from **1** to **8**, thus giving **9** the vibrations of all the numbers, with **9** being the end. This number finishes residue from the past.

NEGATIVE
It would be well to check the goodness of your diet regularly, for many people will drain your energy as they seek counsel from you. Do not deplete your energy. The opposite of charitable attention is being unforgiving and the opposite of trust is being indiscreet. Your Mutable sign could make you changeable from one week to the next. Selfishness and stinginess rear their ugly heads if you have problems forgiving an unkind gesture.

Colour: Yellow-gold—for perfection, the desire to make everything perfect, even people.

Element: Fire—for warmth, cuddling up to. People gravitate to you as they feel your warmth and caring.

Musical Note: High *D*—for accomplishment.

DESTINY NUMBER 11

Master Numbers carry a higher vibration than the single digits. You'll notice that **11** reduces to a **2**. Check both vibrations to see which level you are on. The **11** is the idealist, the one who must have perfection in all he does. This complements your birth sign as you also want perfection. Your ambitions, your dreams and your desires can be put into action with **11** if you have the courage to put them forward and push a little. Some **11**s want to stay in the background and not share their knowledge, for they feel that everyone knows all they know. This is not necessarily true.

If you join up with a **22**, a **1** or a **5** you would have a great team, for these three numbers would get the energy of Mercury going.

This striving for perfection in yourself and your ideals assists you to project your radiance to others so that they accomplish more in quantity and raise their quality of production.

With your sensitive nature you could become the clairvoyant, seeing visions and translating them for yourself in order to help others. Be sure you really want what you start out to learn. Transcend the views of the everyday world and see clearly what reality is.

NEGATIVE

If **11**s go too far in their idealistic search for perfection they can turn into fanatics, like the person who washes his hands every few minutes. This, of course, has a deeper base of emotional upset, yet demonstrates a habit we can get into. The zealot is here, the one who wants everyone else to be perfect! And on the other side is the one who doesn't really care which way the wheel turns and who loses self-direction. The lowest vibration is dishonesty and miserliness.

Colour: Silver—for attraction.
Element: Air—for the idealist.
Musical Note: High *E*—for magnetism.

DESTINY NUMBER 22

This is another number compatible with your inner nature, the number of the cultured person. You are the one who is neat, says the correct thing and acts like a perfect lady or gentleman.

Your direction in business could take an international flair—government, politics or national fame in the entertainment world. Joe Kennedy, Henry Ford and Shirley McLaine are all representatives of **22** Virgos.

Entertainment certainly requires physical mastery of the self, for you function in front of thousands of people. Ford knew what he wanted and invented many ways to get there; Joe Kennedy was a world mover in his time. So don't downgrade the Virgos of today, they are powerful people, especially with a **22**, for they have mastery over themselves.

In order to take advantage of this powerful number you have to think big, act big, and take control. Assume the leadership in industry or finance; take the responsibility, you can do it.

22 is universal power on the physical level. It sets the record straight for all the countries of the planet. Spiritually you could be a strong force to build and support a belief system that is based on logic. Your magnificent dream of peace and prosperity for everyone is inherent in this dream.

NEGATIVE
Indifference to mankind—the big talker but little doer. An inferiority complex can be a withdrawal from society or it could indicate a loud competitor for attention. The lowest vibration of a **22** would be viciousness or an involvement with black magic.

Colour: Red-gold—for practical wisdom. Use the things you have learned for practical application.
Element: Water—for cleansing. Clean out the fantasies from your life and see reality.
Musical Note: High *F*—for physical mastery.

DESTINY NUMBER 33

This is an intense emotional vibration to handle; divine wisdom extends to every emotional plane, from grief to anger, love to enthusiasm. Your desire for truth could lead you to examine and understand these divergent emotional variations. Understanding will lead you to expertise in handling emotions for yourself and consequently for others.

The human race expresses emotions. The beginnings of these emotions are centred in our experiences. How did we react to grief, loss or love in the past? This colours our reactions today. Your sensitive nature can deal with these thoughts in a positive way.

Your Mutable sign can adapt to situations which have highly personal connotations. You would be good as a counsellor, bringing order and peace into many lives, providing you have learned how to handle your own emotions first.

You have a wide selection of companions as you can be attentive and warm and show your firm, passionate side.

33 is a combination of the idealist **11** and the practical **22**. This means that your concepts would be hard to challenge because you work your ideas out in a very practical way to appeal to most people.

NEGATIVE
The opposite of warm, loving emotions is cold, uncaring emotion. There are negative emotions that emphasize a withdrawal from the human race. We cannot shirk our duty to our fellows by becoming irritated at their foolishness. The most serious negative vibration would be trying to control others through negative vibrations, repressing others and not allowing them their time and space.

Colour: Deep sky-blue—for intensity.
Element: Water—for emotional mastery, flowing with or controlling the stream.
Musical Note: High G—for emotional healing. Help people to heal their negative vibrations.

DESTINY NUMBER 44

Your mental prowess is highest in this number. We use logic to weigh one idea against another. There is two-valued logic ('right or wrong'), three-valued logic ('right, wrong and maybe') and simply 'my side, your side and the correct side'. If we take a quantum leap we get to infinite-valued logic, 'righter' or 'wronger' at one time than another—i.e. there is always scope to be better or worse.

You have the ability to use one of these processes as you judge your opponent. Your quick, intelligent mind can bring the slower thinkers to a decision.

44 is a combination of the idealistic **11** and the **33** which is emotional mastery. This means that the creative, idealistic ideas you have are put forth with emotion (which you can control) and feeling to accomplish your goals (**44**).

44 is also the combination of two **22**s, the physical mastery over yourself. **44** stands alone as the powerful manifesting number for material goods. Social service or one of the healing professions would suit your compassionate nature in this number.

Your spouse or lover needs to be someone who can keep up with your penetrating intelligence or give you loving support. You won't mind keeping the home fires burning as long as you have trust and agreement in your relationship.

NEGATIVE
There will be confusion in your mind if you do not know how to evaluate a problem to change a situation. Feeling that your ideas must be the best could make you reluctant to compromise.

Colour: Blue-green—for tranquillity.
Element: Earth—for mental mastery.
Musical Note: High *A*—for mental healing.

DESTINY NUMBER 55

The subtle glow of the red-violet light is contained in your life force energy. Your compassion for others can shine forth this light to give assistance to those who need this vibrant physical energy. At this level you can become a channel, bringing light and knowledge from the higher dimensions into your consciousness and teaching those who are ready to receive these inspiring messages.

Think of **55** as being a combination of **22**, the physical master, and **33**, the master of emotions. **55** brings these two together with the life essence which means that you can learn how to control the emotions of yourself or others in a practical way. Look at where you are and where others are when exposed to events to which there is a reaction. Keep your cool (which you usually do) and just look at how you and others handle the situation which is theoretically under fire.

Alternatively you can think of **55** as being the combination of **11**, the idealist, and **44**, the mental master. The idealist provides the creative inspiration that the mental master sets into viable form. Then **55** gives life to the project. So you can be creative and practical as you put your project into action.

NEGATIVE
The higher we rise, the harder the lessons are. This is the victim, working to decrease knowledge, burning books, repressing the ideas of others, refusing promotions to deserving employees, supressing action toward expansion and invalidating others as well as himself.

Colour: Red-violet—the abundant life energy.
Element: Air—for spirituality. Discover the way of the masters. Meditate on your colour.
Musical Note: Chord of G—for spiritual healing.

DESTINY NUMBER 66

Use the *Research and Discovery* method (page 10) to see if this powerful Master Number is hidden in your birthdate. **66** is love energy, the full realization that you cannot love others until you love yourself and can outpour this feeling to others.

66 is truly the cosmic mother vibration, the double six leading to the nine: $6 \times 6 = 36$; $3 + 6 = 9$, which is brotherly love for all mankind. We are not talking about sex, although that is an important part of loving; we are referring to the ecstasy that comes over us sometimes in meditation, giving us the feeling that we are truly connected with the cosmos, the *Oneness*.

Your eagerness to right the wrongs of people and society is not an ego trip in this number; it is an awareness of the needs of others. You can show and teach others the lesson of love and sharing.

NEGATIVE
A negative **66** would gather many people into his camp by selling them on the idea that 'this is the only way to salvation'. This **66** would use the love energy to enslave others, make them do things 'in the name of love' that go against their moral codes. Another negative vibration is repressing love for yourself and for others, keeping family and friends chained to you with 'you don't really love me!'

Colour: Ultra-rose—the fullest expression of love on this planet. Meditate on this colour, it will fully open your heart chakra if all the other laws are followed which have led you to this initiation.

Element: Fire—for burning away the dross, getting rid of unwanted attitudes, habits that keep us from progressing, or indulgences that cloud our aura.

Musical Note: Any chord struck in harmony.

LIBRA

22 September to 22 October   CARDINAL/AIR

The **Scales**   *Ruler:* **Venus**

This masculine sign represents the soul turning from the 'me' consciousness to 'us'. Libra is about relationships, sometimes windy and stormy and sometimes warm with passion. He leaps into the air to gain perspective, seeing both sides of the challenge. Libra, the Venus Lover, not wanting to take sides in an argument, is the pacifier.

Golden Libra's colour of intelligence shines on friends and enemies alike, though Librans seldom admit to having enemies. They prefer communicating and patching up quarrels after they have perhaps precipitated them.

Librans are good listeners and good talkers, too. Classed as the beautiful people, handsome men and pretty girls, they smile even when angry.

They are really busy people who expend so much energy that you get out of breath just watching them, then they balance vigour with lethargy—activity with dreaming—and therefore keep body, spirit and mind balanced. They know when to quit and refresh themselves with sleep.

Don't ask your Libra child to move out before he is ready. He likes the security of home and will quickly find another 'nest' if forced to leave too early.

This Cardinal/Air sign shows deep emotions, empathizing on one occasion with your problems and on the next not really seeming to care, probably off in some distant fantasy world of his own making.

Librans like the truth: they make good lawyers, psychologists, mediators and insurance brokers. Just don't hurry them as they like to examine both sides of the problem before coming to a conscientious decision.

PARTNERS

A Libra lover or partner is an exciting adventure. You are gentle, attentive and intelligent. You prefer quality, harmony, music, poetry and the proper use of words. You take time to make up your mind about the opposite sex—but remember that your ruler is Venus, the planet of love, and you are all lovers in your own way.

VENUS

The ruler of love and beauty brings devotion and harmony to any relationship. There is gentleness and courtesy in the Librans who express this powerful love of mankind, lovers, partners, beauty and home. Love can move mountains of indifference and strife. On the negative side Venus can be overly sentimental or even evasive of commitments.

CARDINAL

This is Libra's aspect of force manifesting in matter—fast action, impulsiveness and strong ambitions. Librans act first and argue later. This is creativity on a mental level.

AIR

These are the virtues brought forth from former lifetimes. This is knowledge gathered from experience, study and intuition. Judgement and intelligence balance the scales.

NEGATIVE VIBRATIONS

Beneath all this charm and diplomacy is an iron fist in the velvet glove. When you make up your mind it is difficult to persuade you otherwise, for Libra is a mental sign, the sign of intelligence. You want to be liked by everyone, yet are secretive about personal matters. You can switch sides in an argument but will deny indecisiveness.

NUMBERS

The *number* that is connected to Libra's birth sign increases or decreases Libra's energy. Wherever you find Libra in your chart look at the influence your Destiny Number has on this house in your horoscope.

DESTINY NUMBER 1

You have a creative streak with this Destiny Number that shows brilliance. Your plans and ideas may not agree with the status quo but will be wild and wonderful and make you seem like you just arrived from another planet.

Injected into your concept is a sort of logic that is hard to escape and the people around you may look puzzled for a while and then say, 'That's a good idea; why didn't *I* think of that!'

You are the searcher, looking for the truth that is hidden from the public eye; the investigator, the detective, the philosopher who gathers books around him, seeking that nugget of enlightenment. Then you explode into sparks of energy and physical activity, determined to run farther, act better, paint more accurately and rise to the epitome of your talents *now*! And strangely enough, you do just that. You stimulate yourself and others.

Here is the creative businessman with innovative ideas, the writer—you can write really well if you try. Put your dreams on paper for others to see.

As a lover or spouse, how can you fault that charming smile and soft approach, the tender caring, the flowers and the unexpected gifts so apropos of the occasion of your innermost desires?

NEGATIVE

Your air sign lets you fly high, and sometimes it could get lonely up there with your rarefied ideas and plans. You might have to go after your ideals by yourself and not let 'authorities' impinge on your visions. Others may try to guide you into thinking 'their' way or try to hold you from going forward; watch this.

> **Colour:** Red—for energy, the Cardinal thrust.
> **Element:** Fire—the innovator, the burning desire.
> **Musical Note:** C—the self-starter, self-motion.

DESTINY NUMBER 2

As a **2** you become sensitive to the moods of your co-workers and can patiently co-operate with them as you all go about the everyday world. You may still retain your ideas and ideals yet you are able to see other people's side of the problems that come up each day.

It may be difficult for you to come to an agreement with yourself about what to do regarding decisions, since you balance one opinion against another, seeing clearly how peace can be obtained, yet are unwilling to put forth the solution for fear of hurting someone's feelings. Compromise from both sides could be the answer. You are the diplomat, the one who loves to have things run smoothly without chaos or arguments. Men and women sitting down and reasoning together for the good of mankind is your ideal.

Your air sign can catch the butterfly of inspiration, bring it down to the peace table where your Cardinal energy ignites the inspiration and passes it to those who will listen and act.

This consideration and love for others shown by your Venus side will shine on your lover or spouse. Select one who realizes that you cannot do your finest work in a messy office or home. You need order and calm as a **2**.

Your ability as a peacemaker may not bring you great rewards in this lifetime, yet you will know that you smoothed the road so that all **1**s, **8**s, and Leos can march in triumph.

NEGATIVE
If you will not listen to other viewpoints then justice cannot be served. Everyone has a right to their day in court to express opinions. Your Libra conscience seeks justice, so listen a little to the other side. Sensitivity about yourself can bar the way to truth.

Colour: Orange—for balance and harmony.
Element: Water—dealing with the emotions.
Musical Note: *D*—for harmony and tranquillity.

DESTINY NUMBER 3

Your usual happy nature is evident in this number. There is joy in living, eating well, playing hard, and working steadily at and with the things you love. Use your charm to captivate your guests, entertaining them and spreading good feeling.

Communication is the keyword for **3**, and this means listening as well as talking—listening with your inner ear to *really* hear what a person is saying with his heart.

3 has an interesting combination of the creativeness of **1** and the diplomacy of **2** inherent in the structure of the **3**, this latter number wanting to take these abilities and move them forward into the goals you propose for yourself.

This is the life in which to socialize, make contacts that will help you in business. Learn to move easily among many different kinds of people. Many **3**s are in the entertainment field as directors, actors, TV executives, commentators, chat show hosts and other roles where there is a stage, a microphone and someone to talk to.

Another facet to your nature is being a good counsellor because of the communicative factor in **3**. Your leaning toward philosophical matters could put you into a religious or metaphysical field, learning about the mysteries of life so you can use them to assist others.

Choose a partner who holds excitement for you. The stolid homely type would conflict with your gregarious nature in the **3**.

NEGATIVE

The applause of public life could bring on conceit and exaggeration of your abilities. Be a shining light, not a temporary 30-watt bulb. A lower tone **3** would turn to jealousy and intolerance.

Colour: Yellow—for expression.
Element: Fire—for energy.
Musical Note: *E*—for feeling.

DESTINY NUMBER 4

Your devotion to duty is inherent in **4**. You are appalled at unfair treatment of your co-workers or your superiors. You want justice at any cost. This feeling carries through to your personal relationships to the point where you sacrifice your own goals in order not to hurt someone, like keeping a spouse or lover beyond the time when happiness was there. You may postpone decisions on separation from your partner rather than make a clean cut.

Your business ventures will be advanced by your personality. Female Librans make good models and beauticians. Both sexes could succeed as solicitors or politicians. Your professional life will be enhanced by a firm commitment to your spouse.

You may be faced with handling property matters and paying attention to smaller business economies. Get your finances in order, cut and prune the dead wood from your company: Unproductive people are such a drain on your finances.

Love is demonstrated by the order, loyalty and quality that you show. You have no trouble manifesting love and you do show it to others generously. Let those around you see your deep love for mankind also.

NEGATIVE

You could be over-cautious in your dealings with others and become withdrawn and rigid in your opinions. Concentration is your keyword so that your organized life can become a reality and not a burden which is formed of chaos. Proceed one step at a time, on one project at a time, if too many decisions are coming your way.

Colour: Beautiful, healing green—project this colour from your heart.
Element: Earth—the stable person.
Musical Note: *F*—for construction, building, and making your life mean something.

DESTINY NUMBER 5

Librans are usually interested in the arts. Plays, music, drama, paintings and good books absorb your waking hours. This number gives you a broad viewpoint from which to travel.

Your demand for personal freedom may keep you from listening to ways to plan your life, but that is okay, as you will find your own way. You have many choices—you are the traveller, lighting here and there, the messenger, bringing light and life to any company as you entertain with story, song and anything which will keep the party active.

This restlessness continues even when you reach the top of your profession, for you can see miles ahead of anyone else into the future.

You could become a terrific writer—novels or books about those places you have visited (in fact or in your dreams). Adventure calls and you go, sampling the essence of life, yet you need some roots to go home to.

Libra 5s are more spiritual than they realize as they can remember all the things they have seen and things they have learned—and apply them when necessary.

It is better for you to team up with someone who can go to strange places with you for companionship; these could be your roots. Carry your love with you like a snail carries its house wherever it goes.

NEGATIVE

Inconsistency is the bane of the 5s. They can get into a quandary and not know what they want, unable to choose a direction, sitting and sulking. This turns into blaming others and indulging in self-pity. Being Librans they soon snap out of it and come back to their sunny selves again. Don't be afraid of changing conditions; flow with them.

Colour: Turquoise—like a refreshing breeze.
Element: Air—the breath of life.
Musical Note: G—denoting change.

DESTINY NUMBER 6

This harmonious Destiny Number agrees with your concept of staying healthy. Work hard, play hard and then collapse for a while. People seeing you lazing around the house when the garden is overgrown and full of weeds will want to scream at you for wasting your time. The when you are fully rested you go out, cut the grass, weed the flower beds, sweep the path, trim the hedge, and then ask your partner for something to do as you are bored. There just doesn't seem to be a happy medium for your moods.

This number helps keep you equalized, if that is what you want, keeping your scales balanced so that you don't tip one way or another.

Your emotions run high in this number as it is symbolic of the cosmic mother who nurtures all things. You may weep over a dying plant, then throw it out the next day to make room for a new one. This change of character is not quite like the Gemini who becomes a different person from time to time. Librans go deeply into their emotions yet stay the same loving and fair-minded person.

You would make a wonderful parent and a loving spouse. Home is where the heart is. Let your Venus love come through to all those around you.

NEGATIVE

If you get anxious about your family you might start telling them what to do. And they don't like it one bit because they will be all different numbers and signs, which could confuse you a lot. Take pride in your family and your business ventures without being arrogant. Take care of the small things and the big things will take care of themselves. When you are down you could turn cynical, suspicious of others' actions.

Colour: Royal blue—for stability. Meditate on this colour for balance.
Element: Earth—for responsibility.
Musical Note: *A*—for receptivity and harmony.

DESTINY NUMBER 7

When we stand at the crossroads—good or evil, right or wrong, go this way or that—we need to use the inner wisdom of **7**. Since this is your Destiny Number you can bridge from the known to the unknown by gathering knowledge from books, lectures, meditations, etc. This perfect occult number is called the *eye of the needle*, when we stand at the gateway between mundane and esoteric knowledge.

This number gives you the opportunity to analyse your past successes and mistakes so you can build a secure future. Reverse the mistakes and make them the building blocks for a firm foundation. What is your real purpose in this life?

On the esoteric level, **7**s are the mystics who can heal spiritual gaps in a person's aura. This permits healing of the physical body. Remember that permission must be asked of the person *you* feel needs healing. A person may prefer to take ownership of his problems instead of understanding what caused them in the first place.

Your partner needs patience to understand your 'in-depth' contemplation or mood. This need for quiet is not compatible with responsibility to family unless you have other numbers in your chart that indicate your love for children. You always need roots and someone to come home to.

NEGATIVE
The temptation is to remain above the cares and tribulations of life when you are working on this side of **7**. You just don't want to be bothered. Of course, this is no way to increase your knowledge or elevate yourself. You can't be charming all the time; just don't confuse mysticism with aloofness and neglect of your friends.

Colour: Violet—stands for reverence.
Element: Water—flowing with your knowledge.
Musical Note: *B*—for reflection on the past.

DESTINY NUMBER 8

'There is a tide in the affairs of men which, taken at the flood, leads on to fortune' (Shakespeare). Your Cardinal sign means action, direct and to the point; sometimes it can mean impulsiveness and impatience. **8** is power on the material level for most people. It means using your energy to attain high positions in government, entertainment or business. Many people of power and wealth will come you way to ease your path toward the fulfilling of your dream of success. Cultivate those who can help you gain your purpose in life—think big and take opportunities which can advance your position.

On the esoteric level you can reopen your third eye, turn on your psychic ability to discriminate between fact and fancy. Meditation could bring in the power to see auras, and further meditation could teach you how to read these auras.

If you choose the arts you can become famous as an artist, dancer, sculptor, or in any field you choose because you have grace and rhythm and exhibit this to the public. It may be a little difficult to believe that you have this kind of talent but when you realize that you can do many things that others cannot, nothing can stop you from accomplishing your goals. You have only to make up your mind (and you have strong mental powers) to act, sing, become head of a corporation, run for public office, etc.

The opposite sex will be drawn to you, attracted by your grace and your success.

NEGATIVE
Jealousy can rear its ugly head as you try to outdo someone else. This seldom works. You can be great without having to be competitive. This high-powered Destiny Number has great rewards and great pitfalls. Watch your companions along the way.

Colour: Rose—for love.
Element: Earth—for achievement, material gain.
Musical Note: High C—for achievement.

DESTINY NUMBER 9

This compassionate number is suitable to your loving nature. Many religious leaders have this number as they wish to reduce the suffering of mankind. Your sincere desire to help those less fortunate than yourself goes beyond your personal desire to serve. Your energies are put to use in social services or in charitable gifts of your love and money. You are the one who literally will give the shirt off your back to help a friend.

You love to give expensive presents to your lover or spouse, yet these gifts are purchased with deliberation so that the gift fits the recipient and the occasion as well.

This number also means success and achievement in this lifetime as you finish your tasks. So many people like to begin a project, then get bored and never finish. When you begin something after much deliberation, you are dedicated to keeping it going or finishing the job, depending on the type of job it is. When a cycle of work is finished there comes a surge of energy to lift your physical and emotional spirit.

9 is a total of all the numbers from **1** to **8**, thus giving **9** the vibrations of all the numbers, with **9** being the finish line.

NEGATIVE
People will drain you of energy if you let them. This drain could turn you from a loving Libra to a selfish, inconsiderate person. Letting others take advantage of your good nature is a form of dissipation, because it makes you feel noble, and this could be habit forming. Assist others with kindness, but don't get bitter if they refuse your friendship at a later date. People hate to be indebted to a friend. Let others do something for you to balance the energies.

Colour: Yellow-gold—for perfection, the desire to make everything perfect, even people.
Element: Fire—for warmth, cuddling up to.
Musical Note: High *D*—for accomplishment.

DESTINY NUMBER 11

Master Numbers carry a higher vibration than the single digits. You'll notice that **11** reduces to a **2**. Check both vibrations to see which level you are on. The **11** is the idealist, the one who must have perfection in all he does. Your idealism lies in a situation where right would be served on both sides of the equation or problem; the scales must balance for you. This balancing would be the interpretation of perfection for you, everyone getting a piece of the pie, everyone being satisfied with the ruling.

You would make a fine judge with this number, a social worker, and would do well in any job requiring a tempering of decisions. Diplomacy in political situations or settling disputes in the family would give you the feeling of a job well done.

Some **11**s want to stay in the background and not share their tact and imagination with others. Team up with a **22** and you will have the dreamer of a perfect world (**11**) with a partner who can bring it into reality (**22**).

Your intuition is extremely well-developed. This, combined with your mental agility and excellence of performance in those professions and hobbies you should choose, could send you right to the top of whatever occupation you concentrate on.

NEGATIVE

Here are the fanatics who have turned their need to create a perfect world into an ego trip. They want everyone to join them. If you don't join their society etc. you are purged from their sight—and that could be a little drastic. Be idealistic without becoming cynical and aimless.

Colour: Silver—for attraction.
Element: Air—for the idealist.
Musical Note: High *F*—for magnetism.

DESTINY NUMBER 22

22s discipline body and mind. You are able to do tremendous feats in sports and in the arena of business where a clear thinking process is required to arrive at a sensible solution. Your direction could take on an international flair, government position, fame in the entertainment world or wherever a master organizer is needed.

22 is universal power on the physical, practical, level. In order to take advantage of this energy you have to think big, act big, and take control of a situation where leadership is needed. You can be the head of a large corporation, a manager of big business, head of the household or builder of beautiful structures.

In your spiritual life you could be a strong force to bring others into a belief system that is founded on logic and balance—as much right and fairness for both parties as possible; or different systems could be analysed to bring forward the best points of each one.

Usually this Master Number carries the mark of good health as you are too busy to bother about small complaints—and just tell your body to heal itself. It does.

NEGATIVE

You may become discouraged when you are unable to bring a satisfactory conclusion to you huge efforts in whatever you decide to do, and then withdraw from society. This monk-like existence is not for you, since you are the lover of the zodiac. Put your loving spirit into high gear again and have another go at it. You really cannot be indifferent to mankind. Be a doer, not just a talker.

Colour: Red-gold—for practical wisdom, using the things you have learned for practical application.
Element: Water—for cleansing. See reality.
Musical Note: High *F*—for physical mastery.

DESTINY NUMBER 33

You are suited more to handle artistic lines than for running a business. Your emotional involvement with the beauty of paintings, flowers, nature and all things that have line and colour invite your attention. Words also attract you, which means you would make a good defence lawyer, protecting your clients. Or you would find arguing against injustices to man a fascinating subject.

Think of **33** as being a combination of **11** (the idealist) who wants to have perfection in all things, and **22**, who sees how this perfection can be accomplished if we do not become embroiled in silly disagreements.

The human race expresses emotions. The beginning of these emotions are centred in experiences and what we remember truthfully about them. How do we react to grief? To loss of love? These reactions colour our life today. You may try to rationalize your feelings (balancing the scales) and yet your quest for the truth brings you face to face with yourself. How honest are you in defining your emotions? Use the Venus love vibrations to love yourself as well as others.

Your reactions to the opposite sex can magnetize them into occupying your space. Your large, beautiful eyes show the emotion you feel in your heart.

NEGATIVE
There is a healing quality in **33** that would be turned off if you decided that you do not care about people. Your gifts would be negated and it would be difficult to raise any positive emotions or feelings that would radiate goodwill. Also, do not work on others' emotions to their detriment.

Colour: Deep sky-blue—for intensity.
Element: Water—for emotional mastery.
Musical Note: High *G*—for emotional healing.

DESTINY NUMBER 44

You have a keen mental approach to problems, always weighing the pros and cons, trying to find the truth. The scales, representative of your sign, can become unbalanced with attachments to one way of life while closing your eyes to other outlets to your personality. There are many paths up the mountain to enlightenment. Total dedication to your life's work is commendable, but leave a little time for the expansion of yourself and your spirit.

We use logic to weigh one idea against another. There is two-valued logic ('right and wrong'), three-valued logic (right, wrong and maybe') and simply 'your side, my side and the correct side'. If we take a quantum leap we get to infinite-valued logic, 'righter' or 'wronger' at one time than another—i.e. there is always scope to be better or worse. You have the ability to use these processes to evaluate an opponent. Your intelligent mind can bring slower thinkers to a decision.

44 is a combination of the idealistic 11 and the 33 which is emotional mastery. This means that the creative, idealistic ideas you have are put forward with emotion (which you can control) and enthusiasm so others help you accomplish your goals. 44 is also the combination of two 22s, physical mastery over self. 44 can stand alone as the powerful manifesting number for material goods.

Social service or one of the healing professions would suit your loving nature in this number. Select a partner who can give you lots of love and attention and yet can keep up with your quick, penetrating intelligence.

NEGATIVE
You could get impatient with a co-worker; alternatively your spouse is unable to keep up with you physically or mentally (or both). Watch confusing values.

Colour: Blue-green—for tranquillizing vibes.
Element: Earth—for mental mastery.
Musical Note: High A—for mental healing.

DESTINY NUMBER 55

The love and kindness you show to others is a true expression of **55**. This life-giving number is the light of creative love being channelled through you and shining forth to those around you. At this level you can bring light and knowledge from higher dimensions into your consciousness, then teach those who are ready to receive these inspiring messages.

Think of **55** as being a combination of **22**, the physical and practical master, and **33**, the master of the emotions. **55** brings these together with the life essence which means that you can learn to understand how to control the emotions of yourself or others in a practical way. Look at where you are and where others are when exposed to events that become a problem. Just take a look at how these events are handled. Do you talk your way out of a situation, rationalizing your feelings, or do you look the event squarely in the eye to see the truth? How do others react?

Alternatively, you can think of **55** as being the combination of **11**, the idealist, and **44**, the mental master. The idealist provides the creative inspiration that the mental master sets into viable form, and **55** gives life to the project. So you can be creative and practical as you put your project into action.

Your partner cannot help but see this beautiful love that you contain and share.

NEGATIVE
On this side of the number you become the victim of life; working to decrease knowledge, burning books, repressing the ideas of others, refusing promotions to deserving employees, suppressing action toward expansion and invalidating others as well as yourself.

Colour: Red-violet—the abundant life energy.
Element: Air—for spirituality. Discover the way of the masters. Meditate on your colour.
Musical Note: Chord of *G*—for spiritual healing.

DESTINY NUMBER 66

Use the *Research and Discovery* method (page 10) to see if this powerful Master Number is hidden in your birthdate. **66** is love energy, the full realization that you cannot love others until you love yourself and can outpour this feeling to others.

66 is truly the cosmic mother vibration, the double six leading to the nine: $6 \times 6 = 36$; $3 + 6 = \mathbf{9}$, which is brotherly love for all mankind. We are not talking about sex, although that is an important part of loving; we are referring to the ecstasy that comes over us sometimes in meditation, giving us the feeling that we are truly connected with the cosmos, the *Oneness*.

Share your viewpoints with others and teach others how to complete the circle of love. You have a lot of love to give and share: You could become a counsellor, psychologist or vicar; or you could go into social work or an organization like 'Greenpeace'.

NEGATIVE
A negative **66** could gather many people into his camp by selling them on the idea that 'this is the only way to salvation'. This **66** would use the love energy to enslave others, make them do things 'in the name of love' that go against our moral codes. Another negative vibration is repressing love for yourself and others, keeping family and friends chained to you with 'you don't really love me!'

Colour: Ultra-rose—the fullest expression of love on this planet. Meditate on this colour, it will fully open your heart chakra if all the other laws are followed which have led you to this initiation.

Element: Fire—for burning away the dross, getting rid of the unwanted attitudes, habits that keep us from progressing and indulgences that cloud our aura.

Musical Note: Any chord struck in harmony.

SCORPIO

23 October to 21 November   FIXED/WATER

*The **Scorpion, Eagle, Phoenix***   *Ruler:* **Mars/Pluto**

The scorpion is the arachnid that stings when disturbed or attacked. Scorpio, the birth sign, will sting others with his sharp tongue. If no-one pays attention to him, he will sting himself. When Scorpio rises above his lower nature he becomes the eagle, the one whose spirit soars above the earth. The eagle also gets an overview of challenges and problems, because he can see all of the puzzle and make order out of creative endeavours suggested by someone else.

Through trials and tribulations, usually brought on by himself, Scorpio can rise even higher out of the ashes of his changed personality. This is the only sign representing the changes that a personality can go through on the physical, emotional and mental planes.

Most Scorpios have interesting eyebrows which flair up when they do not agree with you. Their eyes look as if they are trying to pierce the veil of mystery—they are. They want to know all about you and will tell you how to solve your problems. While this may seem dictatorial, consider; they could be right. They have the courage to help you face reality.

It's useless to attack a Scorpio with insults; they roll right off—*but* he *remembers* and some day he will get you back.

We need the Scorpios of this planet, for they have the courage to surmount tremendous obstacles, the will to move ahead, and dedication. These tough and determined people can rise above the pettiness of gossip to bring an entirely new concept to personal relationships or impersonal problems. They symbolize the regenerative planet Pluto—death of the old, birth of the new. If people really listen to a Scorpio, they will find sincerity and truth in his statements.

PARTNERS

Select a partner with a passion to equal yours or one who is capable of understanding your nature. A super-sensitive sign or number cannot survive your intensity. You are loyal to your chosen one even though you do enjoy looking. You have high standards for others but go your merry way just being your own outspoken self. Richard Burton was a fine example of a lover, both in his private life and in his dramatic roles.

MARS

Scorpio uses the Mars energy in a concentrated, subtle way. A lot of this energy is used up in fighting himself. He (or she) is jealous of his partner, his job and his friends.

PLUTO

Here is where Scorpio shines like a newly-minted coin. Youthful looking (no matter how old), enthusiastic Scorpio has bright ideas (some sex-orientated) for reforming the world. This is the sign that is forward-looking, although Scorpio can become involved in the mysteries of the ancient.

FIXED

This quiet force is persistent and usually low-key unless your wants are immediate. Then watch this sword-swinging dragon fighter: You will never deviate from your chosen path unless you want to.

WATER

Scorpios can gain control of the emotional nature by sheer will. Hidden emotions need to be brought to light and cleansed in order to rise to full power as the phoenix.

NEGATIVE VIBRATIONS

Beneath all this force and sexual attraction can beat the heart of a marshmallow. No mystery is unsolvable to Scorpio, though he keeps his own counsel unless triggered into volcanic action.

NUMBERS

The *number* that is connected to the Scorpio birth sign increases or decreases his energy. Wherever you find Scorpio in your chart, look at the influence your Destiny Number has on this house in your horoscope.

DESTINY NUMBER 1

Your ruler Pluto and **1** give you the energies to transform yourself and others through creative thought and action. Billy Graham, a typical outspoken dynamic Scorpio, has attracted millions to his meetings and assisted many to look at present lifetimes and transform themselves into better people.

You have many facets to your nature that can help others remould their lives. While you may be brusque in the telling, you temper this with a guide to action on the positive vibration. You emphasize the positive energy in order to renew others. You can renew yourself, also; heal yourself by programming the positive energies in your body.

Develop a positive point of view if you haven't done so already and people will admire you and respect you for your uncompromising leadership. This takes courage, of which you have plenty, to stand up for your ideals. Your unruffled exterior convinces many of your sincere intent to resurrect the 'word of honour' values that have been lost in much of our society.

Your Mars energy, combined with **1**, gives you the fire of ambition and inspiration, the creative brilliance of a keen mind that forges ahead, shattering the obstacles in your path.

The opposite sex will be attracted to your magnetic personality and exciting views on many subjects. You can keep almost anyone interested in your stories and adventures.

NEGATIVE

It get a little lonely up there on your mountain top (the eagle) but you have a good view from this vantage point. Don't let these wonderful energies give you an inflated ego. Arrogance never attracted anything but lack of co-operation. You might have to carve your own pathway to your goals. Others may try to hold you back from accomplishing your purposes.

Colour: Red—for energy, the active thrust.
Element: Fire—the innovator, the burning desire.
Musical Note: C—the self-starter; self motion.

DESTINY NUMBER 2

This may be the hardest number to deal with, as it is a sensitive number requiring lots of patience. This is not the lifetime to eagerly strive ahead with ideas. This number will bring you success if you can sublimate your Mars energy by co-operating with others in a combined effort to reach your goals. This is the number of the diplomat, requiring much imagination, and compromising your fixed ideas of right and wrong. You may have to settle for 'maybe'.

By using your charm and magnetism you can make this number work for you. Katherine Hepburn brought her charm to the screen, as did Richard Burton, and we are still enjoying the films of these wonderful **2** Scorpios. They also have an **11** in their destiny. Research your birthdate to see if you have a hidden talent, an **11**. If you do, you will know that you have star talent in whatever is your endeavour.

You like to have things move smoothly, even if you insist on your own way; you want men and women to sit down and reason together for the good of mankind. Your abilities may not bring you quite the rewards you expect in this lifetime, yet you will know that you were instrumental in bringing peace settlements to a conclusion.

The water energy of this number will assist you with the flow, and peace will reign in your household. You are always attractive to the opposite sex, so you have no worries.

NEGATIVE
Impatience must be put aside in this lifetime while you exercise your best manners to get what you want. If you become overly sensitive about your personal feelings you could sink into self-delusion, blaming others for your failures.

Colour: Orange—for balance and harmony.
Element: Water—dealing with the emotions.
Musical Note: *D*—for harmony and tranquillity.

DESTINY NUMBER 3

Knowing that you can transform an idea into action gives you certainty with your plans. You can communicate well and be the charming, inspirational person that all Scorpios on the second and third level (eagle or phoenix) can be if you remain positive. The power that this number gives you can be turned into conceit when you succeed in bettering your friends and associates time after time. The lower level attitude of a Scorpio is 'let the buyer beware'.

Since communication is a keyword for this number you can use this magnetic quality to deliver your ideas, as well as listen to others. You give the impression of being very sure of yourself which inspires people to follow you. If you become uncertain of your direction, use your magnetism to draw people and ideas to you for, again, you can transform ideas into workable actions. Use drama and comedy relief to get your ideas across.

With your keen sense of knowing when to delve into the unknown, you would make an excellent counsellor in matters which concern emotional relationships.

Your spouse or lover should be interested in many of the lighter things in life such as music and the theatre, so that you both can enjoy the emotional side of life. All kinds of active sports interest you as they give you an emotional 'high'. Even winning at Monopoly or Trivial Pursuit can satisfy your desire to be 'on top'.

NEGATIVE
Do not cloud your reputation with wastefulness and deceit. This is the number (on the negative vibration) of the intolerant person who can become jealous of other people's successes.

Colour: Yellow—for intelligence and expression.
Element: Fire—more energy.
Musical Note: *E*—for feeling.

DESTINY NUMBER 4

Physical or mental work doesn't inspire fear in you. You have immense powers of concentration and the ability to organize your life in such a fashion that your tasks are easy. You think about projects before starting them. This deliberation actually allows you to get more done because you are using your mental prowess instead of your emotions.

You like to have your things put back in their proper place, your toothbrush hung just so, even your daily routine planned so it does not encourage interruptions.

You are the devoted worker with ambition that will carry you far because you are not hiding your efforts. Many workers do their job well but are not as flamboyant and as expressive as you are about your successes. Since you expect others to be as careful as you are, this could cause conflict with your co-workers—they may call you a boss or a martinet.

Your spouse or lover better keep things in order, too, or it could cause a lot of grief in your household. You are meticulous in the care of your body, feeling that cleanliness is really next to godliness.

This attention to detail would make you valuable in any profession where this quality is equated with skill. You could be an economist, accountant, surgeon or writer. On the esoteric side you have the power of healing in your hands if you choose to work with higher beings. Your magnetism pulls in the healing rays on the etheric body.

NEGATIVE
If you insist on being right all the time you won't make many friends. Maybe you *are* right most of the time—this can be conveyed in a graceful manner if you really think about how to do it. Don't be so self-disciplined that you become rigid.

Colour: Beautiful, healing green.
Element: Earth—for the stable person.
Musical Note: *F*—for construction.

DESTINY NUMBER 5

Adventure, sensual experiences in love and a release from emotional upsets in former lifetimes can be yours with this Destiny Number. This vibration gives you the freedom to travel physically with joy, mentally with new insights and spiritually in depth. With 5 you can adapt to new situations in minutes, see what is happening and make decisions that are right for you if you flow with your water sign. Your 'fixed' ideas may get shaken up a little, but with 5 just realize that you have other opportunities.

As you move from place to place in any of the three kingdoms, (i.e., physical, mental and emotional) you will need a spouse or lover who is able to move with you for the excitement that you want. You may also choose a partner who is stable and who can keep your radical schemes more down-to-earth.

You will meet many people from different social levels; cultivate those who can further your objectives. Take advantage of the variety of these affairs to keep yourself free of heavy entanglements. You can sell yourself very easily as you are the greatest salesman in the world with a 5 vibration. Your magnetic gaze can almost hypnotize your client into buying your products.

NEGATIVE

The danger in 5 is gullibility. As a Scorpio you can be 'taken in' by sensual approaches and personal affairs. Also, the fear of change may crop up, though that is not very likely, as you can handle it. You may want to stay in your own little niche where you can exercise your authority rather than move on to new challenges.

Colour: Turquoise—like a refreshing breeze.
Element: Air—the breath of life.
Musical Note: G—for changeability.

DESTINY NUMBER 6

Your magnetic personality can bring many people together—to discuss peace plans for the world or for relationships in business and personal affairs. You could also blow it if you insist on going your way exclusively. If you have become the eagle who flies high and can see the overall scattered jigsaw puzzle that needs to have the key pieces placed exactly, then you will have no problem suggesting innovative ideas. Your co-workers will supply the adjacent pieces or the ideas that correlate with your own concept of the finished puzzle. Then harmony will reign.

Artistic talent could show up in this number, as well as the ability to make people laugh, painting pictures that lure the onlooker into the feeling of the painting, and writing novels of sensual experiences that end in an explosion of beautiful harmony. You can touch others' hearts with your messages of harmonious endeavour.

Marriage is attractive to you. Children are important, for you want to educate them in the ways of the world. Since you delve into many mysteries that constitute harmony, you will want to share these discoveries with your family.

This is the nurturing number, taking care of things, people and projects. Create harmony as well as you can, use your Mars energy to propose *new* enterprises instead of hassling over the old. Use your Pluto energy to regenerate and transform an old issue that you have to face and change.

NEGATIVE
Creating harmony does not mean interfering where you are not wanted. Scorpios are very apt to tell people what to do and how to manage their lives, even when no-one asked.

Colour: Royal blue—for stability. Meditate on this colour.
Element: Earth—responsibility to self and others.
Musical Note: *A*—for receptivity, harmony.

DESTINY NUMBER 7

On the esoteric level, 7s are the mystics who delve into mysteries to discover many ancient treasure troves of knowledge. Your Pluto energy can transform these mysteries into workable and understandable form. As you discover and resurrect these mysteries, write about them so posterity can make use of these channelled messages.

7 is the bridge from the known to the unknown and the courage to reach for the unknown. This number gives you the courage to explore your past successes and mistakes so that you can build a more secure future. Reverse the mistakes and make them building blocks for a secure foundation for the bridge to your goals.

Your spouse or lover needs to understand your search for ultimate understanding, your moods, your impatience and your abrupt comments. You need peace and space to contemplate your desires. This is not very compatible with the responsibility that family brings, unless you have other numbers that tell you about harmony in your numeroscope.

You stand alone in your idealism and want others to agree with you for you are far-seeing. Others may want to go their own way and do their own thing without agreeing to your principles. This produces conflict within yourself. Why seek to change all the world when the change is in yourself?

NEGATIVE
Since you can heal spiritual gaps in a person's aura, be careful about *playing* the game of the mystic. This could get you into deep trouble and will not further your ambition to be the seer to surpass all seers.

Colour: Violet—which stands for reverence.
Element: Water—flowing with knowledge.
Musical Note: *B*—for reflection on the past.

DESTINY NUMBER 8

You have great physical stamina and co-ordination between your physical actions and your brain. This primal energy can be valuable in sports, your chosen profession or in your hobbies, any and all of which require the use of your body and your mind. There are many vocations where this energy can be used to its fullest extent, such as high positions in government or entertainment.

Your powerful emotions can be used for good in the realm of the healing arts. Learn to see or feel auras so that you can evaluate a person's energy flow. **8** gives you the opportunity to open or re-open your third eye to give you the mystical information that you will need in your healing work should you choose that path.

On the material side, this Destiny Number gives you success in your endeavours—material goods of fine quality, money, power, fame and glory. All these are okay if you get them through the constructive use of your energies and not by corrupting yourself and others. This corruption would backfire on you in some way, either through the loss of money etc. or illness. Keep yourself inviolate from truth.

How can such a vigorous, purposeful person not attract the opposite sex? Carry a big stick to fight off all those who wish to take you under their wing and 'protect' you! Choose your partner wisely, one who recognizes your power and purpose and will not detract you from your goals.

NEGATIVE
Successful people need rewards too, so be careful of your companions. Many will seek to undermine your energetic usefulness through jealousy. If you are not a healthy specimen, look carefully at what you are doing to yourself through diet, bad attitudes or lack of exercise.

Colour: Rose—for love.
Element: Earth—for achievement, material gain.
Musical Note: High C—for achievement.

DESTINY NUMBER 9

Brotherly love, the compassionate caring for your fellows is the essence of this number. This is the person who is charitable toward others, undertanding that none of us is perfect, only striving toward perfection. Your sincere desire to help those less fortunate than you goes beyond your personal desire to serve yourself. When you use the vibration of this number on the positive side, you touch a responsive chord of understanding in others.

This is the number of the finisher, the one who gets his projects into motion *and* gets them done. This applies to your thoughts and ideas which can be put into concrete form. When these cycles are complete, a surge of energy comes to lift your physical and emotional spirit.

9 is a compilation of all the numbers from **1** to **8**, thus giving **9** the vibrations of all the numbers; **9** is the finish.

Align yourself with a partner who understands that you are 'on call' for service to your friends, no matter what the hour. You have come to teach the law of love—and also know what you must love (easy for *you*) in order to be loved. This does not mean that you would neglect your family, it is just that you have so much compassion for the human race.

NEGATIVE
Trust and be trusted; people will confide in you, and on the negative side you could become a gossip and tell tales out of school. Selfishness could rear its ugly head if you have a problem forgiving an unkind gesture. Just let it go; revenge may be sweet, but suppose you become diabetic? Rise out of your need to strike back. Become the phoenix soaring high above the need for retaliation.

Colour: Yellow-gold—for perfection, the desire to make everything perfect, even people.
Element: Fire—for warmth.
Musical Note: High *D*—for accomplishment.

DESTINY NUMBER 11

Master Numbers carry a higher vibration than the single digits. You'll notice that **11** reduces to a **2**. Check both vibrations to see which level you are on. The **11** is the idealist, wanting perfection in all he does. This striving for perfection in yourself assists you to be correct in your profession, whether you are an artist, inventor, scientist, philosopher or diplomat. Each of these professions needs exactness and attention to detail.

This is a doubly creative number. Your zeal to carry your projects to fruition will help you to complete the creations you start. Some birth signs are great at starting things but do not like to finish enterprises. You have the fire of Mars to help you go forward with vigour.

Your ambitions, your dreams and your desires can be put into action for you have the courage to push a little when things get to a stalemate. Some **11**s want to be the power behind the throne instead of being in front of everyone taking the credit. **11**s know who do did the work and planning—they did!

This is the number of the clairvoyant, the one with ESP, who can discern things about a person without being told.

Your spouse or lover will soon discover that you like to have things neat and orderly and kept in place. Choose someone who has these qualities; you do not like chaos in your home.

NEGATIVE

If you go too far in your search for perfection you can turn into a fanatic. Here is the zealot, the one who wants *everyone* to be perfect! Another vibration which is almost opposite is the aimless person who really doesn't care which way the wheel turns, a loss of direction. The lowest vibration is dishonesty and miserliness.

Colour: Silver—for attraction.
Element: Air—for the idealist.
Musical Note: High *E*—for magnetism.

DESTINY NUMBER 22

In order to take advantage of this powerful Master Number you need to take control of the situation, think big, act big, and assume leadership that you can certainly handle. You can be the chief in any profession concerned with industry and finance. You are the builder, material power on a physical level.

22s are the master builders. They have authority over themselves in a physical way and can build their bodies to be the way they want them to be.

This universal power can be used to get the record straight in goverment, politics and dealings with other countries where a strong man or woman is needed to cope with situations. Your direction in business could take on an international flair as you look into the business of the world.

Spiritually, you can be a strong force who has built your belief system on logic and a dream of peace and prosperity.

Select a partner who can support your viewpoints without being subservient. You will need a companion who can go right along with you in your endeavours, one who will be well-groomed and whom you will be proud to stand next to when you attend these glittering parties.

NEGATIVE
Indifference to mankind; the big talker not doer, the big noise-maker. The higher you go the harder you fall when you turn to negativity. Or you could go the other way and become withdrawn for a while, licking your wounded pride because your project did not turn out the way you desired. The lowest vibration of the 22 is viciousness and black magic.

Colour: Red-gold—for practical wisdom. Use the things you have learned for practical application.

Element: Water—for cleansing. Clean out the fantasies from your life and see reality.

Musical Note: High *F*—for physical mastery over self.

DESTINY NUMBER 33

This is perhaps the hardest Destiny Number for a Scorpio to handle, as it is very emotional and Scorpios are traditionally emotional, full of energy. Divine wisdom extends to every emotional level, from grief and anger to love and enthusiasm. Your interest in delving into the how and where of things could lead you to examine these different emotional vibrations and come up with a deep understanding of how to handle emotional upsets.

With this knowledge you could go into psychology as a teacher or practitioner. The beginnings of these varied emotions are rooted in our experiences. How *did* we handle grief or loss of love in the past? This colours our reaction today. Your Pluto energy will assist you to dig deeply into reasons and actions which are tied into emotional upsets from childhood or even from a former lifetime.

You have a wide selection of mates and lovers with this number as your sensual, emotional nature is riding high. It can also roller coaster up and down as you gain and lose love. When you acquire the understanding of why this happens, the curve flattens out and it is easier to ride with it.

33 is a combination of the idealistic **11** and the practical mastery of **22**. This means thta your concepts would be hard to challenge, because you have worked your ideas out in a very practical way that appeals to many people.

NEGATIVE
Scorpios are more apt to fight their way uphill to their goals rather than withdraw and be sorry for themselves. They may be oblivious to others' feelings and even twist the meanings of words in order to get their own way. On the lowest vibration, this number indicates crime or mental cruelty, repressing people's ideals.

Colour: Deep sky-blue—for intensity.
Element: Water—for emotional mastery.
Musical Note: High C—for emotional healing.

DESTINY NUMBER 44

Your energies and mental prowess are highest in this number. We use logic to weigh one idea against another. There is two-valued logic ('right or wrong'), three-valued logic ('right, wrong and maybe'), and simply 'your side, my side and the correct side'. If we take a quantum leap, we get to infinite-valued logic, 'righter' or 'wronger' at one time than another—i.e. there is always scope to be better or worse. Your quick, intelligent mind can use any of these processes; you can bring others who think or deliberate more slowly to come to a decision. This is the computer-type mind, with a good memory button that can retrieve facts instantly for use right *now*!

44 is a combination of the idealistic **11** and the **33** which is emotional mastery. This means that your creative, idealistic ideas are put forward with emotion (which you can control) and feeling to accomplish your goals.

44 is also a combination of the two **22**s, physical mastery over self. **44** can stand alone as the powerful manifesting number for material goods (**44/8**). Those of the opposite sex attach themselves to successful people. Your spouse or lover should have an intelligent mind as well as a beautiful body, for you will be going to many important places and want to be proud of your selection.

NEGATIVE

Most of the negativity rises from not getting your own way in this number. Your energy output is so great that you can steamroll over everyone without actually listening to others' opinions, thereby sometimes missing the actual message. On the intolerant and repressive side is the bigot, the oppressor.

Colour: Blue-green—for tranquillizing effects. It might be well to meditate on the colour.
Element: Earth—for mental mastery.
Musical Note: High *A*—for mental healing.

DESTINY NUMBER 55

Scorpios already have abundant life energy and this Destiny Number increases the life force. Have you tried action sports? You could go to the top of your profession in any sport which requires a lot of energy and endurance. You could also move ahead rapidly in business and finance, providing you have the training in the fundamentals of whatever profession you select.

Your flair for the dramatic could help in such professions as a barrister, actor, teacher, pioneer—one who has the courage to go out into the wilderness (physical or mental) to discover new lands and inventions.

Think of **55** as being a combination of **22**, the physical master, and **33**, master of the emotions. **55** brings these two together with life essence which means that you can learn to understand how to control emotions (yours and others) in a practical way. Look at where you are and where others are when on dangerous ground. Keep your cool and look at how others handle a situation which is theoretically under fire. Then you can step in to solve the problem.

Alternatively you can think of **55** as being the combination of **11**, the idealist, and **44**, the mental master. The idealist provides the creative inspiration that the mental master sets into viable form. The **55** gives life to the project. So you can be creative *and* practical as you put your project into action.

NEGATIVE
The higher we rise, the harder the lessons. This is the victim, working to decrease knowledge, burning books, repressing the ideas of others, refusing promotions to deserving employees, suppressing action toward expansion, invalidating others as well as self.

Colour: Red-violet—the abundant life energy.
Element: Air—for spirituality. Discover the way of the masters. Meditate on your colour.
Musical Note: The chord of G—spiritual healing.

DESTINY NUMBER 66

Use the *Research and Discovery* method (page 10) to see if this powerful Master Number is hidden in your birthdate. **66** is love energy, the full realization that you cannot love others until you love yourself and can outpour this feeling to others. **66** is truly the cosmic mother vibration, the double six leading to the nine (6 × 6 = 36; 3 + 6 = **9**) which is brotherly love for all mankind. We are not talking about sex, although that is an important part of loving; we are referring to the ecstasy that comes over us sometimes in meditation, giving us the feeling that we are truly connected with the cosmos, the *Oneness*.

Your eagerness to have everyone love everyone else is not an ego trip in **66**. It is an awareness of the needs of others for love. You can teach and show others the lessons of love and loving.

NEGATIVE
A negative **66** would gather many people into his camp by selling them on the idea that 'this is the only way to salvation'. This **66** would use the love energy to enslave others, make them do things 'in the name of love' that go against our moral codes. Another negative vibration is repressing love for the self and for others, keeping family and friends chained to you with 'you don't really love me!'

Colour: Ultra-rose—the fullest expression of love on this planet. Meditate on this colour.

Element: Fire—for burning away the dross, getting rid of the unwanted attitudes, habits that keep us from progressing and indulgences that cloud our aura.

Musical Note: Any chord struck in harmony.

SAGITTARIUS

22 November to 21 December   MUTABLE/FIRE

The **Centaur**   *Ruler:* **Jupiter**

Friendly, gifted, lucky Sagittarius! Your energy flows outward and upward into the future, reaching for more enlightenment as you sometimes leave physical duties behind. If you feel guilty about not getting the house clean or your desk cleared, you could become more and more frustrated with your unfinished cycles. This frustration can lead to blaming others for your inability to handle all the exciting adventures you wish to explore.

'If you would hit the mark, you must aim a little above it,' says Longfellow. And you do just that, aiming higher and higher, reaching for the stars, the promise of fulfilment. And fulfilment you receive, for you work at it; when one goal is reached you strive for another. No matter what trophies you bring home you always know you can do better next time.

Your wit and drive usually brings you to the winner's circle and those who have not been hurt by your careless (and well-meaning) remarks applaud your successes.

It is hard for you to remain in one position or one place for long, especially inside a house; you long for the freedom of the outdoors, the beach, the meadows and anywhere you can be surrounded by lots of space.

In mythology Hercules had to perform twelve labours; in his seventh, the Centaur (representative of man emerging from his animal self) shot his arrow at the attacking birds. These birds represented the last vestiges of man's little personality which held him back. Man was set free to expand into his true spiritual self.

It is hard to catch Sagittarians and hold them in marriage; they prefer to go galloping after love. You are a sunny, open-countenanced person who is truthful. You can play the clown or the knight errant or use your clever wit to pin your lovers to the floor with plain talk on their imperfections.

PARTNERS
Don't tell a Sagittarian—ask. They do not take to being bossed although they like a firm hand on the reins of love and marriage. Wishy-washy lovers are not for Sagittarians; they pull well in double harness when they realize they have to pull together.

JUPITER
Is known as the planet of benevolence, idealism, compassion, generosity and optimism: it showers the good things on all within Sagittarius' range. Sometimes extravagant and self-indulgent; turns to cynicism when frustrated and negative.

MUTABLE
This is the Sagittarius aspect of force manifesting in matter. This indicates flexibility, changeableness, openness to suggestion, interest in people, involvement in personal relationships. The joiner scattering forces; the warrior.

FIRE
These are the virtues brought forth from former lives. They are energy, enthusiasm, wisdom, understanding, inspiration and joy of living.

NEGATIVE VIBRATIONS
Direct as an arrow and sometimes as hurtful, they say things in a way that injures another's self-image, then try to remedy this by saying what was really meant and getting their feet as crossed up as a horse who has run into barbed wire. Sagittarians do not really mean to hurt, it just comes out of their mouths that way; then they are astonished that the person took it the wrong way and try their best to make it up to them.

NUMBERS
The *numbers* connected to Sagittarius' birth sign increase or decrease Sagittarius' energy. Wherever you find Sagittarius in your chart, look at the influence your Destiny Number has on this house in your horoscope.

DESTINY NUMBER 1

In your search for enlightenment you surge ahead, taking every seminar to which you have access, to find the answers to your intelligent questions. Did we mention your library? Stacks of reference and 'how to' books to keep you informed. Your enthusiasm and creativity is at its highest in **1**.

Your search for knowledge is insatiable in whatever field your interest lies. Create, invent, design and conceive the untried. **1** gives you the impetus to do this. You may not have the stability or the interest to finish what you started, but that is okay as you can turn the job over to a **4** or **2** Cancer or Taurus and they will complete it for you. A **9** Virgo will even do it with love.

Find some time for yourself as you reach out in your relaxation period for these fresh ideas. Your higher mind will assist you to open the channels.

Emotionally you are on fire with your ambitions. You even plunge into romantic entanglements with a recklessness that stops just short of commitment to a life-long partnership. Catching you for a mate is like lassoing a wild horse (the centaur). You just don't want to be penned and unable to roam the field at will. However, once you are caught (with love and sincere attention) you usually remain loyal, for to negate your choice of partner is to deny your own intelligent powers of selection. You did want a permanent relationship, didn't you? Your arrow (Cupid's this time) found its mark.

NEGATIVE

This is arrogance, knowing more than your peers and letting them know how you feel. It is not deliberate, it just slips out—you have the answers to everything! You really do not mean to be bossy or tyrannical, it's just that you have all these books which say what you *should* or *shouldn't* do.

Colour: Red—for energy. Project this to others.
Element: Fire—more energy. Ensure a healthy diet.
Musical Note: C—the self-starter.

DESTINY NUMBER 2

Your creative mind has a rare quality that detects the truth underlying the lies in others' statements. People can be lying deliberately and you will be more than willing to 'set them straight'. If they are lying subconsciously you can carefully lead them into revealing their true feelings.

This is the mark of the excellent psychologist or counsellor if you can recognize this in yourself. A lot of patience is needed to listen to the tales of others. You would much rather be roaming the glades and forests of nature than be roaming in other people's minds for any lengthy period.

The patience that this number gives you subdues the fire of your ambitions so you can work with other people and their ideas. Co-operative, rhythmic, peaceable and patient are adjectives you can assign to yourself. You can become the diplomat who affects compromises between countries or individuals, providing you do not get careless in your speech and attitude.

This Destiny Number will help you retain your cool with your family and friends when your ideas or your discipline is questioned. Your partner will soon learn not to push you too far as your temper when unleashed is something to behold.

NEGATIVE
It will he bard to sublimate your Sagittarius ego in order to work in harness with others. Being over-sensitive about yourself can turn objective criticisms into personal affronts. Don't delude yourself about your importance or you will become covertly hostile, a feeling which can only be suppressed for so long.

Colour: Orange—for balance and peace.
Element: Water—dealing in and with emotions.
Musical Note: *D*—for peace and tranquillity,
    soothing the fevered brow of discontent.

DESTINY NUMBER 3

This is one of the best Destiny Numbers for Sagittarius as it emphasizes good fellowship, love of entertaining and the gathering of friends and family. Your democratic attitude brings you friends from every walk of life. You are usually surrounded by princes and paupers, neither of whom compromise your love of freedom: you treat them both alike.

On the serious side, you have the potential of becoming a counsellor because of your intuitive ability. 3s are willing to contend with other people's vibrations in order to bring them to a better understanding of themselves and their attitudes. You can use drama and comedy to get your ideas across, as well as the use of analogies or the retelling of some of your own experiences that can help others understand their own problems.

Communication is the keyword for 3s. The combination of the 1 of creativity with the 2 of diplomacy leads to communicating on a very high level of understanding. Learn how to interpret your dreams and elevate yourself by paying attention to their lessons. 3s can pick up the vibrations of those around them, act as a catalyst, and then project these ideas and vibrations to other people through their ability to amuse and entertain. This is the number of the extrovert, one who appreciates a little applause.

You love and give much attention to others. Your spouse or lover should appreciate your efforts to hold everything together with love and humour.

NEGATIVE
Guard against overacting. Since you have the ability to pick up the rays of others make sure you shine on your own personality. Watch that you do not 'take over' the spotlight and invalidate others' talents.

Colour: Yellow—for expression.
Element: Fire—for energy.
Musical Note: *E*—for healing.

DESTINY NUMBER 4

Your concentration is on security. Your financial protection will come through hard work and focusing on your ultimate goals. There is potential success and achievement in this number if and when you put your energies into whatever you decide is your life's work. Application of your energies is important even though Jupiter is ready to give you the blessing of abundance.

Find a profession that you enjoy in order get the most out of this lifetime; no need to go grubbing along in a job that you hate. Since you want freedom and independence and are willing to work hard to attain these two goals, choose wisely and think of your work as play time. You could rise to the top of your profession if you take the objective viewpoint—look at your job from a bird's eye view and get an overall picture of where you are going and what you are going to do about it. You are willing to keep 'your nose to the grindstone' if you see that promotions are possible and rewards are coming.

This number is loyalty personified, being ready to adjust to your partner's wishes provided they will listen to your side of the story.

4 is also the number of manifestation. You can make your goals and purposes happen in your lifetime.

Should you become interested in the healing professions, use your hands to inject healing energy in massage, holistic healing or reflexology.

NEGATIVE
Rigid opinions and inflexibility is the trap of this number. Relax a little; unwind.

Colour: Beautiful, healing green.
Element: Earth—the stable person.
Musical Note: *F*—for construction, the builder.

DESTINY NUMBER 5

Most Sagittarians love the freedom of movement, moving from one place to another, and this number emphasizes this quality. It unsticks you from the mundane occupations and ordinary jobs which are uninteresting to your restless nature. Your sociable side would be happiest in positions where you would meet and deal with lots of people. You can become easily bored with routine, preferring changing scenes, different people and jobs which provide a variety of experiences.

This is a sensual number, giving you more than one love affair, which you handle very nicely, thank you. and your partner will be a person who keeps your interest. Sometimes your need will cause you concern and heartache, yet you cannot complain about being bored. It is change that you are interested in. Try a Scorpio **5** or an Aries **3** if you want challenge and adventure. These two signs and numbers can keep you guessing. Frustrating, isn't it, when you are seeking freedom?

If you think of all the numbers which have led up to **5**—the creativity of **1**, the diplomacy of **2**, the intuition of **3** and the loyalty of **4**, you have an overview of the essence of life itself, giving you the *choice* of many directions.

NEGATIVE
If you are now leading a monotonous life take a careful scrutiny at the past years to discover where you took the particular path that you now tread. You can change your vocation, your attitudes and your environment to get out of this rut. What do you really want?

Colour: Turquoise—like a refreshing breeze blowing away the cobwebs of your mind.
Element: Air—the breath of life.
Musical Note: *G*—denoting change.

DESTINY NUMBER 6

Self-realization is possible since you have access to the doorway of your higher mind. Love opens the door and **6**'s energy flows forth to encompass those all around. You enclose your family and friends in arms of love and caring.

This love can be used to bring in the healing vibrations that can be sent out to those who are in need of balancing their body. Healing takes place when the patient understands the cause of the discomfort and is willing to change his attitude toward the cause.

Your understanding of human nature can help you settle disputes and bring harmony to relationships. Your attention to minutiae and your intelligent observation of people and circumstances could equip you for positions in some type of personnel work. You are or could become a judge, reporter, nurse, physician or teacher. These suggestions are only potentials; other numbers in your chart would point accurately to your abilities.

The rough spots in your life can be gilded over by applying your spontaneous wit and humour, though sometimes people laugh at your inept jokes because they love you.

NEGATIVE
All this love and caring can turn into interfering where you are not asked or wanted. The cosmic mother that you represent in a **6** wants to take care of everyone and most people want to learn to do their own tasks and make their own mistakes. Your relationships with your loved ones can be intense at times, both positive and negative, yet it is usually of short duration. Your fire sign burns brightly but briefly like a rocket. Your Mutable sign flows gently downstream until it hits a hot rock of frustration, then watch the steam rise!

Colour: Royal blue—for stability; meditate on this colour.
Element: Earth—responsibility to self and others.
Musical Note: *A*—for receptivity, harmony.

DESTINY NUMBER 7

7, the symbol of the search for metaphysical knowledge, brings the Sagittarian to a high point of intelligent questing for inner wisdom. Sagittarians must find out about the mysteries of life and beyond, or they will be unhappy in this Destiny Number. There are so many theories to explore, so many paths to travel and so many ways to study the experience they go through.

You can become the mystic working with and through other people to discover what makes us all tick, why we react to different stimuli. Your conclusions, uttered with truthful abandon, can anger or correct the recipient of your advice. Truth is not that easy to accept for most of us.

For yourself, look inward at your motivations. Are you 'helping' others for your own self-satisfaction or in order to make things better for them? If it *is* sincerely to help others, you also will receive the reward.

7s are the bridge from the known to the unknown, from the mundane to the esoteric. Sometimes they even have to build their own bridge to get where they want to be.

Give love and joy to your family. Love begets love. Your inner wisdom will tell you when the right person comes along to share with you.

NEGATIVE

An overwhelming amount of knowledge floods your brain making you want to hide. You may want to boast and brag about how much you know. Remaining aloof for a while will give you space to get your act together. The lowest vibration of this number is to suppress knowledge or suppress people and keep them from succeeding in their vocation.

Colour: Violet—for reverence.
Element: Water—for reflection, mirroring your attitudes.
Musical Note: *B*—for reflection.

DESTINY NUMBER 8

This is the number of prosperity. Choose your weapons; fame, glory, power—even money! Use these vibrations wisely. Money—the acquistion of, the handling of and the spending of—can bring happiness, and it can bring harm; it depends entirely on your attitude toward your prosperity.

Large corporations need **8**s to organize and delegate positions of authority to others so that the wheels of commerce keep moving. You have an intelligent mind and you can use this ray to determine your direction in life, no matter what your earthly age. Think carefully about your future so that your plans and goals have meaning and purpose as you move forward in your chosen path.

You can be at the head of large corporations, deal in business and industry or go into government positions of power. Watch your verbal *faux pas* as you forge ahead. You don't mean to hurt anyone, you are programmed to tell the truth—and the truth will make you free, say the sages; sometimes it can free you from your job or position and put you out in the cold. However, you would rather be right and truthful than sacrifice your ideals.

Your fire sign is heaped with burning coals of ambition in this number and Jupiter will offer many rewards for your dedication to your true purposes.

Another side to this number is opening or reopening your third eye to the revelation of your spiritual side to gain power over yourself; pass on your love and vitality of soul.

NEGATIVE

If you discover you can sway, coerce or pummel others into going your way—against their principles—your ego will get away from you and occlude your prosperity. Become a greedy, grasping person and you will lose all you gain. You would make a great con-artist as you love to scheme.

Colour: Rose—the colour of love.
Element: Earth—for achievement, material gain.
Musical Note: High C—for striving.

DESTINY NUMBER 9

You are truly in your element with this number of brotherly love. You chose to serve mankind this lifetime and free yourself from personal restrictions. This is the number of the true humanitarian if you wish to follow the path of serving.

Think of **9** as being a combination of all the single digit vibrations; the creativity of **1**, the diplomacy of **2**, the courage of **3**, the loyalty of **4**, the variety of **5**, the nurturing of **6**, the inner wisdom of **7** and the power of **8**. All these vibrations, used with love, can change the human race, elevating it to a higher dimension of thought and action.

Your destiny is to deal with people, to serve them in whatever profession you select. Counsel them, encourage them, help them and use your gifts of communication to bring compassion and love to them.

This emotional drain will not be as drastic as it can be in other signs because your ruler, Jupiter, is the planet of benevolence and mercy. However, it is always good to remember that you also need kindness to balance your polarity—give some, get some.

You can also become excessively generous with your money and your time.

NEGATIVE
When dealing with those in trouble, the trap is becoming a 'do gooder' who begins to look with scorn at those unable to handle their own lives. Your friendliness can keep you from the trap of selfishness. The lowest expression of this number is immorality and bitterness.

Colour: Yellow-gold—for perfection, the desire to make everything perfect in love.
Element: Fire—for warmth. People gravitate toward you for comfort.
Musical Note: High *D*—for accomplishment, the finishing of your projects.

DESTINY NUMBER 11

This is the first Master Number after all the single digits from **1** to **9**. All Master Numbers carry a responsibility, for they are higher vibrations of the single digit to which they reduce: **11** = 1 + 1 or **2**. So **11** should be written **11/2** to show that a person could be vibrating on either or both levels.

This idealistic number taps the subconscious that holds the dream of perfection that *is* now and *will be*. Your native intelligence can build the confidence that you need between the idea and the realization of the dream.

The centaur aims his arrow high, seeking the target of fulfilment of his goals. Many of your concepts are foreign to the doubters of life and living so you gallop over these sceptical evaluations, racing to your goal line, the mark you have set for yourself. Then holding your trophy high you seek other commitments. This could mean crossing the goal line into another kind of game. Or it could mean turning your back on your successes to seek a new meaning to life.

Your inner flashes of intuition could light the path for many to follow in the material and the spiritual world.

Your constant search for the perfect partner is difficult as perfection is seldom in the physical, mental *and* emotional package. We all have little habits that are leftovers from former lifetimes.

NEGATIVE
Your search for perfection can turn you into a fanatic if you fail to see the reality of the nature of the human race. Each person is working toward whatever goal he has set for himself. **11**s are intuitively brilliant, their goals inspiring; however, their fame can overwhelm them if it turns to greed and self-superiority.

Colour: Silver—for attraction.
Element: Air—for the idealistic dream.
Musical Note: High *E*—for magnetism, the drawing together of people and ideas.

DESTINY NUMBER 22

22 is the practical and physical master who has control over his own destiny as it applies to the material world. You have the idealism of **11** plus the ability to put your dreams into action.

Your international direction could put you into the highest offices in the nation. You have the opportunity to make significant contributions that would reshape the shadows of things to come in politics, government, industry and art.

In order to fulfil this powerful destiny you need to think, big, act big and move into the inner circles of power in whatever country you choose. Everyone sincerely hopes that you use this power to help mankind.

You may try to exert this mastery over your spouse or lover, so beware! Look at the challenge a partner who does not always agree with you can give. A submissive mate is a rather out-of-date ideal.

22 reduces to **4** for those who are not ready for this heady vibration, yet **4** is a manifesting number, getting you what you want, also known as the work number—and work is your middle name. You can turn work into play as you put your ideas into motion.

There is power here over your physical body to heal yourself. You really do not have time to be sick; life is too exciting to bother with bed, unless bed has more interesting facets...

Choose an intelligent partner or you will be frustrated as you climb upward.

NEGATIVE
Follow through with your great plans or you will become known as the big talker and not the big doer. Reach further than your fellows or you might become frustrated.

Colour: Red-gold—for practical wisdom.
Element: Water—for cleansing.
Musical Note: High *F*—for physical mastery.

DESTINY NUMBER 33

Being or becoming the emotional master, which this number represents, requires study of the emotions. There are many books and philosophies which can enlighten you; wander through bookshops and libraries and be aware of the book titles which seem to jump out at you. Study these books to see what your guides are trying to tell you.

As you find yourself understanding emotions and where they come from, you will also find yourself evaluating yourself and others. Just don't be too harsh on yourself. Remember that you are in a learning process.

Think of **33** as being the combination of the **11** (the idealist) and **22** (the practical master). This means that you can put your idealism to work in a very practical, logical way that others will understand. You can acquire, or already have, the patience to be the counsellor who understands about the human foibles and how to evaluate these emotional tones.

Use your wit and humour to soften the emotional blows struck in anger and frustration. Enthusiasm for your work, your loves, your family or your private life can fire others with the desire to make this world a better place in which to live.

NEGATIVE
If you try to control others with the whip of emotions, you can fall into the trap of revealing your own hidden fears, which could erupt at the moment you least expect: 'A soft answer turneth away wrath'. A factual answer to an accusation will confound your accuser. Why not try it?

Colour: Deep sky-blue—for intensity. Your feelings are on the surface and show in your actions.

Element: Water—for emotional mastery, flowing with or controlling the stream of consciousness.

Musical Note: High *G*—for emotional healing. Heal emotions, don't excite them into performing evil. Negative emotions lay us open to suggestion: suggest the positive solutions to problems.

DESTINY NUMBER 44

This number of the mental master colours your Sagittarian nature. You can bring abundance to your co-workers by using the good sense and intelligence that you chose for this life.

Intelligence (the ability to learn and know) uses logic in this number to point out our mental processes. Logic is a product of our mental processes. There is two-valued logic ('right and wrong'), three-valued logic ('right, wrong and maybe') and simply 'your side, my side and the correct side'. If we take a quantum leap we get to infinite-valued logic, 'righter' or 'wronger' at one time than another—i.e. there is always the scope to be better or worse. You have the ability to choose any of these logical processes since you can handle different levels of consciousness at one time. People may think that you are drifting off into fantasy as your eyes glaze, but you are only pulling in the different levels of perception in order to solve the immediate problem.

Your spouse or lover may find this a hard vibration to handle unless they have power of their own which matches the desire to succeed. Compromise will be necessary with such a partner. Subservient lovers may seem peaceful at first but you like the challenge of winning over an able person.

44 is a combination of **11** (idealism) and **33** (emotional mastery). **44** is also a double **22**, the physical master, power over self. **44** can stand alone as the powerful manifesting number on the material side. How about the law, medicine or some healing science as a profession?

NEGATIVE
There is the inherent threat of rigidity in this number, the attitude that 'I am always right because I am always right'. Sometimes the negative side shows through by trying to twist the ideas of others to gain fame and fortune.

Colour: Blue-green—tranquillizing.
Element: Earth—for mental mastery.
Musical Note: High *A*—for mental healing.

DESTINY NUMBER 55

One way to reach the enlightenment you have been searching for is to spread the awareness and knowledge you have. Share all this with your friends. When we have reached this number, we have the potential of giving life energy, rejuvenation, to ourselves and others if this is done with love.

Reinforce your friends' positive attitudes by paying attention to them. If you reward them with complaints they will drift away.

Think of **55** as being a combination of **22**, the practical master, and **33**, the emotional master. When emotions are controlling you, think of how you can be logical about the situation and breathe life into the solution. Count to three, take a deep breath and look around to see if all this is real when you are faced with a problem.

You are of great value to your community and can go far as a religious teacher, educator, reformer or writer, or in any profession which takes you into areas of need so you can lift people out of depression. Your wit, humour and general friendliness make inroads into these areas of suffering.

You can also think of **55** as being a combination of **11**, the idealist, and **44** the mental master. The idealist wants everything perfect and the mental master can help bring order.

55 is the one who injects life into a project, can handle the upsets and emotions which occur, and on the side teaches those around about friendship and loyalty.

NEGATIVE
Everything said about Destiny Number **1** also applies to **55**, both positive and negative. The Master Number has the power to move people around and get them to thinking in a certain way, regardless if it is right or wrong. Be careful about invalidating anyone.

Colour: Red-violet—for life energy.
Element: Air—for spirituality.
Musical Note: Chord of G—for spiritual healing.

DESTINY NUMBER 66

Use the *Research and Discovery* method (page 10) to see if this powerful Master Number is hidden in your birthdate. **66** is love energy, the full realization that you cannot love others until you love yourself and can outpour this feeling to others.

66 is truly the cosmic mother vibration, the double six leading to the nine (6 × 6 = 36; 3 + 6 = **9**) which is brotherly love for all mankind. We are not talking about sex, although that is an important part of loving; we are referring to the ecstasy that comes over us sometimes in meditation, giving us the feeling that we are truly connected with the cosmos, the *Oneness*.

Jupiter, the vibration of optimism and generosity, and your fire sign bring energy, enthusiasm and love to a roomful of people. They gravitate toward you as if you were a magnet. You can sway their opinions toward your way of thinking, so be careful how you handle this power. State your own opinions (as opinions) and then be unafraid to march with those who are seeking justice and equality.

NEGATIVE

A negative **66** would gather many people into his camp selling them on the idea that 'this is the only way to be saved'. They would use the love energy to enslave others, make them do things 'in the name of love' that go against our moral codes. Another negative vibration is repressing love for self and for others, keeping family and friends chained to you with 'You don't really love me!'

Colour: Ultra-rose—the fullest expression of love on this planet. Meditate on this colour.
Element: Fire—for burning away the dross.
Musical Note: Any chord struck in harmony. This sound can change the cells in your body if promoted with love.

CAPRICORN

22 December to 19 January   CARDINAL/EARTH

*The **Goat***   *Ruler:* **Saturn**

No birth sign can win against Capricorn. You can wave your arms around like windmills, shout, and in general try to cower Capricorn but when you are all through and exhausted, Capricorn is still there quietly suggesting that perhaps you could try *this* way or *that* way—and you do.

Think of the mountain goat that climbs higher than other animals, not because he is stronger, but because he is clearly made to scale heights undreamed of by his human superiors.

With this ability you would expect to find Capricorn sweating and striving to get ahead in business, etc. No, you'll find him quietly sitting in the corner entertaining heads of state or the important people with his sly humour. Capricorn gets ahead (even collects them) by learning how to move steadily upward to his secret goals.

Capricorns seem to be as steady as the earth in which they plant their feet, but don't be fooled: they may seem to move slowly but they get there before you do. They have a way of seeing through a lie and turning it into an asset. They do not lie, cheat and steal, they out-manoeuvre their competitors. They have the tea hot and ready and the door ajar for when opportunity comes to call.

There is a streak of sadness in their eyes (when they are not twinkling) although their gaze is steady. Their hands concoct beautiful art; their voices are soothing; and you may think, 'Here's an easy conquest'. A short time later you find yourself (and your furniture or belongings) out on the street—or that Capricorn has tripped away to conquer another mountain.

Capricorns are romantic (buy them Gothic novels) but are not demonstrative in public. They love to love.

PARTNERS

You marry for love and attention, and if you catch a rich one, well, they *are* just as easy to love! Your heart is warm and receptive, you just don't wear it where it can be bruised publicly. A Capricorn man, if you can catch him, usually winds up in bed with his wife no matter how many loves he seeks before those words 'I do'. A partner will never be bored with this earthy person with an impeccable sense of occasion.

SATURN

Saturn, the investigator and teacher, sends you to books and authorities to find out the 'how', 'when' and 'where' of things, then you have flashes of insight to invent new ways to approach them. You test your dreams before committing yourself to anything. Sometimes Saturn makes you a little severe in your judgements, but you will never back-track—you'll just climb higher and look younger with every year that passes.

CARDINAL

The action is fast, direct, and to the point, especially your humour. Your pointed remarks shift the content of the conversation—the slow-minded people remaining in stasis until the joke or the intent shifts down to them. So many times you can be labelled 'sarcastic' when all the time you are speaking tongue-in-cheek about the present norm.

EARTH

Practical, materialistic, Capricorn plants ideals in the solid earth of reality, protecting these ideals from the buffeting winds of illogical reasoning.

NEGATIVE VIBRATIONS

Guard against overmanipulating people on your climb to success. Stepping-stones should be your accomplishments and not your friends.

NUMBERS

The *number* connected to the Capricorn birth sign increases or decreases the energy. Wherever you find Capricorn in your chart, look at the influence your Destiny Number has on this house in your horoscope.

DESTINY NUMBER 1

'I will not reason and compare: my business is to create,' said the poet William Blake. And so you do. Your creations are sometimes wonderfully wrought objects for admiration. At other times your creations are thought-provoking concepts. You plant the seeds of thoughts and then sit back and watch them grow. You admire success and even court people who have attained this pinnacle. You are not the jealous type since you generally see way ahead, perhaps taking the same path as your successful friends. Yet you clearly see the pitfalls of those who have been rash in their judgements; you are not out to make enemies and fight in public. You prefer the comfortable route; avoid gambles and steadily create your own power to rise to the top of your profession.

This number may be a little hard for you to handle until you understand the vibration. It introduces an element of chance, for the creation of something takes you off the beaten track. Your courage and good logical sense keep you in balance.

Your spouse or lover will need to be an understanding person and also be able to see your independence. As a woman, you are progressive, self-determined to rise in your profession, and individualistic in your pursuits. As a 1 Capricorn male, you are aggressive and determined to rise to a high position in whatever field you choose.

Neither males nor females with this number would be bombastic in their pursuits. They quietly go about their business, rolling over any opposition until they get their own way. This creative manoeuvering would be a delight to the onlooker who could perceive what is really going on.

NEGATIVE

Arrogance can rear its ugly head and detract from your accomplishments. On the other side of the negative vibration is indecision and never making a firm commitment.

Colour: Red—for energy. Project this to others.
Element: Fire—more energy.
Musical Note: C—for the self-starter.

DESTINY NUMBER 2

This is a good number for Capricorn, for you (already) have almost unlimited patience in your quest toward your goals. 2 is the number of patience, or (negatively) impatience.

Like the spider who sits and weaves its web in the corner, usually unnoticed by the brilliant high-flying other species, you patiently wait until the prize falls into your net. There the simile ends, for you do not paralyse your prey, you merely want to catch someone who will become involved in your projects. Your tact and diplomacy can then convince the opposition or the non-believers to believe in your solution to your problem. After all the shouting and arguing, your calm attention to the facts is evident as you lay out the entire programme. Then they listen.

This is the compassionate number, the one you chose to smooth the road to far-reaching goals. Your sensitivity to the vibrations of others helps you solve the problem at hand, all the time making others feel that *they* found the solution. You know that you can never take public credit for your 'under-cover work', but you know also who found the solution. Then you take one more step up the ladder of success.

Your partner, children, and family take precedence over your business life as you have very close emotional attachments to your loved ones.

NEGATIVE
You may not receive public rewards for your peaceful endeavours but there is no reason for self-depreciation because you really are the keystone other people touch for luck. Negatively, self-delusion is the trap for you, moving into covert hostility if you do not get your own way.

Colour: Orange—for balance and harmony, the vibrant colour of the sun at dawn and sunset.
Element: Water—dealing in and with the emotions; soothing the fevered brow of discontent.
Musical Note: *D*—for harmony and tranquillity.

DESTINY NUMBER 3

Many 3s are entertainers. You are too, but in a very different way than we usually picture the person 'on stage'. Your humour is subtle, your social interaction quiet and magnetic, and your personal style an intriguing 'laid-back' charm.

Your interest in clothes, jewellery, art and ornamental objects is confined to quality. You may have only one or two pieces of jewellery, but they are genuine and not plastic. Your home reflects this selection of quality for you acquire fine fabrics and interesting pieces of sculpture.

You could be a writer since you have skill with words, and skill with other languages, too. If you kept a journal for a while, go back and re-read it. You might be surprised at the positive joy of living that emanates from the pages.

Think of 3 as being a combination of the creative 1 and the tactful 2, which leads to the expressive 3. This is a strong number, forming a triad of strength which helps you understand the strengths and weaknesses of your co-workers.

Your spouse or lover should be delighted with you as you bring joy and fun into the relationship. Your family likes to have you around as you bring sunshine into the house, brightness that is steady not flashy.

Somewhere, sometime, you will reach the microphone to communicate your ideas and ideals to the public. You could be the fashion editor, the TV commentator, the host of a chat show, or involved in some media that requires imagination.

NEGATIVE
Guard against overacting. You have many friends and admirers, so don't turn them off with your own importance. You need steady, basic friendships to keep you on an even keel. Jealousy, intolerance and conceit is the temptation of this number.

Colour: Yellow—for expression of emotions.
Element: Fire—for energy.
Musical Note: *E*—for feeling.

DESTINY NUMBER 4

You are the practical person who is not afraid of hard work and routine. So few of the birth signs are willing to see the advantages of work and organization in their lives—you are one of the lucky ones. Work becomes play when you really like what you are doing. You can organize and systematize an office, a business, game or a home. When this is done you have ample time for yourself and your hobbies.

Your loyalty is unquestionable. You are the honest, conscientious manager whose dedication helps build the business. You also like to see or touch the things that you are responsible for, preferring concrete form rather than ephemeral fantasy of dreams.

If you enter into sports you can train your body (and your mind) to be a precision instrument of dynamic power. Your self-discipline is admirable.

Another avenue that few people consider is a time-and-motion officer, someone who takes apart the separate actions on a job to determine where efficiency can be improved.

Your partner will be lucky as your home will be clean and neat, everything in its place. You use a minimum of effort, as you think about your tasks first, organizing them in your head before going into action.

NEGATIVE

The conservative energy in **4** makes you less flexible in handling resources like money. You may want to hang on to it instead of investing it for a greater return. Relax a little, unbend some of your rules and regulations when you see them turning you into a rigid martinet. As a Capricorn you need love and attention, and this rigid aura could turn others off. If conflicts arise do not waste time trying to get even.

Colour: Beautiful, healing green—project this to people from your heart.
Element: Earth—for the stable person.
Musical Note: *F*—for construction.

DESTINY NUMBER 5

This is a very interesting number for you, for it frees you from a stuck position in some other lifetime. You now have the freedom to experience various opportunities which will occur at unexpected intervals. You are not as earthbound as other Destiny Numbers.

There is travel on the material plane, visiting familiar and strange places on this planet. There is also travel in the metaphysical world if you so choose to explore the unknown, the exotic and the design of the future. Your ability to sift through fantasy and fact and reach a clear picture of where you are going is a valuable asset.

5s can also handle a number of jobs at once. Your technique would be to know exactly where everything is at any given time.

This is a sensual number, giving you more than one love affair, shedding them when they are no longer useful to you. 'I use' are the keywords for Capricorn. The definition for these words can be understood as a kind of manoeuvring for position.

Your partner will have to be an interesting person: when no longer interesting, you start looking around again for more exciting adventures.

This **5** denotes change, movement, progress and drive. You can take a **1**'s creative idea and change it into an improvement on the original.

NEGATIVE
Monotony is frustrating for you; seeking variety can lead you into unhappiness if you start to depend on stimulants for a 'lift'. Over-indulgence, irresponsibility, restlessness and unpredictability are things to watch.

Colour: Turquoise—use this soothing colour.
Element: Air—the breath of life.
Musical Note: *G*—denoting change.

DESTINY NUMBER 6

Many famous people are **6** Capricorns. If you take particular note of how these people attained their popularity and notoriety, you can better understand yourself and your emotions.

This is the doorway to higher mind through self-realization and harmony. **6**s can create peaceful areas or can interfere with the rightful order of things, bringing chaos. They are full of pride in themselves and their family—an understandable emotion. They are suspicious of others and can become cynical about their work or their profession.

6s have so many good things going if they remain on the positive side of the number: harmony, good judgement, carefulness and balance. They make excellent judges and mediators. With the combination of **6** and the birth sign Capricorn, they instinctively know how to handle money and finances. They also know how to move power around to get their own way.

Some famous Capricorns of this number are former President Richard Nixon, who could have been one of the strongest Presidents of our age, Howard Hughes, the financier, Cary Grant, the actor, and the beautiful Ava Gardner.

It seems that the actors and actresses already knew that the world is a stage (like other Capricorns) and in addition they fully realize that they are the 'actors' on that stage, not the manipulators of the world.

6s love their family and remain loyal to their partner if they can stand the chaos of separation. There is a lot of love here.

NEGATIVE

6s prefer harmony, but also tend to tell their friends about the cause of the friend's problems. Don't interfere if you are not invited to participate in problem situations; you may have heard only one side of the argument. Egg is better inside the face than outside! Cynicism and domestic tyranny are the lowest vibration of the **6**.

Colour: Royal blue—for stability. Use this colour.
Element: Earth—meaning responsibility.
Musical Note: *A*—for harmony.

DESTINY NUMBER 7

This is a different kind of freedom number. 5 unsticks you from incidents in your past and 7 gives you the freedom to move ahead into the future.

With this number you can analyse where you have been, your successes and your mistakes. Then you can put this all together and come up with a better way to live your live from now on. You have the inner wisdom to search for the metaphysical or psychic side of life.

You can apply your own experiences and your philosophical bent toward proving the solutions to mysteries you discover. Develop your mystical approach, work alone in your own efficient way to channel your energies towards scholastic knowledge. You can be the bridge from the known to the unknown.

Then share this knowledge with others. Give love and joy with a caring heart. Your spouse or lover will be one who can understand your search and temporary need to be alone to meditate and cogitate on the ills of the planet.

In your work you are efficient, exact, intellectual and studious, searching for the correct word, the apt phrase, the dignified rebuttal to popular misconceptions. You should be a specialist in whatever profession you choose. Many priests and religious leaders have this number.

NEGATIVE
If this intelligent mind becomes confused, you become sceptical of the knowledge you received. Then you may invalidate yourself and others with sly asides, humiliating others and their ideals. On the lowest level this is the person who does not want another to succeed. He turns to malicious gossip when promotions are given to fellow workers.

Colour: Violet—for reverence.
Element: Water—for reflection, mirroring your attitudes.
Musical Note: *B*—for reflection.

DESTINY NUMBER 8

Finance, business, industry and government are the best outlets for this ambitious number in Capricorn. This does not mean that you have to get out there in the public eye and make yourself or your wants visible. You are the quieter sign that climbs steadily to the top, just like the mountain goat we have already talked about. While others are expounding their grandiose plans, you just keep pegging away at securing your future by making wise investments and handling your money and promotions.

8 is power on several different levels. It is prosperity for whatever endeavour you choose. Do you want fame, glory and power like Muhammed Ali? He was successful and plotted his path to success, manoeuvring into a role of his own choosing, knowing what was best for him. **8** is material freedom, executive ability and personal achievement.

Of course you will attract the opposite sex. Doesn't everyone love a successful person? The only thing that will bother you is the question 'Do they love me or my money?'

Another side to this exciting number is the opening or re-opening of your third eye; the revelation of your spiritual side. Pass this knowledge and love on to others.

NEGATIVE
Sometimes **8**s discover they can sway others to their own way of life or belief systems and create injustices instead of justice. They let their ego get away from them and when they fail they blame others for their inability to handle this power. Con artists are traditionally supposed to have a heart of gold; sure—hard and metallic. Wouldn't it be better to have a warm, caring and empathetic heart?

Colour: Rose—the colour of love.
Element: Earth—for achievement/success.
Musical Note: High C—for striving.

DESTINY NUMBER 9

This number of brotherly love can free you from personal restrictions. It is the number of the true humanitarian, the server of mankind.

Whatever profession you follow will be an expression of benevolence toward your fellow man or woman. Your destiny is to deal with people. You can do this by becoming a solicitor, a counsellor, a vicar or an artist. There are so many jobs and professions that require the expertise of the Capricorn insight.

Watch your diet and vitamin intake; you also need warmth by being around friends who appreciate you and tell you so. Good music and conversation is a must for you, because you can become drained by giving too much attention to those who need your services. Find a quiet time for yourself, a peaceful corner where you can recharge your batteries.

Success and achievement are also inherent in this number. Finish anything you start and you will find yourself with lots more energy.

Since your attention is on mankind in general, you may not receive the personal love that you desire. If you are lucky enough to find an understanding spouse or lover, they will understand your involvement with people and societies.

NEGATIVE
When dealing with those in trouble or when searching for equality, you can become the 'do gooder' who looks with scorn on those who are unable to handle their own lives and ambitions. Too much strain on your resources could make you inconsiderate and irresponsible. Blaming others for jobs you did not accomplish will not elevate your spirit.

Colour: Yellow-gold—for perfection, the desire to make everything perfect, even people.
Element: Fire—for warmth. People like to cuddle up to you.
Musical Note: High *D*—for accomplishment.

DESTINY NUMBER 11

This is the first Master Number of all the single digits from **1** to **9**. All Master Numbers carry a responsibility for they are higher vibrations of the single digit to which they reduce; for example: **11** = 1 + 1 = **2**. So **11** should be correctly written **11/2** to show that a person could be vibrating on either or both levels. This holds true for all the other Master Numbers.

This idealistic, intuitive number brings you flashes of insight and taps the subconscious, dreaming of perfection that was and is to be. Between insight and reality is the courage to face the real world. The confidence that you have in yourself spurs you on to better things. This is the artistic genius, the inventor who gazes out of the window and envisages castles in the air. Sometimes the castle remain right there unless you team up with a practical partner who can bring the dreams to completion.

Finding the perfect or ideal spouse or lover is a little difficult since perfection is seldom on the physical plane. We all have habits that are ingrained from our various experiences. You'll keep searching though, compromising here and there. You are intelligent enough and intuitive enough to know you are not perfect, but the search is so much fun!

NEGATIVE

Since **11**s are intuitively brilliant and their goals inspiring, their fame can overwhelm them if it turns to greed and self-superiority. They can become fanatical about goals or can easily go the other way, clasping their knowledge to themselves.

Colour: Silver—for attraction.
Element: Air—for the idealist.
Musical Note: High *E*—for magnetism.

DESTINY NUMBER 22

You know how to put your abilities into motion; you can occupy the highest offices in the nation if you so desire. You can control large corporations, work in the diplomatic field, or handle some international post in a foreign country. Calm assurance is an asset to government, or would be if we could find and promote some 22 Capricorns. You would not be apt to promote yourself, as you prefer to be the power behind the throne. You are the adviser to the people out front.

You have control over your physical body, can heal yourself, usually because you are too busy to bother about being sick. This number represents physical mastery. You would be terrific in sports, go right to the top of whatever you chose. However, mental games are more your speed: you prefer to outwit your opponent rather than use brute force. Tennis or golf would be good sports for you.

22 reduces to 4 for those not quite ready to accept this powerful vibration. Yet 4 is a manifesting number—you get what you want.

You may try to exert your authority over your spouse or lover, so watch out. If you catch a Leo or Aquarian you might be butting your head against a brick wall to get your own way. Try a little wit and humour to endear yourself to your selected partner.

NEGATIVE
If you do not reach farther than your fellows, you could become frustrated. Follow through with your grandiose plans instead of being the big talker and not the doer.

Colour: Red-gold—for practical wisdom, using the things you have learned for practical application.
Element: Water—for cleansing. Clean out the fantasies from your life and see reality.
Musical Note: High *F*—for physical mastery.

DESTINY NUMBER 33

Most Capricorns know more about emotions than the average person, for they are good at observing human actions and reactions—and not getting involved in the process. They know how to push certain buttons on people to get the proper response. Used correctly, this signifies great ability to quell riots, subdue quarrelling factions and bring balance to disagreements by using wit and humour. This takes the pressure off tempers. Capricorns use little stories that are analogous to the situation to get people laughing. These stories bring up such vivid pictures that the opponents see the futility in winning the battle and losing the war.

Wouldn't it be wonderful to know how to categorize emotions so we could use one to bring out the desired response? A **33** Capricorn does and it is a marvel to behold.

You can also think of the **33** as being a combination of **11** (the idealist) and **22** (the practical master), the person who gets the dreams of **1** on the drawing board.

Since you know how to handle emotions you should not have much problems getting the partner you select.

NEGATIVE
If you try to control others with your whip of emotions you could fall into the trap of fomenting your own fears. These fears could erupt at the moment when you least expect them to. 'A soft answer turneth away wrath.' A factual answer to a loaded question takes your expertise and leaves your opponents hanging on the ropes.

Colour: Deep sky-blue—for intensity. Your feelings are on the surface and show sometimes.

Element: Water—for emotional mastery, flowing with or controlling the stream.

Musical Note: High *G*—for emotional healing. Heal emotions, don't excite them into performing evil. When we are triggered into our negative emotions by fear, we are open to suggestion.

DESTINY NUMBER 44

This is power on a national and international level. If you choose to operate at this level, you can rise to unlimited material heights. Your mind clicks along like a computer, digesting information that culminates in answers both correct and far-seeing. No one plays with your brain waves, however, for you see through their games. You do not reflect negative energy back, yet have far more fun twisting it just a little and letting it percolate back into their lives, using the wiles of humorous persuasion. They never know what changed them.

You are truthful, but a person who wants an answer from you must ask the correct question. You use logic and common sense to get what you want. And you succeed.

44 is a combination of **11** (idealism) and **33** (emotional mastery). This creative ability is under your emotional control and leads you to mental mastery with power over yourself (and others, if you wish). **44** can also stand alone as the powerful manifesting number on the material side. How about using all this talent for healing the minds of those who have been hurt and invalidated in this lifetime?

All this mental mastery does not stop you from attracting many suitors. They all want to hang on to you for the challenge and excitement you provide. Capricorn men are loyal, and while they are not romantic lovers, they do not burn themselves out early in life—they just keep going until the end.

NEGATIVE

Sometimes you might need assistance from someone more knowledgeable than yourself. If rigidity in your personality sets in, it will be difficult for you to accept advice. The lowest vibration of a **44** is vindictiveness, getting even, and controlling people through mental cruelty.

Colour: Blue-green—for tranquillity.
Element: Earth—for mental mastery.
Musical Note: High *A*—for mental healing.

DESTINY NUMBER 55

This number gives you the essence of life in abundance. All the good things you have read in Destiny Number **1** (page 166) apply to **55** many times over. The creative principle is at work here to bring you abundant *life force*, physical stamina, a healthy creative mind and receptive spirit.

When a **55** walks into a room it seems to light up and people want to be around the life energy a **55** radiates. What a joy to make love to this joy-filled person!

You can assist others by helping them gain, regain and reinforce their actual being by just being *there*. People are magnetized toward you as they sense your love and light.

55s have the combination of **11** and **44** to express their lives; idealism (**11**), plus mental mastery (**44**) leading to the explosion of life (**55**). Also think of **55** as being a combination of **11** plus two **22**s, idealism expressed in physical mastery twice over.

Separating **55** into **22** and **33** gives you physical mastery over self with emotional mastery over self *and* others. It means knowing when to push the correct button to bring into existence the things that you know to be good for mankind.

In business you will inject life into the project. Your enthusiasm will carry many workers forward so they can actually produce more than they realized. Martin Luther King, Jr, was a typical **55** Capricorn, leading his people in peace, using his life force to inject spirit into his campaigns.

NEGATIVE

Not every **55** wants to handle this high vibration, and this doesn't matter. The **1** vibration that is a reduction of **55** gives you the creative ability to invent whatever kind of life you desire. Just don't detract from another's life force or you will become a victim of life.

Colour: Red-violet—for abundant life energy.
Element: Air—for spirituality.
Musical Note: Chord of G.

DESTINY NUMBER 66

Use the *Research and Discovery* method on page 10 to see if this powerful Master Number is hidden in your birthdate. **66** is love energy, the full realization that you cannot love others until you love yourself and can outpour this feeling to others.

66 is truly the cosmic mother vibration, the double six leading to the nine; $6 \times 6 = 36$; $3 + 6 = $ **9**, which is brotherly love for all mankind. We are not talking about sex, although that is an important part of loving; we are referring to the ecstasy that comes over us sometimes in meditation, giving us the feeling that we are truly connected with the cosmos, the *Oneness*.

Your reverence for your spouse or lover is visible in your protective attitude. Let no one malign or gossip about your chosen one or the heavy hand of Saturn will be felt on their shoulder.

This loving protection extends to your business life. After the five o'clock whistle has blown for other people, you need to stay and clean up the last odds and ends of the day, just to make sure that tomorrow you will have a fresh start. Your office will be comfortable, your desk will have a flower in a vase brought from home, and if you have no room for your family picture one can be sure to find it in your drawer.

Your love spreads to all things large and small, animals and plants as well as people. As keeper of the love flame, share this with many others and teach them how to accomplish the circle of love around the world.

NEGATIVE

Using the love energy to enslave others, or make them do things 'in the name of love', or even repressing the love that you feel, is the negative vibration of this number.

Colour: Ultra-rose—fullest expression of love on this
   planet. Meditate on this colour.
Element: Fire—for burning away the dross.
Musical Note: Any chord struck in harmony.

AQUARIUS

20 January to 19 February   FIXED/AIR

The **Waterbearer**   *Ruler:* **Uranus**

We leave the past behind and enter the future world of Aquarius. The Waterbearer is carrying his pitcher from the well of knowledge to the river of spiritual rebirth. Aquarius only looks back for information that can serve the future. As we move forwards into the Aquarian Age we leave the house of restriction (Pisces) for that of intuition and knowledge.

Aquarians are the rebels of the zodiac; they don't like to be told what to do because they are individualists and want to go their own way. Curiously enough, this usually turns out to be the right way, as they see ahead into the future. This psychic 'seeing' is creative genius at work. They are imaginative, creative, more interested in their chosen work than in people—unless they are in a humanitarian profession.

Their keyword, 'I know', can be frustrating to others and not win them any close friends. This does not bother the Aquarian as he is too busy exploring new avenues of thought to bother defending his ideas.

Aquarius really has two rulers which split his friends into two camps; one set will be conservative and proper and the other will be the casual type who prefers to sit on the floor. Saturn rules the former, and Uranus, the planet that shatters our outgrown concepts of life, rules the latter.

These shattered, outmoded concepts set the spirit free, a rebirth takes place, and Aquarius soars to new heights, taking everyone along who is willing to face the unknown future.

When Aquarians are evolved they become humanitarians; they feel love for their fellows and want to do something to increase our ability to govern ourselves (not depend on handouts), increase our self-esteem and find our true identity.

PARTNERS

Don't grab or cling to an Aquarian. He wants attention only when it is called for, like a hurt finger, but don't hover too long. Aquarians think they want a partner who is submissive, but the challenging signs and numbers spark their intuitive ability, raising it to greater heights or self-examining depths.

URANUS

This planet has the vibration of the unexpected, the explosive power to break apart the patterns that have been set for an age. It brings the creative, scientific and idealistic vibrations to view. Ask an Aquarian *how* he knows something and the answer will be, 'I just know'. This intuition can be frustrating to the person who has to know *why*. Uranus is the reformer, freedom-seeking, independent and impersonal; the awakener.

SATURN

Is the tester, the stabilizer, the teacher and the responsible one. It is dependable and diplomatic.

FIXED

The four Fixed power signs are Taurus (dormant until stimulated), Leo (active), Scorpio (hidden and subtle) and Aquarius (higher wisdom). Courage is needed to discipline and bring forth the positive rays of these power signs. These agents of karma can be destructive as well as constructive, depending on the elevation of the individuals.

AIR

Inspiring, creative, courageous, positive, acting on the mental plane, gathering knowledge, intuitive.

NEGATIVE VIBRATIONS

Detached, cold, uncaring, irresponsible, rebellious, wilful, disorganized.

NUMBERS

The *number* that is connected to the Aquarius birth sign increases or decreases your energy. Wherever you find Aquarius in your chart look at the influence your Destiny Number has on this house in your horoscope.

DESTINY NUMBER 1

The moment of creation is yours, for you see far into the future. Maybe you are bringing the inventions and the ideas of the future back to our present time. Whatever you are doing, you keep the lives of others exciting and fresh.

Repetition and routine are not for you although you get all your jobs done. No one can figure out how you do all these things. They are unaware that you have a little help in the time warp—you can change time to suit your needs.

While you are filing those cards or sewing that dress or making a pitch for a sale, you are planning what you will cook for dinner or which tie to wear to the theatre. There doesn't seem to be a minute that your mind is blank or relaxed.

You listen carefully to your clients in whatever profession you enjoy (and believe me, you have to enjoy it or you will never engage in it), while the other six layers of your mind pull in the correct questions to ask, the correct answers too, besides remembering that the car needs filling up, and where did I put those income tax papers? This sounds like Gemini but is totally different; Gemini handles all these in the air, Aquarius handles them by getting them done and finished. Aquarius looks cool and unexcited, seems to have unlimited time to talk (remember the time warp) and gracefully moves the minds of those he meets.

The Waterbearer pours love to the world and people, bringing a nodding acquaintance of the clown to reality. When the pitcher is empty Aquarius sits by the well contemplating as the healing waters fill the waiting receptacle. Again he brings life back to the present and busies himself.

NEGATIVE
It's lonely out there. Hostility can enter the chamber of self if arrogance and ill-will is unrecognized.

Colour: Red—for energy.
Element: Fire—more energy. Ensure a healthy diet.
Musical Note: C—the self starter.

DESTINY NUMBER 2

Here you have the inventiveness of Aquarius coupled with the patience of **2**. People are lucky to have you in the office, in business or in government. You bring calmness to any decision-making board. You are an objective peacemaker.

With your leadership ability and gift for thinking on your feet, you could become (or indeed are) one of our great statesmen. Diplomacy is needed for the '90s more than ever while the entire world is not at rest.

You have the power to concentrate on the smallest detail that involves decisions which affect people, yet your mind leaps ahead to solutions more quickly than your associates. Your patience and willingness to stay with the challenge wins people over to your side.

Since you can bring harmony into a chaotic situation, you would make a good adviser to those in high government positions or heads of corporations. Your intuition gives you the right answers but you still want to put two and two together for the logical approach.

Hopefully, your partner is an understanding person who realizes your leadership and peacemaking abilities are valuable.

NEGATIVE
2s do not expect public rewards for they are the keystone of the arch which holds up society and business. If you become overly sensitive about your well-being and yourself, you could negate all the good that you can do. Keep your objective attitude and go about your business.

Colour: Orange—for balance and harmony, the vibrant colour of the sun at dawn and sunset.
Element: Water—dealing in and with the emotions; soothing the fevered brow of discontent in others.
Musical Note: *D*—for tranquillity.

DESTINY NUMBER 3

You are receptive to new and exciting ideas which can be used to entertain people. This is the number of the entertainer who uses jokes and parables to get the message across to the audience. One side of this number is the fun side of Aquarius, the deliberate exaggeration of events that, told in story form, make people laugh—and than make them think. On the other side of this number is the serious person who wishes to communicate the humanitarian expression of love. This love encompasses others in a personal, yet impersonal, way that permits the recipients to react in their own fashion.

3s have quick minds, and are receptive to interesting concepts. Their reactions are clean and as quick as a rapier thrust, cutting away the unnecessary talk and arguments. They pick up the vibrations of those around them and then, acting as a catalyst, bring these ideas and attitudes together and aerate them for discussion. 3s are not the peacemakers that 2s are: 3s bring communication to bear so that peace can be made a possibility.

Your spouse or lover will have a fascinating time being your partner, never knowing what you will dream up next. Your creative individualistic traits are imaginative, whisking you into the future with a rapidity that takes away your breath.

NEGATIVE

Since you want to shatter the old concepts as quickly as possible, sometimes you throw the baby out with the bathwater. Tradition is not that bad, it provides stability. Breaking new trails is exciting and fun, but there may be aggressors ahead, so be a little cautious. Your urge to be of service functions within a certain structure—include the wishes of others as well as your own far-seeing vision.

Colour: Yellow—for expression and intelligence.
Element: Fire—for energy, breaking the bonds that constrict society.
Musical Note: *E*—for feeling.

DESTINY NUMBER 4

You work well in big business and in work that requires organization and concentration on the future goals of the company or corporation. Make the most of the opportunities that come your way by using your Fixed sign to keep you practical. Your ideas seem practical to you, but may seem pretty strange to your colleagues. Explanations may be due in order to get them to see the potentials of your plans. Delegate someone to take time to do this, for your attention is on the next month's or the next year's production and it would be like going backwards to explain everything that it is possible for your company to accomplish.

This is a powerful manifesting number for you; you decide what you want and when you want it and nothing else matters. Pay attention to your psychic side for it knows how to keep you out of trouble. You have a kind of radar that picks up conversations that are going on around you. From these conversations you can tell how the company is doing and what the employees are doing.

Another great aspect of 4 is the healing quality that you have in your hands. Massage would be too limiting for you, so work on the etheric body if you decide to take the responsibility for this kind of magnetic healing.

Your spouse or lover should appreciate your ambition and courage to forge ahead against all opposition. You will always be a good provider (possibly in two or more homes in radically different places!).

NEGATIVE
You could become rigid in your opinions if you do not take time off to dream a little about the future. You could become so engrossed in your projects that you lose sight of the fun part of life.

Colour: Beautiful, healing green.
Element: Earth—a stabilizing factor.
Musical Note: *F*—for making things strong.

DESTINY NUMBER 5

This number is truly in the spirit of your birth sign. It means travel to many different places where new opportunities await you. It also means travel in your studies and your mind, using your air sign to bring you adventure.

This creative mind number can take someone else's original idea and change it into something else or something even better. You are not afraid to try the new ways, new inventions and new methods that someone proposes. However, you will make it your own by improving it a little here and there.

You love surprises, for you must have variety in your life. If you get bored you get into mischief. By taking advantage of all the different ideas presented to you, you can profit financially, mentally, physically and spiritually. It may be a little difficult for you to accept someone else's ideas, for you like to promote your own, but you are really too smart to let opportunities go by.

Through this number and your ability to look at your work objectively you can become one of the world's greatest salesmen (or women). You will not do it in the fashion that is suggested, but you will come up with an approach that surprises everyone at the meeting when they announce that you have won this month's award—again!

You need a partner who will be delighted with your changeable habits: Taurus is too grounded and a Leo would want first place.

NEGATIVE

Seeking variety can lead to unhappiness if you think you have to have an adventure every day. Your ruler, Uranus, does want to blow the status quo apart so think before you throw everything to the wind.

Colour: Turquoise—for a refreshing breeze.
Element: Air—the breath of life.
Musical Note: G—denoting change.

DESTINY NUMBER 6

This number of self-realization matches the Aquarian birth sign. Aquarians are probably the most self-realized persons in the zodiac. They know themselves and are honest about it, honest in their own way. They will tell you the whole story if you do not push them too hard. Just listen and their dreams and expectations are right up front. They can chart their zig-zag way up the hill of life with perfect aplomb while others steer a straight course encountering obstacles along the way. Aquarians weave around the obstacles as easily as an accomplished skier skirts a protruding rock, unless it looks so interesting that they have to stop to examine it. They like mystery and will probe until they find out whodunnit!

This is a number concerned with home and family. Aquarians may forget to do the dishes—but they may entertain the local children with hand puppets. Aquarians need privacy at home—and will give their partner privacy as well.

This is something that your spouse or lover has to get used to. Aquarians are friendly with everyone, and while you think you are getting the undivided attention you deserve, you find that this same attention will be given to the waiter or a friend who just dropped by your table. Male Aquarians make good husbands if you catch them; female Aquarians will be faithful (but still interested in many other people).

This is the number of the cosmic mother—one who cares for and nurtures people, plants and animals. But this nurturing will be Aquarian in nature—like serving popcorn for breakfast. If you are morose or serious, you will never enjoy the warmth that this type of Aquarian can bring to a relationship.

NEGATIVE
Careless, interfering, anxious and prideful.

Colour: Royal blue—for stability.
Element: Earth—for responsibility.
Musical Note: *A*—for receptivity, listening to others with empathy.

DESTINY NUMBER 7

This number gives you the opportunity to use your life for a different approach than one would expect from an Aquarian, and this is looking backward at the past. Most Aquarians are only interested in the future with a little sprinkling of what is happening now.

However, you can garner wisdom from actions taken long ago if you would be willing to discover the mysteries that are hidden there—and you do like mysteries. You could take the mystical path tracing your past lives from the beginning to now and even going further by tracing the lives to come.

Wisdom is the keyword for this number. Seek hidden truths as you contemplate the metaphysical side of life and which path to follow for the time being. Perhaps you will be a priest, guru or social worker. You may wish to teach young people, to spread information about the world as it could be.

You have always wanted to be free, and 7 doubles this desire. This can take an emotional tone when you struggle to release yourself from old habit patterns. Yet your realistic outlook tells you that all these experiences are just learning experiences to go through. Sometimes you can see where you are repeating incidents, thereby clearing up the emotional content very quickly.

Study; bridge the gap between the known and the unknown, between the mundane and the esoteric.

NEGATIVE

Refuse to humiliate others when you are in a downward mood. This does not happen very often, for you would rather withdraw from the fray. You may seem aloof and uncaring to others but that is your way of gaining a little space for yourself.

Colour: Violet—for reverence.
Element: Water—for reflection.
Musical Note: *B*—for reflecting your moods.

DESTINY NUMBER 8

Here is all the power, glory and money you want, if you decide to swing along with this number. You will find your-self being invited to take leadership to direct people and nations where there is a monetary concern for their welfare. If you are flying high using your Uranus energy for breaking apart the status quo—or if you stay in never-never land—you are not putting your good mind and stewardship to practical use. You are not fully aware of your great possibilities if you cannot use your energy for practical things.

Power can be used for good to bring others to the realization that situations can be handled with sanity. Teach how others can learn to handle their affairs with justice and love, sharing instead of trying to work everything out 50:50.

On the esoteric level, you can open your third eye. This includes becoming aware of other people's energy and how it assists you to handle this flow. You could learn to see auras and assist others to discover where their energies lie.

This is a practical number. You seek rewards on the material level, things you can touch and see. Your spouse or lover should realize this and not try to change you, for it will not work. You will find your own pathway.

NEGATIVE

Here is the schemer, the one who loves glory, fame and attention without really deserving it. If you have put in lots of study or meditation or whatever you do to see into the future, and then achieve your rewards, that is good. If you have walked over others to gain money, position, glory and fame, then you are really not entitled to the adulation or the trophies. This is a tricky number for it promises much and only delivers if you are deserving and patient.

Colour: Rose—the colour of love.
Element: Earth—for achievement on this third
   dimension, this earth; material gain.
Musical Note: High C—for research.

DESTINY NUMBER 9

This is one of the best numbers for you as it contains the humanitarian aspect, the same vibration that your birth sign sends out to people. This all-encompassing love radiates from you and inspires others to reach their highest potential.

You can go beyond bias towards your own ideas. In time you transcend your belief system in order to incorporate the ideas of others that you find compatible. This is brotherly love, recognizing that all people are in need of love; all have unique experiences which compel them to act as they do.

Your emotional attachments to others may be brief, but intense, as you move from one person to another. These intense relationships may end abruptly and frustrate others. In time they will realize you have no desire to possess them. Free them, so they can be their own masters.

You can be an immense instrument for good by working in the mainstream of life, whether it be in an office, a manufacturing plant or as a priest and confidant.

Awareness and success are keywords to remember, for this number means completing your tasks, getting the job done without depending on other people.

NEGATIVE

You can carry the banner of goodwill, acute perception and willingness to co-operate if you do not try to make people into your image. Although you have all this love, no one is perfect (yet), and trying to change people may also be a form of judgement ('you're not as good as I am so I'll improve you'). People will copy what you do—not what you say.

Colour: Yellow-gold—for perfection, the desire to make everything perfect (in your opinion). At least take time to look at the other person's viewpoint before you go striding off into battle with no one to support you. You can change things with love.
Element: Fire—for warmth. You attract people.
Musical Note: High *D*—for accomplishment.

DESTINY NUMBER 11

This is the first Master Number after all the single digit vibrations **1** to **9**. All Master Numbers carry a higher vibration and a responsibility to others than the single digit to which they reduce. For example: **11** = 1 + 1 = **2**, so **11** should be written correctly **11/2** to show that a person could be vibrating on either or both levels.

2 is the peacemaker, **11** the perfectionist who dreams of a perfect world with strife ended and a circle of love surrounding the planet. This dream may not seem practical to those who surround you. The **11** perceives unrest and an identity crisis that affects his co-workers. You can use your brilliant mind to understand the greed and the need that others have for self-glorification.

Sometimes you may be reluctant to do this, because when you know something you feel that everyone knows it—and this isn't necessarily so. Share knowledge with your trusted friends for they will help you find the right solutions to complex problems.

You could receive flashes of illumination which light the way for many to follow. Use your charisma to enlighten and change the consciousness of those who would fight your ideals. You can help heighten the consciousness of humanity.

NEGATIVE
Since you are intuitively brilliant and your goals inspiring, your fame could overwhelm you if you lose sight of your goal of internal and external peace. Or you could keep all these wonderful exciting concepts to yourself, refusing to share them with others, thereby enriching no one.

Colour: Silver—for magnetizing other people for support of your ideals.

Element: Air—for the idealist who builds castles in the air; don't knock it—everything starts with a dream.

Musical Note: High *E*—for magnetism.

DESTINY NUMBER 22

International direction, universal power on the physical level, managing or owning major corporations, becoming the nation's foremost diplomat, and many other possibilities are your destiny if you choose to exercise the powerful number in your chart.

Your Uranus ruler can knock apart the outmoded ways of doing things and then you can institute efficient methods which will bring prosperity to your business.

You need to have and keep a healthy body for all the pressure that seems to come your way. Select and use a sport that gives you release from the strain of these pressures, a hobby that is absorbing for the few moments you get for yourself. This sort of unhooking of your mind from the problems of the day gives you freedom to roam in reverie and receive visions of what will help you solve major problems.

Your self-mastery can be used to show others how discipline can be employed to improve themselves and conditions as far-reaching as the uplifting of our planet's vibrations. You can get people together to work to better their situation.

Look at **4** to see how you can manifest your desires. Become the manager of a bank, the MD of a firm, a foreign diplomat or curator of a museum. You appreciate the finer things in life.

Your native honesty (remember President Lincoln?) and intelligence will carry you farther than you ever dreamed if you follow the positive vibrations of this number.

NEGATIVE

You may feel that something is missing if you do not follow your dreams and reach farther than others in your work-day world. Also if you do not follow through with your grandiose plans you will be labelled the big talker and not the big doer.

Colour: Red-gold—for practical wisdom.
Element: Water—for cleansing.
Musical Note: High *F*—for physical mastery.

DESTINY NUMBER 33

Your objectivity towards life can conquer the emotional content of this number. You do not usually get embroiled in other people's problems or games, as you are wont to dismiss them. Rather than get enmeshed in petty discussions, you can stand on one side looking on, knowing the answers but not giving advice unless you are asked. Of course, all this means that you have a good understanding of how the emotions work for and against people.

Think of **33** as being the combination of **11** (dreamer and perfectionist) and **22** (the practical solution) to put these dreams into motion with feeling. **22** knows the plan can be perfect if effort is applied in the right direction. You can lead the way to sane solutions and be the highly motivated peacemaker, bringing the cool wind of logic to heated emotions. Using a little humour can lighten the situation and you are good at telling stories which pinpoint the solution to arguments.

Take a look at **6** to also understand the underlying basic need to nurture the dignity of others and not their emotions.

Your lover or spouse will eventually get to know you have no desire to control, you just want to have peace or passion when you want it.

NEGATIVE
You are apt to withdraw into your inner sanctum if the heat in the kitchen becomes too hot. You will not brood, as Cancers do; you simply withdraw to think about more pleasant things, planning for the future. Many people will not understand this attitude and scold you for it. The lowest vibration of this number is trying to control others through their negative emotions—fear, anger, grief, etc.

> **Colour:** Deep sky-blue—for intensity.
> **Element:** Water—for emotional mastery. Learn all you can about this.
> **Musical Note:** High *G*—for emotional healing.

DESTINY NUMBER 44

If you thought **8** was powerful, just look at this number and what it brings: This is double power and is the Master Number of the mental body. The *mind* is a complex structure containing receptors (the way we see and perceive things), reactors (the way we react to different stimuli) and analytical functions. The mental body uses this analytical portion of the mind.

You can approach a challenge through the analytical doorway; look at the facts, use your inherent vision to forge ahead in your thinking to discover certainties and uncertainties. What is real and what is unreal? What are the facts? What are the lies?

33, on the other hand, approaches challenges through feeling and reacting emotionally. Think of **44** as being a combination of **33** and **11** and you get a different twist. The dreamer and idealist become very emotional about having to sort out the facts (**44**) to get the job done. You can also think of **44** as being a combination of the double **22**. You have the ability to lead with your far-seeing intuitive concepts.

NEGATIVE

This amount of power would be difficult for some birth signs to handle; you are already a leader, however, for you know where you are headed and can handle power if you do not become rigid in your opinions with the attitude, 'I am always right'. Maybe you are, but this does not endear you to your friends or your partner. You cannot get the job done with arrogance.

The lowest vibration of this Master Number is trying to control others through mental cruelty. Here is the psychotic who controls people by using a mask of righteousness to sway opinions his way.

Colour: Blue-green—for tranquillity. This colour calms the intense fire of ambition and helps put your desires in the right perspective.

Element: Earth—for mental mastery.

Musical Note: High *A*—for mental healing.

DESTINY NUMBER 55

This is *life energy* in abundance—you have the task of shining light and life on others. Look towards the future and enthuse others about upcoming events and inventions. At this level you can be a channel, bringing light and knowledge from higher dimensions into the consciousness of those who are ready to receive this inspiration. As light from the sun beams down to the earth, breaking through the prism of consciousness to become warmth, intelligence and tranquillity, so a **55** (if willing) acts as a prism to bring understanding to us from higher dimensions.

Think of **55** as being a combination of **22** and **33** added together wherein the practical mastery of things on this plane of existence works with mastery of emotions to bring a moving life-energy force into existence. This can elevate the consciousness of all those you contact with this energy.

Or think of **55** as being a combination of **11** and **44**, wherein the dreamer designs a world of his own and makes it take form through the double powerful energy and command of **44**.

NEGATIVE
This could be a person burdened with karma on the wrong or inactive path. If you choose to look forward in a positive manner instead of wallowing in self-pity, the light and life energy will come to lift you out of the darkness.

Colour: Red-violet—the abundant life energy.
Element: Air—for spirituality. Discover the way of the masters. Meditate.
Musical Note: Chord of *G*—for spiritual healing.

DESTINY NUMBER 66

This powerful number radiates love energy and can be found by using the *Research and Discovery* method on page 10. This Master Number carries the pulsation of love for everyone.

Love extends from the self to others, and you know you cannot love others unless you know and recognize the perfection of your own soul. This is not an ego trip; it is a full realization of outpouring love through the acceptance of karma-free relationships in the soul. The inner self receives a vision of perfection and yearns for this love relationship with the soul mate and the supreme being.

66 is truly the cosmic mother, whether you are male or female, the double six leading to the nine, i.e. $6 \times 6 = 36$ and $3 + 6 = $ **9**—brotherly love.

You are here to keep the love flame going and we don't mean sexual activity, although that is an important part of loving. We are speaking of the joy in this total universe that is ours for the asking.

66 reduces to **3**, so read about that number also. Some people vibrate on one level or another or they may seesaw back and forth from outpouring this love energy or merely in entertaining people with wit and humour. That is love also.

NEGATIVE
This love energy can be used to enslave another. Jealousy can rear its ugly head (although with you this is seldom), and you can be determined to get even. You can refuse love or even become selfish and possessive of your partner, your friends, and your possessions.

Colour: Ultra-rose—meditation on this colour will open the heart chakra.

Element: Fire—for burning away the dross, contempt, frustration, hate, and bringing forth the imprisoned love to share.

Musical Note: Any chord struck in harmony.

PISCES

20 February to 20 March   MUTABLE/WATER

The **Fishes**   *Ruler:* **Neptune**

Pisces, symbolized by the fishes swimming upstream and downstream at the same time, can be thought of as a person who has a hard time making up his mind. Or he can be searching in the past and in the future in his soul's quest.

This compassionate sign is the most sensitive in the zodiac. Pisceans feel deeply, and woe betide the spouse or lover who wounds their pride. Their moods swing from indifference to bitter sarcasm; from charm to irritation; from bewitchment to resentment—and not too slowly either. Pisces would be more comfortable paired with a **4, 5, 7, 8** or **9** because these numbers have calm, introspective and adventurous souls that will not trespass unwittingly on the Piscean sensitivity.

Many people call Pisces the scrap pile of the universe. Little bits and pieces of all the signs are stored in Pisces, which gives them an understanding of many different kinds of people. Pisceans always want to be somewhere else in the universe. They instinctively know there is a better place.

The positive vibrations of this sign show a wisdom far beyond that of the average person. It seems Pisceans are tuned into some other planet that is far advanced over ours. We could call this psychic or clairvoyant ability, yet the Piscean is apt to negate this as being too mystical.

One thing is sure—don't try to cage a Piscean or put him into a position where the work pace is six foot square and he's chained to a desk. He seeks freedom to wander, like the fishes, taking his neat, clean and graceful self outdoors and into activities that give him space and peace.

Gentle, emotional, imaginative, dreamy, fearful and interesting, Pisces loves security and gambles on it.

PARTNERS

Pisceans, being the dreamers of the zodiac, can miss their greatest opportunities to make money, make love or make a move towards fame and recognition. When they realize it's time to get on with some sensible goal, they have no trouble at all gaining their objectives. There is another way out: marry for money or find an ambitious hard-working partner.

NEPTUNE

The great mask wearer! This sensitive planet, the ruler of Pisces, shows wisdom, intuitiveness, genius, and contact with other dimensions. The music Pisces enjoys is like falling water, poetic and graceful, producing visions of fantasy. Neptune sinks deeply into the sea trying to hide his intelligence behind the coral of obscurity and illusion. But a snap into reality will bring out the creativity and devotion that Neptune brings to this much maligned sign.

MUTABLE

Flexibility is the keyword: adaptability, tolerance and informality, sometimes prone to negativity, changeability and lack of will, or so it seems. This person can cope with nine grandchildren (all fussy eaters), an **8** Leo for a partner and three boys who tower above them both.

WATER

You would think with all this going backwards and forwards that Pisces are unstable—don't be fooled, for they have compassion for the human race (unless they are totally negative characters) and understand the emotional upheavals others have. They have been there and back and prefer to withdraw rather than fight, and they come out with fewer bruises.

NEGATIVE VIBRATIONS

Self-delusion, fear, enjoyment of self-martyrdom, inertia and oversentimentality.

NUMBER

The *number* connected to the Pisces birth sign increases or decreases energy. Wherever you find Pisces in your chart look at the influence your Destiny Number has on this house.

DESTINY NUMBER 1

This is one of the more ambitious signs of Pisces. This creative influence will open channels to your various talents. You have the possibility of tuning in to the vibrations of any of the other zodiacal signs. For instance: do you want the freedom of thought that the Aquarian has, or the stubbornness of purpose that Taurus acts on? Study the birth signs to understand their vibrations and how people of certain signs act and react to situations. You can draw on a particular sign's vibrations to help you to make a decision. Remember that people of other signs and numbers are also reacting to their various experiences in life.

This is valuable information for all Piscean adventurers. There are bits and pieces of all the other signs residing in Pisces, so you can pick and choose your direction instead of reacting in an undecided manner. This makes an interesting game for you to play.

Develop a strength within yourself so that criticism intended to divert your attention from your goals does not get under your skin. Your personal integrity is acute, you are not really interested in manoeuvring others to do what you want to do. You can get stuck on the point of indecision.

You need attention and encouragement to stay with your projects—projects full of imagination that can inspire others.

NEGATIVE

We sincerely hope you have not been invalidated in your childhood for your imaginative dreams. Your sensitivity can be crushed even as an adult. It may be a little hard to be out there on that newly discovered star; gets pretty lonely knowing that you are right and no one else can understand your visions of truth and beauty.

Colour: Red—for energy.
Element: Fire—more energy. Ensure a healthy diet.
Musical Note: C—for the self-starter.

DESTINY NUMBER 2

You have planted the seeds of imagination and action in your former lifetimes, and in this life you have earned a rest. This time, however, you have a lot to learn about relationships. This compassionate number in your compassionate birth sign could assist you to become a good counsellor.

2s are called the peacemakers as they know how to put one and one together to form an alliance of goodwill. Your cool-headed intuition can tune in to the minds of warring factions and bring harmony into existence. All the time your mind is going click, click with ideas of how to present a solution that would be acceptable to both parties.

You can be (or are) a great trouble-shooter, able to solve both sides of a problem with your charm and disarming techniques. Your solutions to problems may be a little unusual, stretching the credulity of the participants, even eliciting humour in the situation. Then the opponents say 'Wait a minute, that's not so impossible' and everyone gets down to the business of settling the dispute.

Your spouse or lover will appreciate your gentleness and charm (and the flowers, gifts and funny cards). Your sensitivity to their moods endears you to them.

You may not receive the awards of a **1**, but you will know who is the power behind the throne. This knowledge is reward enough for you really do not want to be in the public eye unless other strong signs and numbers are in your chart.

NEGATIVE
Impatience follows you through your life until you realize that waiting for others' decisions gives you more time to organize your thoughts and your rebuttals. You can become over-sensitive about your feelings and attribute general critical statements to be personal affronts.

Colour: Orange—for balance and harmony.
Element: Water—for emotions.
Musical Note: *D*—for harmony.

DESTINY NUMBER 3

You have talents and tend to scatter your energies trying to discover which one to follow. It is a temptation to start several things at once and then decide that you need a holiday from all that hassle. Well, **3**s may be here on vacation after all.

3 is a social number, entertaining and charming your friends and associates into giving you what you want. The problem is to make up your mind as to what you really want!

You have two ways to go (as usual) in your search for success in business. One way would be working for someone, or a company, who can outline the goals and routines for you. You will have your rebellious times but you would tend to accede to their methods. The other way would be to take advantage of the assistance that successful people offer you in your artistic and idealistic pursuits. In either instance you can gain the goals you have visualized if you stay on the positive side of this number.

There are many people in the entertainment field who carry this number. They know how to employ flamboyant gestures, coupling them with the emotional output necessary to television, stage and film careers.

Your spouse or lover will constantly be pleased with your surprises of theatre tickets, long romantic drives, or reservations at the finest restaurants.

NEGATIVE

Guard against changing your mind too often; you could confuse your close associates. Using the energy of your opposite sign (Virgo) brings a more organized attitude. You can pick up the vibrations of others and reflect their attitudes back to them, so be careful about invalidating your boss or your partner. Don't waste your talents.

Colour: Yellow—for expression to the world.
Element: Fire—for energy to express.
Musical Note: *E*—for feeling.

DESTINY NUMBER 4

This number has a stabilizing affect on your birth sign; it will keep you from vacillating in your decisions, as you tend to be more organized in your approach to life.

You can manifest what you want this time around. If you can visualize the creativity of **1**, the diplomacy of **2** and the energy of **3**, all coming together in the **4**, then you can see what 'manifesting' means. Use these energies when you are faced with a decision. You may have to count to four to remember that this time you can use diplomacy—another time you may want to use your creative energy and ignore diplomacy. Since you love to choose, this number could be fun for you.

Another wonderful aspect of **4** is the healing potential you have in your hands. Esoterically you can work on the etheric body if you want to take the responsibility of this kind of magnetic healing.

Your spouse or lover may be a little confused about an organized Piscean, so keep your little secret if you wish.

Your Neptune self is exhibiting the calm waters of a placid sea and can also foresee the stormy waters ahead and be prepared for them. Your tendency is to retreat and dive deeply into your innermost self for security. When you predict stormy waters (or scenes) you can also hide behind the rock of stability, stating ideas and ideals.

NEGATIVE

Many people move slower mentally than you do, so use a little patience to get along with them. While you can see several roads ahead, being Piscean, another **4** may only see one avenue of approach to success. Instead of invalidating the other person, use your charm and persuasion to get them on your side.

Colour: Beautiful, healing green.
Element: Earth—another stabilizing factor.
Musical Note: *F*—for construction, building.

DESTINY NUMBER 5

Travel, excitement, and new experiences which will contribute to your spiritual and emotional growth is inherent in this Destiny Number. The travel can be physical, mental (in study) or even astral, if you are intersted in the metaphysical side of life.

You could profit from these new adventures if you do not withdraw when too many choices come your way. As you seek excitement and become willing to try different approaches to your business or love life, you can make your dreams come true: you are the dreamer and visualizer!

5s do not stand still in the backwater of life. They usually pursue life with vigour, knowing that seeking adventure may succeed or it may not turn out the way they envisioned it. Sometimes, though, the anticipation is more thrilling than the success. When we reach our goals it sometimes seems like the end of an era, and this can be a let-down.

This is a sensual number, relating experiences to the touching, loving and feeling part of you. This reveals the artistic side of Pisces, for you appreciate good music and elevated conversation.

It is also the number of creative mind, taking the 1's original idea and changing it into something else or even something better than the original. Many *improved* inventions have come through 5s.

NEGATIVE

The sensual part of a 5 can increase your intake of food or drink, so it is something to be a little careful about. Fear of change is the essence of this number, the fear of trying anything new and different. The 'essence of life' is negated if you do not take advantage of this exciting number.

Colour: Turquoise—like a refreshing breeze.
Element: Air—the breath of life.
Musical Note: G—denoting changeability.

DESTINY NUMBER 6

This number is a radiation of harmony. You really are not interested in fighting, chaos, things that do not work (like people) and carelessness. This harmonious number brings, you the power of logic so you can adjust to the problems and challenges of this life.

Any profession or job where you can be of service to people would be compatible with this number, like social worker, teacher, physician or personnel manager. In your concern for justice you would make a good judge, lawyer or councillor. You seek facts, not rumours, then carefully analyse both sides of the argument in order to exercise your inner wisdom. You would also do well as a dramatic actor or a musician.

6s like home and family. They create order and insist on it. Their interest in food goes beyond mere eating, for they like to *create* exotic dishes. Their spouse or lover can just turn over the kitchen to the male or female Piscean and read the evening paper while Pisces conjures with the pots and pans.

You take good care of your money as you do your loved ones, so your partner never has to worry about you hiding from work. It isn't that you like work, you just know this is the way to get what you want out of life. If you have an expensive hobby you know you have to work for it.

NEGATIVE
In your concern for justice be careful you do not meddle in other people's affairs when you are not invited. Sometimes your feeling of always being right (when you are in a good mood) could be misconstrued by friends and business associates as an ego trip. Not so. You have carefully weighed the pros and cons before you make a clear-cut decision, so be sure to make this clear.

Colour: Royal blue—for stability.
Element: Earth—for responsibility.
Musical Note: *A*—for receptivity.

DESTINY NUMBER 7

You have always wanted to be free, and this number (on the positive side) does free you to make your own choices. This does not make it any easier, as making a choice is difficult for you; however, the freedom to do it yourself does enlarge your space to operate. No one is going to hamper you from achieving your goals unless you let them.

You don't even have to have goals because this number frees you from your past and lets you move into the future with confidence. It is like crossing a bridge—you see this side and the other and you want to cross this stream. Sometimes the planks on the bridge are rotten so you need to get some new boards to make it safe for yourself by building a new bridge (of consciousness).

7 is also called the 'eye of the needle', seeing from this dimension to another with ease. 7 is analytical, looking at the past to see where your successes and mistakes were, then looking to the future to see how you can do better. When you have this number in any of the numerology categories you need to stop and take a look at what you are doing. You can unstick yourself from habit, from doing things in the same old way, and from your old attitudes.

Your partner will find that you are exciting to live with—living with you will never be dull! A stable 4 or 8 will keep you grounded or provide grounding for your freedom.

NEGATIVE
You can become sceptical of your own abilities and withdraw from the fray. If you become too confused you might try blaming others, even though you know this doesn't work; the compassion in you will bring you up rather short if you try it. At the lowest level of negativity you can become suppressive to others, stopping them from doing what *they* want.

Colour: Violet—for reverence.
Element: Water—for reflection.
Musical Note: *B*—for reflection on self.

DESTINY NUMBER 8

This is one of the most powerful numbers in numerology; it represents primal energy, the power to achieve success on a material level. When a Piscean decides to win he no longer impersonates the dual fishes who are undecided on which direction to swim; he becomes the whale ploughing through calm or turbulent water to achieve a goal. With this number there is no stopping you if you decide to take advantage of this vibration.

You can become the leader and director of a business or several businesses, handling the money situation with ease. **8** is power, money and prosperity on the positive side.

Occupations which require physical stamina would be more appealing to you. You find release in the exercise of your physical muscles, thus sports, yoga, athletic competition and sports car racing would be examples of the out-pouring of your physical energies.

Your spiritual side can be opened also as **8** gives you the opportunity to open your third eye and experience seeing auras, seeing visions of the future and opening the channels to spiritual energy.

Your spouse or lover will need to recognize your desire to succeed. You will always have a good home and an ample bank account if you stay on the positive side of this number.

NEGATIVE

This is the love of money, power and glory which destroys by climbing over others in your rise to the top; ignoring the 'little people' to gain your objectives. This is impatience to get your own way, plotting and schemimg to get ahead. As an **8** you can get ahead without resorting to negative force.

Colour: Rose—the colour of love.
Element: Earth—for achievement, material gain or esoteric enlightenment.
Musical Note: High C—for research into the intuitive esoteric world.

DESTINY NUMBER 9

This is a good number for you as it represents love for all mankind. **9**s are the servers of mankind, the ones who go out on the highways and byways to bring the sheep into the fold.

You would make a good evangelist, speaker, or volunteer in charitable fund-raising efforts. This is brotherly love, recognizing that all people have unique experiences which compel them to act as they do. This all-encompassing love can spread out to all those you meet and inspire them to act in love and compassion for their fellow man or woman.

Your emotional attachments to individuals may be short, but intense, as you move from one person to another. These intense relationships may bring frustration to others but in time they realize you do not want to possess them. You inspire and set them free.

Your destiny is working in the mainstream of life where you can be an instrument for good—social worker, reformer, housing officer, healer or dietician. Any occupation that serves the populace would be good for you. Even drama and singing would bring your love to your audiences.

This is also the number of a person who gets things together from start to finish, completing your cycles of action, jobs and tasks. This ability to finish a job can lead you on to advancement in your chosen profession. Many people start many things but few complete their tasks.

NEGATIVE
You may find that you are being drained of your energies since you spread yourself too thinly over many projects. Your mental side says it can be done, but your emotional side says 'Help!' Watch your financial resources also; your kindness can drain your wallet.

Colour: Yellow-gold—for perfection.
Element: Fire—for warmth.
Musical Note: High *D*—for accomplishment.

DESTINY NUMBER 11

This is the first Master Number after all the single digits from **1** to **9**. Master Numbers carry a responsibility for they are higher vibrations of the single digit they reduce to. For example: **11** = 1 + 1 = **2**. So **11** should be correctly written **11/2** to show that a person could be vibrating on either or both levels. This holds true for all the other Master Numbers.

11 is the number of the perfectionist—your intuition can develop to genius level. Your search for truth can raise your level of intelligence, as well as that of others, if you desire to share your knowledge with them.

Sometimes **11**s are reluctant to reveal what they know since they feel that 'everyone' knows about that. Try sharing some of your knowledge with people who are interested in the same things you are and you will be surprised how much more you know. You may also discover new ways to examine your way of life, your job or your family by exchanging ideas.

Share and exchange knowledge and feelings with whom it may concern to bring a better understanding between you and those who are important to you. You will receive flashes of illumination which could light up the path for many to follow. Your perceptions of a perfect world could influence those around you; we always hope that this is for good.

NEGATIVE

Since you are intuitively brilliant and your goals are inspiring you will draw many people to you. This could overwhelm and trap you, for many geniuses become self-superior and fanatical about their mission in life. On the other hand, you could keep all these wonderful discoveries to yourself, thereby enriching no one.

Colour: Silver—this is for attraction. You can
   magnetize people to your side and support.
Element: Air—for the idealist who builds dream
   castles—don't knock it; it all starts with a dream.
Musical Note: High *E*—for magnetism.

DESTINY NUMBER 22

You are destined to become the head of a big business, take a high government position or in general use your talents in a practical and universal way. You have a responsibility to the times and the tides in the affairs of men and women. You can achieve recognition on a worldwide scale as you make contributions to society.

You need to think big and act big as you seek out the giants of industry who will further your plans. Get in contact with those in power and take your place alongside them. As a Piscean, the compassionate one, you can facilitate the re-building of a good world instead of a repressive one.

You can be a forceful speaker, for your dynamic aura encompasses the audience. You also receive a sort of radar from the audience which helps make a strong line of communication between you and them.

Investigate law, commerce, communications (such as television and radio) and politics to achieve your dreams.

Your spouse or lover will enjoy your romantic approach as well as dinner at the finest restaurants, expensive but appropriate gifts and your undivided attention at the proper times. You need a partner who is aware of your tremendous power.

NEGATIVE

If you cannot follow through with your grandiose schemes you will be known as the big talker and not the big doer. Also, if you do not strive to reach farther than the average person, you may become frustrated, involved in petty work and details. On the lowest vibration, this is crime on a large scale.

Colour: Red-gold—for practical wisdom. Use the things you have learned for practical application rather than fantasies.

Element: Water—for cleansing. Wash away your doubts and see your path clearly.

Musical Note: High *F*—for physical mastery.

DESTINY NUMBER 33

This is the number of emotional mastery. It is the ability to learn about the emotions and how to use them to better understanding.

Your ruler Neptune and the Mutable water sign of your birth connects to the emotions. **33** gives you the possibility of bringing all these factors together and under control; then you can use this knowledge for your own enlightenment as well as using it properly (surely) to enlighten others.

Think of **33** as being the combination of **11**, the perfectionist, and **22**, the physical master who can put your dreams and visions into material form. Use your intuition or 'feelings' to go about doing this or that. Your flashes of intuition will carry emotion with them, which helps to set this information in your mind. Sometimes flashes of intuition are just that, and they disappear as quickly as they appear unless there is feeling in them.

22 knows that the plan can materialize and be perfect if effort is applied in the right direction. Realizing this, a **33** can balance disagreements by using humour to release the tension. All levels of emotion are useful at different times— even anger. We suggest that the emotions not be used to hurt or avenge anyone.

Your spouse is going to enjoy your company to the utmost —you are the gentle or fiery lover, depending on your mood.

NEGATIVE

The trap of this number is trying to control other people through their emotions, getting them angry so they lose control, or frustrating them so they become angry and make mistakes. This, of course, will reflect on you at a later date. Be particular in your choices of goals, for you can sway people through their emotions.

Colour: Deep sky-blue—for intensity.
Element: Water—for emotional mastery.
Musical Note: High *G*—for emotional healing.

DESTINY NUMBER 44

If you thought **8** was powerful, take a good look at this number and see what it brings. This is double power to manifest what you want on the material plane, the mental master who can visualize, analyse and then materialize his dreams and aspirations.

The *mind* is a complex structure containing receptors (the way we see and perceive things), reactors (the way we react to different stimuli) and analytical functions. The mental master uses the latter part of the mind, that analytical portion that uses logic to determine the answers. You can approach a challenge through the analytical doorway, look at the facts, then use your inherent intuition to dissect the certainties and the uncertainties until you arrive at a conclusion. This is analogous to a jigsaw. How do you logically solve the puzzle? By fitting the correct pieces together.

Think of **44** as being a combination of **11**, the idealist, and **33**, the emotional master, and you get a little different insight. **44** would then arrive at the solution through vision and feeling. You would be using your intuitional ability to perfect your project.

Your spouse or lover needs to understand this tremendous power that moves you in several directions. There is tenderness and passion here—what a nice combination.

NEGATIVE

If you try to control people through mental cruelty it will backfire on you. Invalidating others—not listening to their side of the story, refusing to compromise—is a negative manifestation of your energy.

Colour: Blue-green—for tranquillity and healing. This colour calms the intense fire of ambition so that it can be directed into proper channels.

Element: Earth—representing mental mastery.

Musical Note: High *A*—for mental healing of yourself and others.

DESTINY NUMBER 55

As light from the sun beams down to the earth, breaking through the prism of consciousness to become warmth, intelligence and tranquillity, so a **55** (if willing) acts as a prism to bring understanding to us from higher dimensions.

Think of **55** as being a combination of **22** , the physical master, and **33**, the emotional master. Added together you become the practical master of things on this plane of existence and are working to conquer your emotions to bring a moving life force into action. This life energy can elevate your own consciousness as well as others.

Or think of **55** as being a combination of **11** and **44** wherein the dreamer designs a world of his own and is able to see it take place on this third dimension. This is the architect who designs beautiful structures *and* oversees construction, seeing his drawings come to life. We can become (or are) architects of our own lives. We put life into the way we truly want things to be. Think about it. We can put energy into sickness as well as health.

If you follow this course you will be admired for your tenacity, your creativity and your personal integrity.

NEGATIVE
It's a little lonely on this high pinnacle of endeavour, Pisces. If you choose the negative side of this number you are burdened with being on the right path but stationary. This is where victims of life are still walking in darkness, seeing no light or path. Choose to look forward in a positive manner instead of wallowing in self-pity.

Colour: Red-violet—the abundant life energy. Let this life force flow out to all those around you.
Element: Air—for spirituality. Discover the way of the masters. Meditate.
Musical Note: Chord of G—for spiritual healing.

DESTINY NUMBER 66

This is a powerful number and can be found through the *Research and Discovery* method on page 10. **66** radiates love energy; it is a Master Number which carries a lot of power in and with love. This love extends from the self to others, knowing that you cannot love others unless you know and recognize the perfection of your own soul.

This is not an ego trip; it is a full realization of out-pouring love through the acceptance of karma-free relationships in the soul. The inner self receives a vision of perfection and yearns for this love relationship with the soul-mate and the supreme being. You can seesaw between the Master Number **66** and **3**, which is its reduction. Sometimes you feel love and sometimes you just want to entertain people with humour and compassion.

66 is truly the cosmic mother, brotherly love, the double six leading to the nine ($6 \times 6 = 36$; $3 + 6 = 9$). You are here to keep the love flame going and we do not necessarily mean sex, although that is an important part of loving. We are speaking of the joy in the total universe.

NEGATIVE
The higher the vibration, the lower a person can sink if he acts on the negative side of the Master Numbers. This number can be used as a tool to enslave others, having them do things 'in the name of love' that go against our moral sense. Love also can be withheld as punishment or through anger at another person. This love can become selfish, possessive and jealous of friends and lovers.

Colour: Ultra-rose—meditate on this colour.

Element: Fire—for burning away the dross, the contempt, the frustration, the hate, and bringing forth the imprisoned love for self and others.

Musical Note: Any chord struck in harmony—bringing the soul in balance. Find the particular chord to which you vibrate.

PART II: PERSONAL DATA

PERSONAL YEAR

The Personal Year Number is the vibration that influences your life in any given year. This is a fine focus of Jupiter, the planet of benevolence and idealism. Jupiter showers you with all the good things in life as long as you recognize what the goods things are. If you are operating on the negative side of Jupiter, it could lead you into extravagance and greediness.

To obtain this number you add your birth *day* and your birth *month* to the year you are seeking. For example: if your birth *date* is 26 April 1932 and you want to find the Personal Year for 1990, do this:

Add 26 (the day) to 4 (April) to 1990 = 2020.
2020 = 2 + 0 + 2 + 0 = **4**

The Personal Year for 1990 for anyone with the birth *date* of 26 April 1932 is therefore **4**. Do *not* use your *birth* year but the year in which you wish to find your Personal Year.

19 (Day) + 4 (April) + 1990 = 2013
2 + 0 + 1 + 3 = 6

1 + 9 + 5 + 6 =

19 (Day) + 4 April + 1956 =

1 + 9 + 5 + 6 =

PERSONAL MONTHS

Still under the influence of that great planet Jupiter, we also find our own Personal Months by adding our Personal Year to the current month or to the month you are seeking.

For example: 26 April 1932 is the birth *date*. We want to find the Personal Month for *July* of 1990. Since we have already established the Personal Year for this birth date for 1990 as **4**, we simply take the **4** and add it to the month of July, which is represented by **7**.

4(Personal Year) + **7**(July) = 11. 1 + 1 = **2**

Therefore, the Personal Month for the birth date of 26 April 1932 for July 1990 is **2**.

Jupiter: *Expansion, Understanding, Friendliness, Abundance, Inspiration, Increase, Spur.*

The definitive words for Jupiter listed above capture the essence of the positive side of Jupiter's vibrations. Understand these words by using a good dictionary as you discover the true meaning for yourself. Meditating on all the descriptive words given in this book will also assist you.

The *negative* side of the **Jupiter** vibration is: *Extravagance, Indulgence, Cynicism, Greed.*

When we talk about the *timing* of your decisions we need to remember that Jupiter has an influence as well as the vibration of the number that you find for your own Personal Month. The interpretations for personal months are given in the following sections. make sure you look under the appropriate Sun sign heading.

ARIES

PERSONAL MONTH 1
This is a time for action, a time to seek new, exciting offers which could enhance your position in your profession, relationships with your partner or with your family or in your search for the health aspect of your physical body, your mind or your spirit. Be sure to check how this agrees with your Personal Year by reading the interpretations in the *Table of Numbers* on pages 282 to 285. By putting the two readings together you will become aware of what is happening in your life and how to determine the forward positive movement you can take at this time. Use your Mars fire to further your ambitions and welcome opportunities that come your way this month. This could mean a change of job, a new lover, a new home or a change of attitude towards your life. Act on your intuition and take charge of the direction in which you are moving. This is an opportune time to make full use of the Mars fire of ambition to find the unusual.

Negative You could become bossy and arrogant over your successes this month, thereby incurring the wrath of your associates, so watch out.

PERSONAL MONTH 2
Good relationships can be formed during this month if your Destiny Number is compatible. Always look at your Destiny Number to see how it goes with your Personal Year and Month vibration so that you are in harmony. Friendships will come to you but it is up to your Aries nature to find the spark to ignite the fire which can cement the real feeling between you and the person or circumstance. You can let a month like this give you a quiet time, a resting period to build up your intense energy. Small issues may assume inflated importance during a **2** month, so delay your decisions until next month if it is at all possible. Jupiter's kindness, consideration for others and optimism is prevalent at this time, so seek understanding of the values of life.

Negative Using this month to be more by yourself to examine your pathway is not a selfish vibration. If your quiet time includes criticism of others and sends you into a depression, indulging in fantasies to detract from another's personality, that is negative.

PERSONAL MONTH 3

Good relationships can be formed in this month also, but the perspective is different—that of communicating to others in your inspiring way. Accept invitations or have friends over for a good time, an evening of play or exhilarating games. Display your talents if you are seeking new friends. Go forward, do not look into the past; you have already lived those lifetimes and it is a time to look to the future, making your plans and securing your goals. It is easy for you to be light-hearted; use this talent to lift others up to this fun level—laughter cures a lot of ills and we all tend to be more serious than we need be. Communication is very important at this time, so listen and talk until you understand just what is going on in your job. This job may concern family or business.

Negative Exaggerations and alibis lead nowhere during this month. Face the facts. If you have become conceited about your accomplishments, try not to communicate this to others.

PERSONAL MONTH 4

This month is an opportunity to put your house in order. This means your physical surroundings, ending the cycles that you started in a **1** year or month if this is at all possible. **4** months also give you a chance to take inventory of your belongings, your attitudes, your relationships and your progress on the path you have chosen for this lifetime. Where are you going? Are you satisfied with the life you are leading or the friends you have surrounded yourself with? When you have completed the inner workings, plan ahead. Organize and analyse the details of contracts, correct errors, put your correspondence and your finances in order. Stabilize yourself this month as next month brings some exciting adventures which fit your vibrant self. Cut and prune away the deadwood to discover the true flower of sanity.

Negative If you have become rigid in your opinions and unwilling to give up 'your way', now is the time to find out why you are inflexible on certain matters.

PERSONAL MONTH 5
Jupiter's influence is really with you this month, for *expansion* is in the air. Adventure, travel and moving in several directions at once is compatible with your energies and should be a fun time for you as you move rapidly into unusual situations. This is a time of activity, creating new images through your Mars fire. In business this is the month to advertise, to contact many people and also open your mind to many different viewpoints—not necessarily making decisions—just experiencing change and more change. Discard your old ideas if they have not been productive.

Negative This can be a restless month where you hop from one circumstance to another, creating havoc instead of acquiring more wisdom. Keep yourself well-groomed, as the tendency to become so involved with your affairs can make you careless and sloppy.

PERSONAL MONTH 6
Home is where we live and it is very important to recognize your roots this month. Attend and serve those closest to you even though it takes patience to listen to their tales of woe. Give your family, whether it be your spouse, lover, children or a group, your loving attention and friendliness. This is a personal time for you to listen to the inner guidance and use this perception to clue into other people's feelings so you can be of some help. This help means not taking on their burdens but assisting them with love to see what their real problem is, and turn it into an asset. Establish harmony with those

around you and protect those who need your energy. Being as self-realized as you are, you can turn to the doorway of higher mind through harmony. Bring yourself in balance and turn on your love when meditating so you can contact your higher self.

Negative This is the month for anxieties and carelessness if you practice pride and cynicism on your family.

PERSONAL MONTH 7

This month you should balance your cheque book and all your accounts. The analytical approach will carry you far this month—insist on freedom from worry. Try to be alone part of the time so you can get your thoughts and desires in balance. Keep yourself in control and don't be sloppy in your appearance, your walk, your words or your surroundings. Dust off those knick-knacks you haven't found time to look at lately, and while you are at it, dust off some of your out-moded ideas.

Negative You may become sceptical and aloof from your friends because of this need to be alone. Don't let confusion over the issues suppress your naturally exuberant self.

PERSONAL MONTH 8

This is a power month for you, a time to take a good look at your money situation. Have you done your homework about how you can make money so that you can collect on your knowledge and your expertise? Is your energy directed toward gathering in your rewards? 8 also symbolizes glory which could be the opening or re-opening of your third eye. The third eye is the director of energy; it is the inner vision—practice the power of visualization to assist the opening. This month will also bring rewards both emotional and material: think big, organize yourself toward the goals you wish to accomplish, aim your sights high and reap your rewards.

Negative Money and power could slip through your fingers if you scatter your energy this month. Try not to become impatient or unjust.

PERSONAL MONTH 9

A wonderful month to clean up your debts, clear your desk and finish your projects so that next month you can begin anew. Complete as many cycles as you can or have time for. This is the month to use that wonderful energetic Mars energy to get things done. Be charitable toward others as you bustle about; this is a good time for public appearances and performances, especially those which are involved with the community and any meetings that concern human affairs. It is time to express your love for your partner in realistic ways, with gifts, unusual treats, love and sharing.

Negative You could find yourself just doing for yourself instead of sharing your love. Sometimes impersonal love—just for mankind—and service bring good feelings. Don't neglect your friendships at this time—centre on others instead of yourself.

TAURUS

PERSONAL MONTH 1
Take charge of the direction in which you are moving. **1** always means creativity and being self-determined to take your own pathway. This is not hard for you to do, for you move in a sure way toward your goals, maybe a little slower than some of the other signs, but you get there by persisting and enduring when other signs would have given up. This is the stubbornness of the bull, using **1** as a creative factor to bring more light into your life. Be sure and check your Personal Year and Destiny Number with your Personal Month to see if they are compatible. Sometimes a number **1** month falls on a **2** Personal Year. This would only mean understanding that you can use your creativity to cement relations in business or in your love life. **2** is the patient idealist.

Negative Watch that your creativity does not take on the colour of arrogance or bossiness. You could delude yourself into thinking that you were better than your co-workers or partner.

PERSONAL MONTH 2
Collect information which can further your plans for the future or the present. It's time for rest and study. Small issues that usually would not bother you can be irritating during this period. It might be a good idea to delay any important decisions that have to do with conflict until next month. Peace should be maintained during this sensitive period. This is also a good time to look at your personal relationships, as a new union is possible. Your channels are open during this month, so you are sensitive to others' feelings and their reaction to you. Your friendliness does attract the opposite sex since you make the space so comfortable and beautiful. Check your Destiny Number to see how compatible this month is with **2**.

Negative Because of the peacemaking qualities that this number brings, you are apt to vacillate in your decisions as you want to please everyone. This earthy constancy and devotion to detail may annoy your co-workers or your partner.

PERSONAL MONTH 3

More forward this month with verve and confidence: There is more inspiration and fun in this month than there has been for a while. Don't brew over your mistakes of the past, just move onward—'today is the first day of the rest of your life'. Express your talents in good company, parties and interesting get-togethers where you have a good time and maybe even learn a little. On the job use your dynamic communicating skills in your charming way. See plays that appeal to your love of slapstick and broad humour. Experiment with exotic foods, candlelight and fine wines to excite the palate.

Negative This is not the time to be intolerant of other people's choices. Don't gossip, no matter how juicy the information; you'll hate yourself in the morning. This would be against your true nature.

PERSONAL MONTH 4

This is a good month to get your work in proper order, organize and categorize the different parts of your job. Sometimes you let things pile up, especially if you are a **1, 3,** or **5** Destiny Number, since your ambition is to run ahead of the pack. Structure the different parts of your work, life and emotional involvement. This may require discipline and dependability—you already have this in your Taurean nature—a **4** influence is just an added impetus to getting your act together. You can also manifest what you want this month because you believe in your powers. Your clarity of thought prefers to see what you are getting into, rather than taking a chance.

Negative There is a definite rigidity to **4** that can affect you this month if you are not aware of the exact nature of **4**. You could become so engrossed in your projects that you do not leave space for fun and lose sight of living your life.

PERSONAL MONTH 5

Now you can break out of the shell or stricture that the previous month brought; if you used last month wisely, then you have a plan to work on and can be a little freer in expressing your ideas. This is also a good month for travel, for looking at the adventurous side of life and the interesting things you could be doing now. In business you could use this outgoing vibration to listen to other viewpoints so you could accept that which is useful to your nature. This sensual number attracts the opposite sex, so take pleasure in the sights, sounds and feelings that arise at this time.

Negative The variety that **5** brings to this month could make you restless and inconsistent. This is against your basic nature and could cause you a lot of frustration. Indulge yourself a little but do not over-indulge to the point where your physical self loses too much of your stable energy. Relax and enjoy; you can do this without forgetting your innate poise and elegance.

PERSONAL MONTH 6

Assist your family and friends to find a loving relationship with you and with each other during this month. Your almost unlimited patience can be focused on harmonious vibes with those around you. Your partner needs extra attention now, and perhaps you need extra loving attention too. In business, use the best judgement you have to arrange matters to your liking. You can bring in higher knowledge by finding a quiet time for yourself to balance your energies. Self-realization comes through the love aspect of your ruler, Venus. Love yourself, feel yourself worthy. Evaluate the advice that will be given to you this month and don't be bullish about it. A few minutes' reflection may bring the understanding that those around you love you and are trying to help.

Negative You could be interfering in others' problems. Your anxiety about them could lead you into making careless remarks. Tread lightly in love.

PERSONAL MONTH 7

A good month for your analytical, refined and studious character. All your columns must balance as you total up the year, your life, your friends, etc. No loose ends for you now. Your inner wisdom leads to better understanding of your fellow man or woman as your seeming aloofness melts a little and your graciousness appears. This could fool a lot of people and they might like to take advantage of your great good nature—not knowing that the Venus aspect can give way to the stubbornness of the bull as you stick your heels down to get your own way again. Buy new and exciting clothes and do not be sloppy in your attire—who knows whom you might meet around the corner this month. 7 is the bridge from the known to the unknown, so cross over with care.

Negative This could be a confusing month if you do not get your quiet time. You don't need to be a loner, just be alone once in a while. Friends whom you do not really trust may turn you into a sceptic for a while.

PERSONAL MONTH 8

An excellent money month for you. Your will and determination will carry you far at this time. Rewards of material significance unrelated to money are coming your way during this month, providing you have laid the groundwork in the past. Sooner or later money will come to you and you will be able to handle it very well. Esoterically this is a good month to reopen your third eye and experience the sensual side of your nature—smell the roses, enjoy the beautiful possessions you have accumulated, see good plays, visit art museums and let this aura of Venus take you 'out of this world'. Be prepared for emotional gains in love: a new experience, a new lover or a renewal of an old one.

Negative Money, power and love could slip through your outstretched horns (the bull) if you are not paying attention to this **8** month. It has power, and the bull has a way of getting his own way, although sometimes it *is* by being thoughtful and giving.

PERSONAL MONTH 9

Since you generally have wonderful endurance, this would be a good month to clean your closets, pay your bills and finish at least some of the jobs you started several months ago. This is also a time to express your love for your partner with thoughtful gifts only you can think of. Your practical attitude needs order and cleanliness in your material life style. Also your mental attitude may need a cleansing, perhaps a little more outgoing friendliness when you are in a group. Many people respect and trust you, yet they may be afraid to upset you, so bend a little.

Negative You could be turning inward at a time when friendship is all around you. Watch your inconsiderate or unkind words if your energy level is not up to par. This is not a time to be selfish or unforgiving if your patience has worn thin.

GEMINI

PERSONAL MONTH 1
This is the month to use the Jupiter influence of inspiration to create the kinds of things that you want for the next few months. You can create material objects or new ideas and plans for the future. We all need this impetus to jar us out of our complacent ruts and give us new and exciting jobs, lovers, friends and challenges. Mercury sets you on fire to invent more avenues to bring light and love into your life. The air is electric with impressions and visions, and if you are not aware of this at least be alert to what is going on around you. Always compare your Destiny Number with your birth number to see how the vibrations compare or conflict. When you understand these vibrations it is easier to work within the structure.

Negative It is very easy for you to 'know it all', vigorously pushing your ideas and plans where many times they are not accepted (in spite of your personal charm). Be factual; castles in the air are fine as long as you are solely responsible for them. Arrogance raises its ugly head when you are centring in your ego instead of knowledge.

PERSONAL MONTH 2
Harmony creates new and expansive ideas which in turn create sensitivity to the challenges of everyday life as well as the problems of mankind. A calm exterior invites communication; an essential element in the solving of problems. This month is a time to retreat a little from your dynamic life and regroup your forces, your health and your attitudes. Delay the important decisions until next month as you gather all the facts pertinent to the challenge you face this month or in the months to come. Your Mercury urges you ahead to make decisions right now, and if this is imperative read all the fine print on the contracts. Check your Destiny Number and see how compatible it is with this **2**.

Negative Since **2** concerns relationships, this could mean a split in business or family closeness. A negative approach could supply the wedge for a division of ideas and emotions this month. Wait until next month before taking drastic action.

PERSONAL MONTH 3

Your efforts at communication rise to the occasion this month. Your confidence is restored, your verve for action is rehabilitated and you move forward with trust in your own abilities. This is also a time for fun. As you pick up the rays of others, you can return them with spirit and an outgoing love. Let your light shine. Quickly adjust any disagreements with your charm and ability to communicate; don't let resentments pile up but have faith in yourself and remember to charm people with wit and merit.

Negative Exaggeration is your stock in trade, yet too much too often can turn off the listening powers of others. They will discount your stories by half. The tendency to alibis may enchant the listeners at the time—but you wonder later why their phones are always busy. Charm (but do not hypnotize) others this month.

PERSONAL MONTH 4

Routine does not suit your nature. Organization is easy for you although you do not want to be stuck juggling papers etc. when you can be free-wheeling in your chosen profession. Delegate your authority to others as you supervise them, but do get your act together this month (even if you have to do it yourself). This is the month to get your affairs in order, get people cracking, pit your wits against those in authority to sharpen your facilities. Your emotional involvements may require a little discipline to keep the communication going, but you are good at that, reading other people's minds and getting them to adjust to your way of thinking.

Negative This **4** vibration could bring on a rigid sense of right and wrong—which is strange for a Gemini because of your quick mind and decisions. This could be a good time to get some rest from your hectic days and nights. Read the small print on a contract so arguments will not ensue.

PERSONAL MONTH 5

This is a fun time for travel, lightheartedness, adventure and perhaps a little self-indulgence. Get yourself some affection to carry you through the high vibration that you throw off: you need attention too. This is a period of change, seeing how the other half is living and if you want to try that for a while, it's okay since you will go back to doing your own thing in the months ahead. This sensual number brings love, new friends and perhaps a new job.

Negative This month also brings inconsistency and a tendency to forget old relationships in the search for excitement. Remember to dress your best as this is the month you might be caught with your best intentions down, unshaven or with curlers in your hair; your worst is better than many others' best though.

PERSONAL MONTH 6

The male energy that is inherent in your birth sign, as well as the male power of **6**, will give you the impetus to handle your own affairs, whether in business or those matters concerning family. This is the period of adjustment, learning to balance the way you wish to go, communicating these wishes to the ones concerned and coming to harmonious agreement. Harmony in loving and living relationships is in the air. If you are redoing your home or apartment, look for harmonizing colours and fabrics to complement you. You need affection too. Your spouse or lover also needs extra attention now. Smooth the rough edges of your love relationship and you will find the best of all possible answers to your need for quiet and peace at this time. This self-realization number gives you the energy to encompass your friends and family in harmonious vibrations.

Negative You could be too strong in your resolves and interfere with other peoples' lives. Just provide the space for your family to grow and express their opinions.

PERSONAL MONTH 7

A good month to analyse and solve problems at home and in the business world. Use your abilities and energies to move forward toward your goals and purposes. Your expertise in dealing with people using directness and charm can swerve people from their most stubbornly-held ideas. This number gives you the freedom to experiment on many levels both material and spiritual. In the healing professions you can assist many by healing spiritual gaps and applying your mystical approach. **7** is the bridge from the mundane to the esoteric, from the known to the unknown—although you always seem to know where you are going even if you have to build the bridge to get there.

Negative You could restrict your freedom of thought and movement if you let too many challenges bring chaos into your life.

PERSONAL MONTH 8

This is the month when you can put all that exciting energy into getting what you want. There will be decisions to make that concern money matters, property and material possessions. Watch your impulsiveness as you reorganize your business life. Rewards of money or trophies for work well done will be coming your way this month. Think big, direct your sights high, aim high. Esoterically this is a good time to re-open your third eye and experience seeing auras or to open the channels to clairaudience or clairvoyance. You like to experiment and the force is with you this month. Contact Aries people for exciting love or business adventures this month.

Negative Your power could slip through your fingers if you refuse to study the possibilities of love or business this month. It is hard to keep you still long enough to bring an agreement with others—in unison—you agree, but it takes a little longer for slower-moving minds. Be patient.

PERSONAL MONTH 9

Get it finished this month, whether it is to spring clean, clear out your desk or end that love affair. This month gives you a clean sweep so that you can begin afresh next month with no unfinished projects dragging you back. If you have kept it together you can enjoy success this month. If you have forgotten appointments, ignored those special to you, and turned your energy back on yourself in selfishness, you can expect rebuffs. You will have to charm your way back into their good graces, a feat that is not difficult for you.

Negative You could be unforgiving and want to strike out at the injustices that you have brought on yourself. If you refuse friendship this month you could turn temporarily bitter. Your exuberant nature usually rights itself shortly and you overcome that loss of money or love.

CANCER

PERSONAL MONTH 1

This is a good month to start a new nine-month cycle of endeavour. The **9** month is the ending of the cycle. Anything you begin this month should be self-determined—not guided by someone else's opinion. Do and plan the things that are important to you; this can be a rebirth of ideas you began in the last cycle and did not finish, ideas that just sort of dropped by the wayside, forgotten in the rush of everyday living. See where those plans and resolutions have gone— perhaps you can re-infuse them with your intuitive energy and bring them to life and fruition. This is the time to start something with enthusiasm.

Negative It is easy to withdraw from conflict, for you want to protect your interests and when they are threatened you gather them to yourself, taking them into the cave of security where no one can attack. You could also turn to your other mood and become belligerent about your possessions, material or otherwise. When asked why you have decided to make no decisions or why you wish to retire from the human race, you sidestep the issue—much like the crab who walks sideways so much it seems to be backing up!

PERSONAL MONTH 2

This is a month for relationships for you; getting along with people, using all the diplomacy you have to bring solutions to your own and others' problems. Harmony creates the climate for settlement of disputes. Watch the fine print when dealing in contracts, leases and money transactions. When in doubt don't do it; this is not a time to have people rush you into a decision. If they try, your water sign could turn to steam and explode the entire plan. Love and marriage is possible during this month for compatibility and peace reigns on the positive side of the number.

Negative Your relationships could turn sour and breakups could occur as your mood fluctuates from loving attention to your chosen one to crab-like and indirect unpleasantries. We're never sure where a crab is heading, as he goes after the prey indirectly until the moment of decision—then snap goes the trap! Knowing your qualities helps you make up your mind—if you are in the mood.

PERSONAL MONTH 3

Life, liberty and the pursuit of communication is the goal this month. More action and more decisions are possible as you are not looking backward to try to discover your failures. Failures are in the past—the future is here and going forward. Look at past experience as a way of learning and move forward! Though you worry about how this is going to turn out you have more energy for decisions this month. Your reflection in the past month has absorbed the necessary details and the Moon is full of promise. Let it shine on you and give you strength.

Negative You are impatient to get your affairs settled. You could become intolerant of those who are squandering your time and become gruff and unpleasant; then your soft heart yields again to kindness.

PERSONAL MONTH 4

Put yourself, your surroundings, your correspondence and your finances in order this month. **4** brings orderliness to your life. Your emotional attachments may keep you piling your bills and letters in neat piles rather than answering them. Get your affairs in order, give them the attention they deserve—who purchased those extras you really do not need? Your partner? What is your agreement about purchases? This is a manifesting number, meaning that you can bring into your life the vibrations you really desire. Try reading other people's minds so that you can anticipate their direction and head them off at the pass. Remember to be loyal where loyalty is paramount.

Negative You might become a little tight with your money when expenditures for sale items would be the safe and sane thing to do. Watch for rigidity of purpose and ideals. Be a little flexible.

PERSONAL MONTH 5

This is a good month for you to take a holiday from your intense application to duty, family or business. Go camping with your family or take them where they can enjoy a different environment and experience relationships with a variety of new exciting adventures. This is a period of change, seeing how the other half lives. You might move to another locale during this period, or even change jobs. A little self-indulgence won't hurt now; care for yourself, love a lot and enjoy the sensual part of your sensitive nature. Have fun. New clothes and new friends lighten our spirit; this can be an adventure, seeking the colours which give us pleasure. Friends are stimulating and are stimulated in turn by your keen observtions.

Negative You might feel like you want to cast off your old friends because these new ones are so interesting—so watch out; next month you might want to see them again. Inconsistency leads to carelessness and loss of friends.

PERSONAL MONTH 6

Harmony might be considered the suppression of emotions to gain the greatest good for the largest number, but one truth emerges in the final analysis when the facts are in—whatever is, is, and cannot be suppressed for infinity. **6** symbolizes harmony, sometimes a desire for peace at any price. Then we may find that we have created a monster which discharges a spate of misunderstandings when pushed too far. **6**s need balance in their understanding of others as well as themselves. This month seek harmony through truth and self-realization—what do I really want—what am I really doing to reach my goals? Get your emotional needs taken care of this month, or you may wind up feeling neglected—which in turn produces other misunderstandings. This is a time for friends and family, caring and sharing.

Negative You may become anxious to solve a lot of family problems and interfere where you are not wanted.

PERSONAL MONTH 7
This is the month where you can dissect your challenges and problems and find solutions. **7** is ready to sit down and tap his own wisdom by analysing the emotions of whoever is engaged in the problem. This can concern money, business, family or whatever area interests you now. Study the reasons so that you can put your supersensitiveness and ESP to the test. In the healing professions you can apply your awareness by healing the spiritual gaps of others by your mystical approach.

Negative You may not want to become involved in other people's problems unless they relate to you in some way. You could become confused with the issues and be hurt in the process by the brusque manners of others. Remaining aloof does not necessarily solve anything.

PERSONAL MONTH 8
Money is important to you, and this is the time to get serious about making it and keeping it or keeping it in circulation to make more money. The harder you work and plan, the more you can accumulate. If you prefer trading, and you are really good at judging the value of an article and how far you can discount that value while inflating yours, this too is possible as you are switched on this month. Power, glory and fame (sometimes even money) are the rewards of work well done. This will bring you a surge of psychic energy, a validation of your own worth—then you go out and work harder than ever. Look for love, too, in this primal-energy-charged month. Soar with your imagination as you open the channels to reopen your third eye.

Negative This power could slip through your sensitive hands if you are not aware of the energy. Usually you are responsive to the mental connections which suggest to you what is really going on. Take any negative viewpoints that are thrown at you and turn them into positive ones.

PERSONAL MONTH 9

Thoughtfulness, love of your friends, concern for mankind are paramount this month. You want the world to stop this violence and can get on with its natural growth of love and caring. You can't handle it all by yourself, so enlist the aid of an **8** or **22** to stand by your side. **9** is the time to finish projects, clean up your act, your prejudices and your attitudes. The attic of your mind gets a little dusty around the edges with neglect. Love and the world loves with you, complain and the world says 'who cares?'.

Negative Your inner self can see the injustices toward yourself, and you want to either dig a hole and jump in it to hide, or you will want everyone to see how you have been mistreated, crying 'Oh, poor me!' and 'No one loves me!' Either way you would wind up alone and really unloved.

LEO

PERSONAL MONTH 1

A new nine-month cycle of endeavour always starts with the number **1** month (the **9** month is the ending of this cycle). This month you listen to your own counsel, your own desires to succeed. This is the month to start something depending on your Destiny Number. Use the interpretation of your Destiny Number to go alone with any and all of the Personal Month interpretations in order to get a better view of where you are and what to do about it. This month could also bring about a rebirth of ideas you had in the last nine-month cycle that you dropped for one reason or another. It is easy for you to be enthusistic and optimistic about your goals. Be a little more specific instead of generalizing and you will be able to pinpoint the direction in which you are supposed to run.

Negative Indecision could detract from your natural disposition to move ahead. Also, fabricating the truth in order to push your plans forward could get you into trouble. The lowest vibration this month is a tyrannical approach to those under your command.

PERSONAL MONTH 2

This is a good month for you to create the climate of calmness for the settlement of disputes. Use your charm and sexual prowess to accomplish your ideals. Sexual does not mean 'sex' in the usual connotation—it means the leonine qualities, the way to attract people and what you want this month. Dress well, expect to meet important people who will further your career, and don't be caught with your underskirt or shirt-tails showing. It would be a good idea to watch all the fine print in every contract, lease, or any money transaction during this time. Do not let this important perusal of detail be left to your employees or friends. See to it yorself that you look over every paper. There is a peaceful aura that reigns over this month and helps make relationships better. A good month for marrige and love. Curb your tendency to force love from another—use flowers, epicurean meals and loving attention to attain your desires.

Negative This **2** month can bring feelings of extreme sensitivity about yourself. There is a little inner voice that questions your ability if your goals are slow in coming. Next month may bring the fruition of these goals if you have smoothed your way this month.

PERSONAL MONTH 3
Now you can forge ahead in a straight line toward your goals. Last month was sort of withdrawal from the fray, now you see the light at the end of the tunnel. Inspirations come faster and are more easily put into operation with a **3** vibration. Communicate your desires to others. Tell them your goals for the business or for your family. The future is here, looking bright; the past experiences have just fitted you for this month and it's time to move foward!

Negative Your inner self, that voice of little courge, may say, 'Things do not look good. The media says,' and so on. This is the time to use your kingship and lead people out of the darkness of doubt much as Alfred Hitchcock leads his readers through the intricacies of mystery stories.

PERSONAL MONTH 4
Since you are determined to succeed, this is one of the best months to put your affairs in order. A lot of details may come up during a **4** month which require close attention. Work toward your projected goals so that you will have time to play a little next month. Concentration is needed. Give attention to your co-workers so they do not detract from your persistence toward your constructive goals. This is also a month which encourages you to manifest what you want to bring into your life. You can't always order the universe to give you money, power, etc., to which you are entitled, so

ask. This is not entirely in your nature, for you prefer to go after what you want.

Negative You could get very pushy trying to climb that ladder of success and step on others as you reach for the top. There is jealousy and violence in this number on the very lowest vibration, so keep your temper in check and give your co-workers a purr instead of a growl.

PERSONAL MONTH 5
Look at what you are doing and see if this is the time for expansion. Any kind of adventure, travel to strange places, change of scenery or change of lovers can bring you some exciting experiences. If you have been planning to expand your business or your family, a **5** month is the proper time to start. It is not a good time for beginning a business, just for enlarging the one you have already started. This is a period of change, seeing how the other half lives. You might even think about moving to another city or state. Indulge yourself as you can. Preen a little, dress well and expect stimulating company; lighten up—you can be the star this month.

Negative You might find your new friends so interesting you'll cast off the old ones. Or you might go to the other way and resist change because everything is working so well for you. Okay. Just don't become rigid in your habits. Remain flexible.

PERSONAL MONTH 6
With your tawny mane thrown back, your engaging smile and hearty handshake, you can charm the hind legs off a donkey. Your warmth, roaring good humour and confidence bring a good feeling to any gathering. You are usually the star, one way or another, but in this number you will be working for the harmony of the group. You'll bring harmony and peace to diplomatic circles or family squabbles if you have to fight

to do it. In this number your family comes first. They would be smart to recognize this power in you and humour some of your erratic moods. Since you want to be first in all things, you feel that you can make your own rules, then you want your family or business associates to live up to them. A lot of teachers and politicians are Leos because Leo is good at rationalizing plans, authorities, laws and decisions. Since you are so able, it is hard not to be autocratic. You really take care of others although you sometimes complain about carrying everyone's load—don't kid yourself—you enjoy it!

Negative You may be interfering where you are not asked, not letting other people make their own mistakes. You disdain help, why not let others refuse it also?

PERSONAL MONTH 7

This is a good month to look back at your successes so you can gain from these experiences. We didn't mention failures as Leos seldom fail in their endeavours. That would be a loss of ego, and how can you lose that when you are the king? You accumulate money, goods and ideas, so pass this to others, sharing your largesse freely, for you know (in this perfect occult number) that the more you give the more you receive. Leos are fun people. You can also use this month for healing purposes by the **7** mystical approach.

Negative You could become sceptical of others' expertise and use humiliation to cut them down to size.

PERSONAL MONTH 8

This power month is loaded with get-rich ambitions and money-making opportunities. All you need is your energetic outlook and commanding bearing to show others how to invest their time, money and vitality to reach whatever goals they have set for themselves. You are very effective in groups or lecturing as you can put forth the ideas in a clear lucid manner, with a little drama thrown in for colour. Power, glory and fame (even money) are the rewards of well-presented and accomplished work. This will bring you a surge of psychic energy, a validation of your own worth, which, as you are a Leo, most people do not think you need; they do not know that underneath you may need all the courage you can muster to get up on the platform and deliver.

Negative You could hover over your employees or your family, not giving them the opportunity to work out their own way of getting the job done. Your ego is hurt if you do not get compliments or rewards of some kind when your work is successful.

PERSONAL MONTH 9

This is the month to ease restrictions on yourself and others in order to achieve the pinnacle you set eight months ago. Finish your most important projects, and if this is not feasible, at least take a good look at what you are doing that is preventing their completion. This is a time for brotherly love, understanding your employer and employees. Take a little time to investigate their motives. There is compassion for children, romantic episodes for couples and humane pursuits for those who pay attention to this **9** influence.

Negative You could become selfish and want to keep all the rewards for yourself, even if you haven't earned them—later your innate honesty would come back to haunt you. Avoid being unkind to people who do not have your ability to charm. Saving money is fine, just be sure that you do not tighten the reins so much you become stingy.

VIRGO

PERSONAL MONTH 1
A new nine-month cycle of endeavour always starts with the number **1** month (the **9** month is the ending of this cycle). This month you listen to your own counsel, your own desires to succeed. This is the month to start something depending on your Destiny Number. Use the interpretation of your Destiny Number to go along with any and all of the Personal Month interpretations in order to get a better view of where you are and what to do about it. This month could also bring about a rebirth of ideas you had in the last nine-month cycle that you dropped for one reason or another; your creative power must have a logical foundation. Abstract reasoning can set your nerves twanging; but if you are given a problem to unravel where you can use deductive reasoning, you can take away the unnecessary obstacles and decipher the pros and cons with ease. In other words, you need a plan or blueprint to follow, or change to trigger your creative responses.

Negative Perfection is a great goal unless you try to put pressure on those around you to perform without error. This could turn into a form of tyranny. Also, arrogance rears its ugly head if you feel invalidated.

PERSONAL MONTH 2
This is a good month for you as it increases your patience with your work day world. **2** months can give you some relief from the nervous strain you labour under, if you will just withdraw a little and stop trying to run everything perfectly. Let a little dust collect while you read an uplifting book. This is not inherent in your nature, yet you can school yourself to believe that there are priorities and a good book could be the thing that will give you the most pleasure while you learn about life on the other side of the coin. Sometimes we get ourselves bogged down in our own 'perfection' and expect

others to follow all the rules rigidly. This is a good month for personal relationships, for lovers and spouses. There is a peaceful aura that pervades over marriage if love is not forced.

Negative You can become impatient with your partner because he/she throws papers and clothes around until the house is a mess! Again, where are your priorities? Keeping your family running smoothly without undue criticism or keeping the house (and business areas) neat for guests? Where is the importance?

PERSONAL MONTH 3
Now you are freer to advance your plans and goals. You are the born scientist, investigating the how, where and when of the mysteries of life and knowledge. Don't be afraid to carry some of your experiments forward this month. Communicate your desires to your co-workers so that there is a bridge of understanding between you and them. Your inner self tells you that you are a very special person and you are; so are many other people. We all have special qualities, and this is the month to bring them to the fore.

Negative You could be indecisive about moving your plans ahead, or planning that fabulous trip. You also could be thinking, 'How will this affect me?' and be more concerned about your ego than the results that could be made if you were unafraid to forge ahead with your plans. Don't delude yourself or you could become covertly hostile this month—especially if you stop yourself from achieving your goals.

PERSONAL MONTH 4
This is the month to establish yourself on a firm base for future growth and stability. Organize your work, your employees or even your boss. You have never been backward about correcting his mistakes, although you do it with tact so subtly that he feels good about himself. Continue to watch

your 'timing' when you are faced with a decision. All of your affairs, whether about home, business, or love, need scrutiny to avoid loss of co-operation between the parties involved. This is a busy month requiring many uses of your good judgement. With all this effort it would be a good time to get enough rest and watch your nutrition. The wonderful thing about a **4** month is that you can manifest what you want if the groundwork has been laid in the preceding months.

Negative You could lose your cool, get angry and upset because things are not going your way. Take a couple of days off to get yourself together and back in the pattern you have set for yourself. You operate best with a cool head and warm hands.

PERSONAL MONTH 5
If you have done a good job of getting your act together last month now you can expand. Buy that beautiful dress or classy shirt and preen yourself a little, because this is the time for adventure. Get out and meet some interesting people. We know that you are shy and would rather observe the actions of others but how about just trying to make the first move! Say hello, ask about the most exciting thing that happened this week. You might be surprised at the answers! You are such a good listener you only need to prime the pump with a question or two and most people will think that you are the most wonderful conversationalist in the world.

Negative You could go overboard and spend too much of yourself or your money. Or you could resist change violently, not coming out of your shell.

PERSONAL MONTH 6
Pay attention to your family this month; closeness with them is desirable without criticism. Use love and give of your inner unselfishness to promote harmony. This is not the time to get upset over small details; they may not seem small to you, but

they may seem petty to someone else. Strike the harmonious note in order to get along with co-workers. You have excellent judgement in these matters and you could bring justice and balance to your personal relationships by using your courteous ways to charm your co-workers or your family. Do not force issues this month, ask for guidance as this is a personal time. Give assistance to those who ask and nurture your relationships; people depend on your seeming tranquillity more than you think.

Negative Your nurturing could turn into meddling where you do not belong. Your sense of fair play usually keeps you out of hot water unless you just *have* to set someone right! Let others make their own mistakes as long as it does not affect your space or your purse.

PERSONAL MONTH 7
How about taking a look at where you hae been for the last six months and see if your goals are on the way to being realized? You are so good at doing the mundane chores that you might be turning your world upside down and mirroring others' goals instead of your own. Your solution is to go around, under, or over the obstacles that are in your way. There is promise ahead for next month since your analytical mind can index your desires, pigeonhole those unusable this month and act on those desires that are immediate—thus smoothing the road to a successful next month.

Negative You could be creating chaos instead of calm. Do not become suppressive or malicious of others.

PERSONAL MONTH 8
All you need to do to make money this month is stay with the careful accounting, to which you are accustomed. Watch the pennies and the pounds will grow. Your careful judgement on investments could move you further towards your financial goals. As an employee you can work without supervision and

your boss no doubt knows your value; speaking up won't hurt! This is the month to ask for a raise. As an employer, carefully select those you wish to promote. Power, fame and glory (even money) are the rewards of well-presented and accomplished work. This will bring you a surge of psychic energy, a validation of your own worth, which you need from time to time.

Negative You could be more demanding of your co-workers than they are able to produce. We have so many experiences in our lives which tend to shape our feelings toward certain circumstances. Catering to the whims of your co-workers is not the solution, though some investigation could increase their productivity.

PERSONAL MONTH 9
This is the time to finish your projects, especially those you began in your **1** month—those of short duration. Take a look at what you are doing that is preventing you from completing certain goals. Clean out the closets in your house or your mind and get a clean start next month on some new and interesting enterprise. **9** also means brotherly love, understanding the problems of your family and those with whom you come into contact. There is compassion for children, romantic episodes for couples and humane pursuits for those who pay attention to this **9** influence.

Negative Avoid being unkind to people who do not have your ability to charm. Use compassion to understand what is really going on. Becoming bitter about injustices will only send you farther down the emotional scale.

LIBRA

PERSONAL MONTH 1
A new nine-month cycle of endeavour always starts with the number **1** month. The **9** month is the ending of a cycle. This month you listen to your own counsel, your own desires to succeed. This is the month to start something depending on your Destiny Number. Use the interpretations of our Destiny Number to go along with any and all of the Personal Month interpretations in order to get a better view of where you are and what to do about it. This month could also bring about a rebirth of ideas you had in the last nine-month cycle that you dropped for one reason or another. Your creative power stems from your innate sense of justice and fairness. You can reason in the abstract sense and philosophical manner to arrive at your conclusions. Create your own plans that you want to carry forward and complete in the next nine months. Plan carefully, then put your plans into action. Avoid decisions that depend on emotions. Be factual.

Negative Indecision could restrain you from reaching your goals. Arrogance can deprive you from accepting others' viewpoints.

PERSONAL MONTH 2
This is a good month for personal relationships; show your love and your good nature to the public as well. They usually like to see your smile or grin as you bring sunshine into their lives. This is not the month to start a business, a love affair, etc. That was last month and the coming month. This is the month to grow within a love that you already have; let it ripen. Confront situations that need to be aired and talked over. This is the month for compromise if patience is used with a lavish ladle. Use your intuition to avoid mistakes in judgement. Co-operation with your boss or your employees or co-workers is needed for your advancement in your chosen profession this month.

Negative You could lose your patience since you love a good argument; not listening to yourself and what you may say that will hurt another person. If your opponent begins to agree with you, you are apt to change sides and argue for a while there. This is confusing to people and will not bring about compromise.

PERSONAL MONTH 3

Now you can go ahead with your plans and bring success to your ventures. Relax a little and stop arguing abut trivia. You can also indulge yourself a little, take a vacation, have some fun, spread humour and goodwill wherever you can. You are a good host and entertain your guests with stories, music or whatever is your special talent! This is a strong month combining the creativity of **1** with the diplomacy of **2** to fulfil your dreams of success (**3**). Get out into the country to explore nature, growing things, and the fragrance of clean air (if you can find it). You need to experience the beauty of our planet in the flowers and grasses, hills and valleys, deserts and lakes.

Negative Your uncertainty disturbs your contentment if your scales get tipped too much.

PERSONAL MONTH 4

If last month was playtime for you, then you are prepared to get back to the old mill and grind away at your regular duties. **4** is usually called the work number; however, if you like to be involved in your profession, your school or your retirement, then that *is* play for you and **4** holds no restrictive bonds. **4** is also the manifesting number, getting what you want, visualizing it happening and making it appear. You can make it appear faster if you have laid the groundwork in the **1** and **2** personal months. Establishing yourself on a firm base for future growth with your lover or spouse and your workday world even if you have to give a little.

Negative You could express the firm side of your personality to the extent of seeming to be rigid in your opinions. You like to argue and will take the opposite side of any argument; just don't try to suppress others' opinions—they might fight back.

PERSONAL MONTH 5

Your adventurous soul goes soaring this month, giving you the changing patterns that you like, although they seem to be hard to handle. There are so many choices presented that it will be difficult for you to decide which is the better one to take. More than four choices over one challenge could make you struggle for air. Get some time alone and away from the crowd so your decisions about the opposite sex can be made wisely. Remember you like cleanliness, beauty and order in your life.

Negative You could get very confused over the exciting things that are happening too fast if they imply disharmony. Instead of the creative mental level of 5 you could become sloppy and withdraw into sleep or indulge yourself in whatever turns you on. Don't be afraid of change—it brings fresh air.

PERSONAL MONTH 6

This is family month, time to pay attention to your spouse or lover, your children (if any) and your brothers and sisters. Use love to promote the harmony you came here to express as a 6. This is the most harmonious number for you as it is the nurturer, the cosmic mother, the one who takes care of people and things. Venus (ruler of your sign) can assist you, through love, to open the doorway to higher mind through harmony and harmonizing your relationships with others. This is not a time to be careless in your work or profession; take meticulous care with details of documents; read the fine print of anything that you have to sign. Do not force issues; ask for guidance as this is a personal time for you. People rely on seeing your charming smile and your radiant personality.

Negative You could become finicky as your temperament vacillates between being anxious about the outcome of your adventures and the calm, all-knowing part of you that knows everything will be all right. Don't interfere this month in places and spaces where you do not belong. Advice is seldom welcome and those who think they want it, want it least of all.

PERSONAL MONTH 7

'Of science and logic he chatters, as fine and as fast as he can; though I am no judge of such matters, I'm sure he's a talented man' (Winthrop Praed: *The Talented Man*). And we are sure that a **7** month holds much talent for logical deductions, using the magic you have to enchant and disarm the unwary—and even the wary. Take a look at your successes and your mistakes of the past six months so you can bridge the gulf of indecision. By looking back, you can look forward to plan the next move in your chess game of business of love, for next month is one of power for you. Be prepared for a good, prosperous month ahead.

Negative You could become sceptical of your talents and withdraw into a sulk if things do not go your way.

PERSONAL MONTH 8

Take care of matters pertaining to material growth, money, possessions, business and finance this month. Now you can reap some of the rewards due from your careful decisions of the previous month. Exercise your charm and ability to weigh in the balance the steps you must take to further your career. You have a good sense of values, knowing what to buy or sell after you have taken the time to ponder the action quietly with no interruptions. If disturbed, you have to start all over again to get your wheels turning.

Negative There is a facet to your nature that most people do not understand. You cannot be pushed into making a decision if you feel that time is needed. You are not usually intolerant but your impatience will loom large on the horizon if there is friction in the ranks of your co-workers. You could lose money and prestige this month if you make hasty decisions.

PERSONAL MONTH 9

Time for romance! Be aware of the opposite sex (as you usually are anyway) for some exciting, albeit brief, episodes may happen this month. **9** is always brotherly love, also taking care of those less fortunate than you. Sometimes just using your smile will change things in the office, for people cannot help reacting to a Venus child with love. Finish as many projects as you can during a **9** month. This number is the tearing down and the terminating of jobs left undone in order to make room for the new and exciting territory still unexplored.

Negative Avoid being unkind to people, animals and inanimate objects. If you play the selfish game you could reap scorn instead of success. Ranting about injustices gets you a good soap box lead, but unless you *do* something about it you are only left with a box to burn. When your scales are unablanced you slide into dissipation, abusing your body through overindulgence. The bitterness you feel will change to sweetness when your scales come back into balance through diet, change of environment or change of attitude.

SCORPIO

PERSONAL MONTH 1

A new nine-month cycle of endeavour always starts with the number **1** month (the **9** month is the ending of this cycle). This month you listen to your own counsel, your own desires to succeed. This is the month to start something, depending on your Destiny Number. Use the interpretation of your Destiny Number to go along with any and all of the Personal Month interpretations in order to get a better view of where you are and what to do about it. This month could bring a rebirth of ideas you acquired in the last nine-month cycle which you dropped for one reason or another. There is a restless energy at work, since your creative ideas are coming in quicker than you can put them into operation. You want results *now*. Remember that it takes a little linear time to get things activated and moving. Plant the seeds this month, begin your new ventures but don't rush your co-workers into making rash mistakes. Let your Pluto energy reactivate and resurrect those important goals in your life; generate energy by talking about them.

Negative You could go the other way by becoming indecisive or hostile to others who are moving ahead.

PERSONAL MONTH 2

Watch your personal relationships this month; they could bring rich rewards to you. Tone down your Mars energy for a few days and see what happens as you observe the actions of others, particularly the opposite sex. Is your boss feeling wild and woolly this month? Don't cross him. If he is another Scorpio he could erupt. If you feel like blowing your top at your boss, wait until you get home and throw rocks at a tree or into the lake to spend your frustrations. Adjust situations that you feel you can handle with calm assurance of your ability to keep the peace.

Negative You could lose the battle if you lose your temper and want to argue about who is right. What you say could hurt another person, and to apologize later is going against your nature. This is not the month to tease others; they could turn on you.

PERSONAL MONTH 3
Holiday time again! Relax a little and have some fun. Spread humour and goodwill wherever you can. You can also indulge yourself a little, entertain your guests with stories as only you can tell them. If you can balance your physical, emotional and mental energies this month you can realize some of your plans which began in your **1** Personal Month. This is a powerful month to move toward your goals. So you have a choice, either take a vacation or put your energies into action to advance towards the goals you have set yourself.

Negative If you scatter your energies in all directions you will not be able to accomplish much this month. Keep your eye on the ball, say what is on your mind (you usually do anyway), because keeping your feelings repressed will only make them explode violently later on. This is a good month to gossip if you *really* want to get into trouble!

PERSONAL MONTH 4
It is within your nature to be orderly; you insist on your tools being put back where they belong. You are not averse to letting someone use the tools of your trade, just *put them back!* This applies to all manner of trades and possessions. Your organized mind wants to reach out for information that *should* be in its proper place. **4** is also a manifesting month for getting what you want. Visualize it and make it appear. You can make it appear faster if you have laid the groundwork in your **1** and **2** months. Try not to be suppressive to your associates; they may be working on a **5** month and want to express their wild ideas for expansion. Maybe there is a kernel of truth in their rantings.

Negative You could become very rigid in your opinions and insist on being right. This inflexibility (without cause) could lessen your chances of success. The arguments you propose could set the pattern for the future decisions that you might want to *change* in the future. Look carefully at the facts before making statements.

PERSONAL MONTH 5

Now is the time for change of plans or expansion of your business or a vacation from past labours. If you have to stick to your vocation, look carefully at the future prospects when taking on new products, or changing your plan of attack. This is not a good month to start a new business or affair. It is a good time to extend your interests, or explore hidden factors, or to experience others' viewpoints. This does not mean that you have to take their advice—you are your own best adviser —just look and listen a little.

Negative There are self-indulgent influences in this month which could make you overdo it. You are a robust, healthy individual, and disease has a hard time staying with you as you are a fighter. Since 5 is the symbol for over-indulgence, just take a look at what you are doing to your physical body.

PERSONAL MONTH 6

This is a two-faced month for it concerns family. You are good to your children and your partner, yet you expect obedience without question. It can be a wonderfully rewarding month if you see that those around you also need to speak their minds while you listen to their points of view. If you continue to be an authority on everything, you will clash with those you love. Your tendency to remember even the slightest deviation from your directions could cause friction. Your water sign could help you flow through these 6 months if you remember to go with the flow. Take time to be extra careful in profession or business. Read all the fine print in any documents that you are responsible for. Do not force issues, but sit back and *think!*

Negative Your usually calm exterior could be bubbling inside with unuttered comments regarding the behaviour of family and associates. Seek the facts. You could be wrong, and you do hate to be wrong. Don't interfere in spaces and places where your authority will be questioned. This will only bring on more problems that you do not need.

PERSONAL MONTH 7
'People will never look forward to posterity who never look backward to their ancestors' (Edmund Burke: *Observations on a Publication*). This is a month to look back on successes and mistakes so that you can build on the former and not repeat the latter. You have a great talent for investigating the mysteries of the past, whether they be involvements in business, family or the occult. You might even take a close look at your dreams during this month to see if there are messages for you.

Negative You could set yourself apart and become the sceptic of all things. A *little* scepticism is all right though.

PERSONAL MONTH 8
This is the month to move into power. Not that you haven't always had the upper hand; this is just *the* time to move. Material growth, money, possessions and financial matters are first on your agenda now. You have a talent for making and holding onto money because you always know where your investments are going. Use that magnetic power to discover the secrets of your rival companies who are bidding for the account or job that you desire.

Negative You could turn to scheming to get your own way, which is not really in your nature. Ordinarily you just know the way to accomplish your desires. Don't get too impatient at delays, you can make the job appear if you do not lose your temper and become abusive with language.

PERSONAL MONTH 9
Ah! Romance is in the air! 'Isn't it always?' says Scorpio. This

could be the time for brief affairs or the ending of one that has been going on for a long time. Well, there are other fish in the sea. Finish those cycles of work that have been put aside for a later date. Now is the time to complete those tasks—better still, just talk someone into completing them for you, as you so ably can when you fix those magnetic eyes on the person you have selected.

Negative You could carry a grudge against someone and this month exercise the option to get even with them. This works for you, but only temporarily, as it backfires at some time in your life. If you play the revenge game you could reap scorn instead of success. You act as though this does not bother you, and yet too much revenge leaves you with no friends. Be considerate and moral rather than bitter and immoral.

SAGITTARIUS

PERSONAL MONTH 1
This is the month to use the Jupiter influence of inspiration to create the kinds of things that you want for the next few months. You can create material objects or new ideas and plans for the future. We all need this impetus to jar us out of our complacent ruts and give us new and exciting jobs, lovers, friends and challenges. Your fire sign helps motivate you to new endeavours and shoot your arrow straight for the stars. The air is alive with visions as well as music. Be aware of what is going on around you. Always compare your Destiny Number with your Birth Number to see how the vibrations compare or conflict. When you understand these vibrations, it is easier to work within the structure.

Negative It is very easy for you to express your knowledge, your plans and your dreams to others. Overwhelming others with creative ideas could turn them off, instead of seeing the enthusiastic person you really are, they might see a braggart. Indecisiveness, bossiness and ill-will this month could cause a lot of trouble in the office.

PERSONAL MONTH 2
Time to go dancing and relax from the workday world. You get tied into doing things for others and need a few favours yourself. It takes a lot of patience to handle family and business plus the hobbies you so enjoy. Friends are always interrupting you, for they know you care about them. Some-times you just want to be yourself. This sensitivity to your friends and family gives your love somewhere to go for they need you. If they did not need you, you would feel like you had been cheated. This month may include some emotional problems that have to be settled. Don't get too sensitive about yourself. Next month will be a lot better for you.

Negative Just keep your cool and become the peacemaker; be the one who brings the warring factions together and provides the calm atmosphere for compromises. Move in perfect rhythm to the sounds of peace.

PERSONAL MONTH 3

Now you can go forward, and if you weren't unkind to people last month you can realize some of your dreams. Communicate, don't let others withdraw from you; find out what makes people tick. You have the ability to get to the bottom of any dispute with your friendly outgoing love. This is the month to entertain. Jupiter is right with you. Use your charm and trust in your own abilities. This is also a good month to display your talents, to be seen and heard. It is easy for you to learn since you work from inspiration and intuition.

Negative Exaggeration and gossip are the *bêtes noires* of the month. The temptation is there to be intolerant of others. Watch your pennies and don't waste your money, time or talents.

PERSONAL NUMBER 4

This is the Destiny Number that gives you the impetus to be orderly, filing your papers correctly, putting all your spices and tins of food in their proper storage places and generally keeping your surroundings looking good. Orderliness is something you have grown into slowly because there are so many interesting things to delve into that there is little time to categorize them all. Housewives (and husbands) begin to organize their work when they abandon temporary living quarters and move into their own home. Why fix up someone else's house? You will just have to move sooner or later and leave that repaired ceiling, those painted cupboards. This attitude holds true with your job or profession. When you make it your responsibility, you become organized. Remain loyal to your commitments this month. Stay with your job or your family until all the facts relating to the disagreement are in. Duty will overrule the need to find a more comfortable space.

Negative You could become violently angry if someone questions your loyalty. You could also become rigid in your opinions to the exclusion of facts.

PERSONAL MONTH 5

This period of change is right up your street. You like adventure and new happenings. Of all the signs, you and Gemini like to juggle a few balls in the air at one time. This can be a fun month of travel. We travel on boats, planes and trains and also in our minds to many different spaces and times. Here is the essence of life and living. This is creative mind on the mental level, seeking new avenues of discovery, playing with ideas of invention and using imagination to promote concepts that improve your product. Take time out to let your visualization come through. A little imagination with your spouse or lover could bring interesting results.

Negative You could become sloppy in your dress, in your speech and with your friends. Inconsistency could lend to self-indulgence in food and drink.

PERSONAL MONTH 6

This is the month to exercise good judgement in all your affairs, business and love. It is also a month for attention to family, giving love and understanding to your spouse and children (if you have any). Communicate your wishes and listen to theirs so you can come to an agreement about important matters. Many things can be done that concern harmony, like redecorating your home or redesigning your wardrobe. Listen to yourself when you speak, and see if you are really using the word patterns you desire; are you using love or are you just talking to keep the air filled with words? You need human contact, especially this month. Cuddle up to your family if they will let you and bring harmonious relations closer. Get satisfaction by being loving or indulging in your favourite hobbies.

Negative You could be interfering in private business of your family where you are not wanted. We love our partners and children and even have concern about our business relationships and do not want to see anyone hurt by wrong decisions. However, it is the prerogative of each of us to make our own mistakes.

PERSONAL MONTH 7

Use your inner wisdom to see the problems that face you then use your outgoing friendliness to bridge the gap between misunderstandings and solutions. You always seek the truth, and in seeking you will be moving towards your goals and purposes. You have nothing to hide but are right there up front. Other people trust you because they see this in you. **7** is always the bridge from the known to the unknown and your direct way of dealing with the things that you want to discover will uncover the knowledge you wish to gain. This number gives you freedom to experiment on many different levels of consciousness and subconsciousness if you keep on the positive side of this number.

Negative You could become confused if you are trying to balance too many problems.

PERSONAL MONTH 8

Your Sagittarian luck works directly and indirectly. For instance, when you aim your arrow towards your goals it flies straight and true. Then again if the vibrations are not right for you the arrow misses the target. However, if you missed the target today perhaps it is because tomorrow is the lucky day for you to get what you want. That letter you were supposed to post is still in your possession and while you are feeling guilty, the stock you were going to buy took a nose dive—saving you thousands. If you just flow with what is happening you will be right there when the money is falling around you this month. It is a good month for a raise, winning something and being successful in your undertakings. On the esoteric side it is a good month to meditate on reopening your third eye. Open your channels to see clearly your spiritual goals.

Negative Your temper is aroused if someone questions your honesty this month. Your blunt approach could make business enemies. You don't really mean to hurt anyone; you just tell them the truth, no matter how hard it is for them to swallow the bitter pills.

PERSONAL MONTH 9
Success and achievement is possible if you have laid a good foundation in the previous eight months. End projects that can be finished. Clean out your files, your drawers and your attitudes so that you can begin afresh next month with some new and exciting adventures. There is also a chance for a little romance this month if you are aware of the vibrations being sent your way. Go out of your way to do something for others; this sympathetic understanding of your friends' problems can provide a way for you to grow in human understanding.

Negative You could become unforgiving if someone slights you. Don't turn this into selfishness or scorn; it would only detract from your outward friendliness.

CAPRICORN

PERSONAL MONTH 1
This is the time of the month to use the Jupiter influence of inspiration to create the kinds of things that you want for the next few months. You can create material objects or new ideas and plans for the future. We all need this impetus to jar us out of our complacent ruts and give us new ideas, lovers, friends and challenges. Your Cardinal energy helps you invent more avenues to bring light and love into your life. The air is electric with impressions and visions. Be alert to what is going on around you. Always compare your Destiny Number with your Birth Number to see how the vibrations compare or conflict. Do this will all your Personal Month numbers.

Negative Lack of confidence in yourself; vacillation between one decision and another; building castles in the air that never materialize; invalidating yourself—all are negative vibrations of **1**. When your ideas are not accepted you feel like you want to run away. Another negative side is the feeling of arrogance, 'knowing it all'.

PERSONAL MONTH 2
This is the month to rest and renew your energies for the month ahead. Your sensitivity to others is at a high pitch and you may react with hostility then regret it later. Delay the important decisions until next month as you gather the facts pertinent to the challenge you face now or in the months to come. If your Cardinal motivation urges you to move ahead, be sure to read all the fine print on the contracts, whether they be for business or love. Make sure that both parties understand the agreements. Make peace, not war, this month; pay attention to the smallest detail and plot your moves. Collect, don't spend. Move in rhythm to the vibrations that are coming your way instead of fighting.

Negative Your subtle humour could turn into mischievousness and thus destroy a relationship with your partner in love or business. Don't play tricks this month but keep your cool.

PERSONAL MONTH 3

Now you can thrust forward, again, after last months withdrawal. Your confidence is restored, your energy level is up and you have the strength of ten. If you prefer to entertain, give yourself the benefit of a social whirl this month—go out and have a good time. **3** always has to do with communication, talking, making yourself understood, entertaining others, performing, receiving applause. In all this social interaction there could be romance or flirtations. You could also make some good business contacts in a casual way.

Negative Your communication could become trivial and superficial to the point of gossip if you are not careful. You could also become careless and waste a lot of this good energy in too many frivolous pursuits. **3** is really a strong number and you can build a more secure future by using the creative factor (**1**) and the diplomatic factor (**2**) which is inherent in **3** (communication).

PERSONAL MONTH 4

Since you like things organized and in their proper places, this month should be a good one for you. The vibrations of orderliness, patience and devotion to duty are with you. It is always easier to flow with the vibration rather than paddle upstream against a strong current. You have a way of hugging the shore (if you have to go against the current) remaining in control and skirting the rocks of harassment. This emotional steadiness is admirable, yet it can do a U-turn and change into ribald humour—especially when you get yourself into strange predicaments.

Negative You could let your earth sign make you a little rigid in your opinions this month. You expect and give loyalty but not everyone is geared toward this principle. Not to worry; you'll either change them subtly or fire them or move away from the situation so that you are not involved.

PERSONAL MONTH 5

Time for some fun, freedom and recreation. This is a good month for travel, visiting strange places and maybe even having a little adventure. This is a period of change, or seeing how the other half is living and whether you want to try it for a while. This sensual number brings love, excitement and new risks. Your Cardinal sign is pushing you to get out there and experience something different. All this travel takes money but you never worry much about that unless you have some miserly signs in other parts of your chart. When you are ready to spend the time and money for what you want you are usually able to scrape it together; money, to you, is only a medium of exchange. Sometimes money doesn't even seem real to you.

Negative This month also brings inconsistency, a tendency to move ahead so rapidly that you forget old relationships. Remember to dress your best at all times during this month as you will be meeting new contacts which may help you in business, and you don't want to be caught unshaven or with curlers in your hair.

PERSONAL MONTH 6

This is the time for balancing and a review of things that make for harmony in the home. Pay attention to your spouse and your children. This is a period of adjustment after the freedom of the previous month. Did you spend too much money on that trip, on clothes or gifts? Now you have to pay for the extravagance. You have a tendency to become over-generous since you prefer quality and it is hard for you to be stingy in your giving. You must have and select the proper gift for the proper time. You also appreciate the subtle nuances of gifts properly selected and offered to you. You need lots of attention at this time. Find some quiet and pursue a peaceful existence this month.

Negative The intense interest you have in family relationships could lead you into interfering where you are not wanted. Nurture, but use good judgement, as you usually do in all the other eight months.

PERSONAL MONTH 7

Time to analyse where you have been and where you are heading. Use your natural ESP and psychic sense to see ahead, using the events which are now shaping your life. You can solve many problems that have been piling up the past few months simply by considering where and how you were successful. Your mental ability is at its highest vibration right now. You can make decisions in business and in personal relationships by using your knowledge of how to do it, then consider some experiments that will affect your plans for the future. If these considerations do not fit your earthy 'I want to know where I am going', analyse some more. The right answer will pop up when least expected.

Negative You usually win if you remain true to your own nature. Don't become too sceptical and aloof from others this month. You may need their input to keep you from being confused.

PERSONAL MONTH 8

You usually get what you want and decide where to put your energies. That takes a little thought for you must now sort out your priorities. This is the month for prosperity—get that job, that advancement, that raise and get withit. It might be more fun to watch the whales from your patio or meditate on top of Ben Nevis, but your practical self says 'Now is the time to get going'. Esoterically this is a good time to reopen your third eye and experience your psychic ability to understand what is happening in the world (as a planet vibration) and in

your personal sphere. You can see the potential of your future
by studying what is taking place now.

Negative Your power could slip through your fingers if you do
not trust your own judgement. The urge to spend unwisely is
the negative vibration of material power this month. Take
control of your plastic money.

PERSONAL MONTH 9
There is love and harmony this month only if you have kept
yourself together and see the potential in Saturn's teaching.
Negative vibrations will set your mind whirling with unresolved plans unless you send out the seeds of positive inspiration and logical planning. Finish your projects; clean out
your drawers; pack away those unused articles; give away
what you can in order to make room for new exciting adventures that are just around the corner. Don't be the butt of
society's admonitions, hammering your horns on the rock of
uncertainty; become the mountain climber who knows where
the crest is and climb, ready to see over the top. Keep your
faith, next month is a **1**, a new start.

Negative You could become bitter over frustrating conflicts.
You do know that you can now manifest what you want.

AQUARIUS

PERSONAL MONTH 1
This is a time for action, a time to seek new, exciting offers which could enhance your position in your profession, relationships with your family. It could also enhance your search for the methods of healing the physical body, mind or spirit. Be sure to check with your Personal Year Number and your Destiny Number vibrations. By putting the two readings together you will become aware of what is happening in your life *now*. Your air sign will assist you to see opportunities ahead for business investiment, new jobs, new hobbies or education. You can create the environment to reach out toward your goals, or you could create new goals. Act on your intuition and take charge of the direction of your search.

Negative You could want everyone else to follow in your footsteps regardless of their wishes. Should you become bossy and arrogant, you will lose the respect of friends and co-workers.

PERSONAL MONTH 2
Small issues may assume inflated proportions this month, so put off your decisions until next month if at all possible. You will need all your patience to handle yourself so that you are not drained of your energies. You could do some of your best diplomatic groundwork (not decision-making) and your need to protect people and your work is uppermost this month. Don't become over-sensitive and rebut opponents with anger. You will lose a lot of ground that way. Collect information that will further your plans. Study those papers, and prepare for exams that are coming up all too soon. Listen to your friends and associates—this is a good time to cement relationships with them and with your close personal tie.

Negative You will be criticized for wanting to be alone—at least part of the time. You can't always be on tap for trifling conversations and deeds but you are right there when important jobs are to be done. Committee work bores you; why not just get on with the job?

PERSONAL MONTH 3

Here is a good month to communicate your ideas and ideals to others. You can inspire people by being 'on stage' with your full personality, telling people that all these impossible things really *are* possible if they will just get out there and do the job. This is a good month for a holiday too. Take time to go fishing, back-packing, hang-gliding or any of the exciting and unusual hobbies you enjoy. Your energy output is so intense your periodically need time to relax. Go forward, don't worry about the past—it is gone. Do not bother about the past except to build on your successes.

Negative You may have become conceited about your accomplishments. If you brag a lot people will soon not invite you to their homes. You can also get caught in exaggerations.

PERSONAL MONTH 4

This is a good month to balance your chequebook, get your finances in order, finish that quilt and asphalt the roof. You notice that I said 'and' for these are jobs that you have put off for the last three months and will now try to get them all done. And you will, for you like doing many things at one time. You can also take stock of your needs for the next year. Where are you going on your holiday? If something else comes up that needs tending to, you can handle that also this month. If you are buying or selling be sure to read the fine print. You trust everyone and you are usually right; however, it is easier to be a little careful than regret it later. This is one of your more stable months, a time to cut and prune the dead wood from your life.

Negative You could be vibrating on your 'Fixed' sign and

brook no intererence with your established routine—whatever that is. At least *you* know what you want to accomplish this month. Don't become too rigid in your opinions; others have a right to theirs too.

PERSONAL MONTH 5

Experiments, extravagance and experiences abound this month. Have fun exploring several directions at once. This is compatible with your energies. You can experience unusual friends, bringing undergraduates home to dinner because they are so interesting. Who knows, they may be studying yoga! Your air sign picks these unusual adventures out of the blue, that is where you reside a great deal of the time anyway. The view from out there is so interesting. You can see the games from a broader perspective while you are out there sitting on your cloud. You could also whip yourself up a million pounds this month if you are in the sales game. Your innovative ideas are in full swing now.

Negative This restless month could create a little chaos for you. Keep yourself well groomed for unexpected visitors.

PERSONAL MONTH 6

Home, family and friends are very important to you now. At some period in your life you will by trying to find your roots, plying your closest relatives with questions about your ancestry. How many kings or pirates? Aquarians have led both these interesting courses whatever previous lives they have experienced. This is a good month to pay attention to your family—have a picnic, make exotic dishes, explain to the children how a butterfly flies, and so on. You have answers for the quixotic questions, that is if you are in the mood. You may give them straight answers, even scientific ones. This is a month for harmony, so don't rock the boat with fanciful ideas or changing the furniture around or changing the routine of the office. You will encounter rebellion if not the deflating of your ideas. However, this never bothers you; you just go someplace else to try them.

Negative This is a month for carelessness and anxiety, if you try to get your family to adhere to your rules. Your rules change from time to time and this could be confusing.

PERSONAL MONTH 7

You could be occupied with humanitarian efforts this month. Your independent nature wants to run the fair, or whatever is going on. Sometimes this works and sometimes it does not, because you cannot turn down an appeal for help. Rather than getting someone else to do it, there you are down on your knees nailing the platform together. This analytical number is right up your street since you like to figure things out. Mostly you have flashes of intuition giving the solution this month. When you are finished with healing others' sore fingers, you turn inside yourself and could spend hours studying Sanskrit or ancient wisdoms.

Negative You prefer to skip and skirt around the edges of serious, studious projects. You can pick the answer out of the air anyway, much to the annoyance of others.

PERSONAL MONTH 8

Your objectivity about money puts you in a good position to acquire it this month. People who grab for money and hold onto it do not have the 'luck' you do because you just know that there is more gold around the corner. You don't necessarily feel you will be 'given' money or prosperity; you are willing to work for it. Contact those in power (your boss, your customers, etc.) for a raise or more sales. The independent part of you knows that you deserve more recognition for your efficient way of managing your job or your profession. Aquarians are usually self-employed or get to the place where they are in command, high on the ladder of success. Esoterically this is a good time for meditation in order to reopen your third eye. You can experience opening the channels to clairaudience or clairvoyance.

Negative Your money or prosperity could slip through your fingers this month if you cannot control the rebel in you. You may want to invest your time and money in chancey ventures this month, and although, in your far-seeing eye, these ventures are okay, they may take a long time to mature. If you want immediate results for your investment of time and energies, take a closer look at what is happening now.

PERSONAL MONTH 9

Your ability to finish your work-cycles and get things cracking and organized is at its peak this month. Clean out your wardrobe, your desk and work a little harder on your attitudes, too. Next month will be a new beginning for you, a fresh start if you can release the things that are holding you back from your full potential. The sea of life is moving out like the tide and you need to let your 'Fixed' ideas go with it. Then inspiration, creativity and knowledge will flood your consciousness in the coming month. Strangely enough, romance is in the air this month also.

Negative Your impulses can run away with you. You may want to wipe out all the past, being uncharitable in your evaluation of others.

PISCES

PERSONAL MONTH 1

This is a time for action, a time to seek new, exciting offers which could enhance your position—in your profession, in your relationships with your spouse, or with your family. Your search for well-being in your physical, mental, or spiritual body is inspired by this number. Be sure to check how this agrees with your Destiny Number and your Personal Year Number. Understanding these three categories will help you understand yourself. Use the water sign to cool down rising tempers at injustices to yourself. Welcome opportunities that come your way; you have the ability to change them to suit yourself. These changes could mean a new job, a change of residence or a change of attitude toward your life. When you get ready to blast ahead nothing can stop you!

Negative You could become bossy and arrogant over your successes or your mistakes, thereby incurring the wrath of your associates. Beware.

PERSONAL MONTH 2

This is the month to take a good look at the friends you have, see where they are headed and if you want to continue the relationship. Sometimes we follow our peer group through inertia. It is just easier not to resist. However, you have an intelligent mind geared to imaginative projects and products. Good relationships can be formed this month if your Destiny Number is compatible. Always look at your Personal Year and your Destiny Number to understand the vibrations of each month. Small issues may assume exaggerated importance so delay any important decisions until next month; you will then be ready to move ahead with your plans that you are now formulating.

Negative Your observation of another's motives may get you down. You may indulge in fantasies about how you are being 'treated'. Then you drop the 'poor me's' and your glum exterior drives people from your presence.

PERSONAL MONTH 3

Good relationships can also be formed this month, but from a different perspective—that of charm: you can charm your way into another's heart. Have a good time this month; relax and let go. This is holiday time for your mind and body. Don't be too concerned about the past or future, you are here *now*. Laughter cures a lot of ills and we all are more serious than we need to be. Communicate good fun to others and it will lift your spirits as well. Listen to what people are really saying; you may be assuming too much by half-listening. On the esoteric side, meditating to bring in knowledge from higher beings is compatible with this number. Experiment and experience.

Negative You could be jumping around from job to job (in your mind) and never settle on any one. Intolerance raises its ugly head as you judge other people for their inconsistency. In your successes you could become conceited and exaggerate your importance.

PERSONAL MONTH 4

When you make up your mind you come up with some splendid ideas. **4**, wherever it occurs in your chart, is the number of organization, getting your act together. This month you will need a lot of patience to sort through the tasks to find the ones which need your immediate attention. Rather than waste your time deciding which of these tasks takes priority, just choose one, do it, and then go to the next. Indecision just builds a higher wall to getting the job done. Most of the fear of decision is the fear of making a mistake because this would destroy your self-image. Other people realize that perfection is hard to come by. Use your practical, intelligent side to build toward the future. All considerations towards your work, hobbies and family must be given careful thought; next month you can move ahead with the choice you have made.

Negative You can become so engrossed with making all the choices that you forget that others around you have wishes also. You can become rigid in your opinions, refusing even to speculate on another way of doing some task. Relax a little.

PERSONAL MONTH 5

Now is your chance to move into situations that you have planned. The force is with you, as they say in *Star Wars*. This is a time of activity; you have remained grounded too long in your present occupation and need a new outlook. You may even see your work from a different perspective. This is a changeable month. You will be meeting new people, looking at new concepts with your vivid imagination. There is also travel. This does not mean that you *have* to travel, just that it is a good month to do it. Maybe it is good for you because your luggage will arrive at the same place and time you do!

Negative You can become very restless, wondering (you wonder a lot) why your act was so together last month and this month things just sort of fell apart.

PERSONAL MONTH 6

This is the month to centre your attentions on love for your spouse, lover and family. This love moves outwards to encompass them; they sense your inner peace. It may take a lot of patience for you to face their shortcomings and listen to their problems, yet you have an inner ear that can hear the underlying cry for help. This is a personal time for you to listen to inner guidance on what to do. What is happening can't be all bad or coming from outside yourself. Perhaps your attitude needs changing. When you are helping others you do not need to take on their burdens; you only need to listen to the real problem and then turn it into an asset with love. Protect those who need your calm assurance. Bring yourself into balance by reaching for love in your meditative period.

Negative You could become so absorbed in other people's problems that you interfere. The caution is to listen—not to advise. Sometimes we want to help so much we turn people off with our offer of assistance.

PERSONAL MONTH 7
You will not be bored this month because there are so many mysteries for you to unravel. There are many authorities on many subjects and the information becomes confusing. Your inner wisdom will lead you to the right choices if you will listen to your inner guidance this month. Being positive or looking on the bright side brings better vibrations than being negative about what is happening around you. This is the time to reflect on things undone, analyse and plan how you can reach your goals. Be ready to move; you can close the gap between wishing for something and actually realizing it.

Negative Your intelligent mind seeks peace and comfort, so you can get confused with all the chaos going on around you. You may want to tear down another's dreams and hopes for a better life.

PERSONAL MONTH 8
Take a good look at your money situation this month to see if you have the opportunity to increase your prosperity in some way. You might have to work more hours, collect that which is due to you, or go after a promotion. You can do this when you set your mind to it. Sometimes the easy way of keeping the peace and letting things slide just doesn't work. This month brings rewards for past efforts. Think about your goals, where do you really want to end up? We know that you are not that interested in becoming a millionaire, but money and power is nice to have for a while. 'The tides in the affairs taken at the flood leads on to fortune,' says Shakespeare, and

they will release a lot of good things for you. If you have everything you want and are interested in the metaphysical world, you can open or reopen your third eye by a direct application of meditation and your energy this month.

Negative Money and power could slip through your fingers if you ignore this positive vibration and scatter your energies in aimless pursuits.

PERSONAL MONTH 9

Look around you and see the material things you no longer need, and how they clutter your life. Take them to a charity shop or a jumble sale. It is a little emotional to let go of souvenirs and things to which we have become attached—yet this is inhibiting your growth. Next month you can start afresh with lots of room to store your new puchases. This is also a good time to do some service for mankind; do some charity work or something for your friends. Express your love for your partner by bringing gifts and unusual treats home. Love and share your thoughts and goals so that communication is smoothed out.

Negative You could be rushing forward, leading the band of do-gooders only to find yourself alone with no one behind you. Watch how your emotions can inspire you—not perspire you.

CHALLENGES OF LIFE

Challenges are obstacles we encounter during this life. We are now concerned with the timing of events that stop you from progressing until you understand just what the obstacle is and what it means.

In the *first half* of your lifetime, you will encounter a Sub (or minor) Challenge which is represented by a number.

In the *second half* of your lifetime, you will encounter a Sub Challenge which is represented by another number.

The Major Challenge, also represented by a number, is with you and your entire life until you solve the mystery. We accepted these challenges when we decided to incarnate on this planet so that we can strengthen the weak links in our destiny. Recognizing these weak links by finding the negative influences of these numbrs will be helpful.

Saturn is the planet known as the *disciplinarian*, the teacher, the door to the initiation and all these good things we shy away from or fear. See Saturn's other side—if you have no game going, no challenge, and life proceeds smoothly straight down the road with the same scenery, where is the spice? Understand the good that Saturn brings us. Saturn is connected to the challenges of life.

FIRST SUB CHALLENGE
Subtract the number of your birth *month* from the number of your birth *day* or vice versa.

SECOND SUB CHALLENGE
Subtract the number of your birth *day* from your reduced birth *year* or vice versa.

MAJOR CHALLENGE
Subtract the First Sub Challenge from the Second Sub Challenge or vice versa. Place all these numbers in your Personal Chart on page 286.

Example: March   17,   1939

$$\frac{3 \qquad 8 \qquad 4}{\quad}$$

5 4	**5** = First Sub Challenge
1	**4** = Second Sub Challenge
	1 = Major Challenge

TABLE OF CHALLENGES

CHALLENGE 1
Many people will try to dominate and control your life. The remedy is choosing your own way without being belligerent about it. Know when you are right and please yourself after considering all the facts. Strengthen your self-determinism and be the daring, creative person you really are. Dependence on others can limit your talents.

CHALLENGE 2
Your feelings are uppermost and you are apt to turn others' opinions into personal affronts. This sensitivity can be very useful if you 'tune' in to people and see where they are. Cultivate a broader outlook on life and learn to be co-operative without being indecisive. Be thoughtful and consider the welfare of others as well as your own.

CHALLENGE 3
Social interaction frightens you and your reaction is to withdraw or become loud and over-react. Each violent swing of the pendulum suggests that you are living in a personal construct without reality. Develop your sense of humour; try painting, dancing, writing or any artisitic sort of self-expression that can bring out the real you.

CHALLENGE 4
This easy challenge is *laziness!* However it can lead you into a rut where it is too much trouble to get out of that comfortable chair to answer the phone. Finish your cycles of activity and you will find your energy level rising. The other side of this challenge is rigidity. Learn patience and tolerance without becoming a slave.

CHALLENGE 5
This 'freedom' number allows us to progress *but* it does not mean doing anything and everything we desire without paying attention to our responsibilities. There are laws of society and universe that tell us to use moderation, not over-indulgence, in sex, drugs, alcohol or food. Organize your life. Recognize duties to family and friends.

CHALLENGE 6
This idealistic number may lead you into thinking that you have the best of all possible answers and belief systems. Your opinions can be dogmatic where personal relationships are at the crossroads. Do not impose your 'perfection' on others. Give willingly of your time and knowledge without suppressing other people's creativity. Turn 'smug' into 'hug'.

CHALLENGE 7
This research and discovery number challenges you to become scientific and analytical. Heed your inner guidance. Develop a patience with existing conditions and make an effort to improve them. Do not stifle your spiritual nature. Your limitations are self-imposed. Cultivate faith in the justice of the general plan of things then seek to better it.,

CHALLENGE 8
Wastefulness is the keyword for **8**. This can be brought about by carelessness or miserliness. A false sense of values, efficiency and judgements can become fetishes in the material world. Use your energies to cultivate good human relation-

ships and avoid greed. Be guided by reason and not by avarice. Honour, glory, fame and money are okay if acquired in the right way.

CHALLENGE 9

This challenge is rare since it carries the lack of emotion and human compassion. It also means judging others and refusing to understand them because of an inflated ego. The time has come for this person to learn to love and empathize with others.

CHALLENGE 10

Here are *no* or *all* challenges. Study the numbers above and see if you react to one. You have reached a point in your spiritual development where you can choose which challenge to release. Smooth the edges, learn and know the vibrations of the independence of **1**; the diplomat of **2**; the emotional thrust of **3**; the diligence of **4**; the expansion of **5**; the adjustment of **6**; the wisdom of **7**; the power of **8**; and the Universal Brotherhood of **9**.

If your Challenges are the same as your Destiny Number, give it very close scrutiny.

LEVELS OF THE NUMBERS

Every number can be expressed on three levels—*Positive,
Negative, Repressive*. This does not mean that a person is
expressing on all three levels. You can evaluate yourself by
observing:

1. How you react in certain situations.
2. What is your chronic emotional tone? Happy, grumpy,
   short-tempered, enthusiastic, fearful, bored, etc.?
3. Check how the interpretations listed below represent
   your overall response to your daily grind:

Positive	*Negative*	*Repressive*
Certain	Apathetic	Despotic
Enthusiastic	Unsure	Tyrannical
Definite	Antagonistic	Suppressive
Specific	Vacillating	Hostile
Searching	Non-feeling	Violent
Transforming	Covert	Stop Motions
Activating	Resentful	Hateful

This is the reason that people with the same numbers react
differently to certain situations and differ in attitude towards
themselves and others. You can choose which level you are
now on and change your level if you wish to change yourself.
You can also change your name or a few letters of your name
to bring in the vibrations of your choice.

TABLE OF NUMBERS

NUMBER 1
Positive creative; optimistic; self-determined; creative mind through feeling; can reach a higher dimension of awareness when preceded by a **10**.
Negative indecisive; arrogant; fabricating.
Repressive tyrannical; hostile; ill-willed.

NUMBER 2
Positive sensitive; rhythmic; patient; loving; restful; a peacemaker; skilled; response to emotional appeal with love; protective.
Negative impatient; cowardly; overly sensitive.
Repressive mischievous; self-deluded; hostile.

NUMBER 3
Positive communicative; entertaining; charming; can acquire knowledge from higher beings; inspirational; an intuitive counsellor.
Negative conceited; exaggerating; dabbling but never really learning anything exactly; gossiping.
Repressive hypocritical; intolerant; jealous.

NUMBER 4
Positive organizing; devoted to duty; orderly; loyal; heals etheric body by magnetism; works on higher levels; endures.
Negative inflexible; plodding; penurious; stiff; clumsy; rigid; argumentative.
Repressive hateful; suppressive; gets even.

NUMBER 5
Positive adventurous; understanding; clever; knows the essence of life; creative mind on the mental level; traveller; creative healer.
Negative inconsistent; self-indulgent; sloppy; tasteless; inelegant.

Repressive perverted; afraid of change; indulgent in drink and food; no sympathy.

NUMBER 6
Positive harmonious; good judgement; loving of home and family; balance; cosmic mother; self-realization; the doorway to higher mind through harmony.
Negative anxious, interfering, careless.
Repressive cynical; nasty; domestic tyranny.

NUMBER 7
Positive analytical; refined; studious; capable of inner wisdom; symbolizes the bridge from the mundane to the esoteric; the mystic; able to heal spiritual gaps.
Negative confused; sceptical; humiliates others; aloof; a contender.
Repressive malicious; a cheat; suppressive to self and others.

NUMBER 8
Positive powerful; a leader; director; chief; dependable; primal energy; can open third eye; money maker; sees auras.
Negative intolerant; biased; scheming; love of power, fame, glory without humility; impatient.
Repressive bigoted; abusive; oppressive; unjust.

NUMBER 9
Positive compassionate; charitable; romantic; aware; involved with the brotherhood of man; successful; finisher; merciful; humane.
Negative selfish; unkind; scornful; stingy; unforgiving; indiscreet; inconsiderate.
Repressive bitter; morose; dissipated; immoral.

NUMBER 11 *Idealist*
Positive idealistic; intuitive; cerebral; second sight; clairvoyant; perfection; spiritual; extra-sensory perception; excellence; inner wisdom.

Negative fanatic; self-superior; cynical; aimless; pragmatic.
Repressive dishonest; miserly; carnal; insolent.

NUMBER 22 *Physical Mastery*
Positive universal power on the physical level; financier; cultured person; international direction in government; physical mastery over self.
Negative inferiority complex; indifference; big talker—not doer; inflated ego.
Repressive evil; viciousness; crime on a large scale; black magic.

NUMBER 33 *Emotional Mastery*
Positive the idealist with power to command or serve; leader who has emotions under control; constructive, emotionally controlled ideas.
Negative erratic; useless; unemotional; not using gifts of sensitivity to others.
Repressive power to work on other people's emotion to their detriment; riot leaders.

NUMBER 44 *Mental Mastery*
Positive universal builder with insight; can institute and assist world-wide reform for the good of mankind; can manifest his postulates.
Negative mental abilities used for confusion of worthwhile ideas; twists meanings of great statesmen and very able people for personal use.
Repressive crime through mental cruelty; uses mask of righteousness to do evil; psychotic.

NUMBER 55 *Life Energy*
Positive abundant life; channels from higher dimensions with ease; brings light into existence; student of action; heals using life force.
Negative karma burdened with inaction on the right path; chooses to look backward and wallow in self-pity.

Repressive victim of life; in darkness; no path visible; withdraws; blames others.

NUMBER 66 *Love Energy*

Positive self-realization through love; this love extends from self to others, knowing that one cannot love others unless one knows and recognizes the perfection of one's own soul.

Negative using love as a tool to enslave another; extreme selfishness and possessiveness; refusing to love when time and person is correct.

Repressive seeing only the barriers to love; repressing loving attention to others; repressing the need to outpour cosmic love to others.

YOUR PERSONAL CHART

Name _____

Birthdate _____

Birth Sign _____

Birth Number _____

Birth Element _____

> This planetary aspect represents the moral excellence and goodness that the soul has achieved in former lifetimes, virtues which will assist a person in this lifetime.

Birth Colour _____

Birth Musical Note _____

Personal Year Numbers:

1988	_____	1992	_____
1989	_____	1993	_____
1990	_____	1994	_____
1991	_____	1995	_____

Personal Month Numbers:

January	_____	July	_____
February	_____	August	_____
March	_____	September	_____
April	_____	October	_____
May	_____	November	_____
June	_____	December	_____

Challenges:

Major _____

1st Sub-challenge _____

2nd Sub-challenge _____

YOUR PERSONAL CHART

Name _____

Birthdate _____

Birth Sign _____

Birth Number _____

Birth Element _____

This planetary aspect represents the moral excellence and goodness that the soul has achieved in former lifetimes, virtues which will assist a person in this lifetime.

Birth Colour _____

Birth Musical Note _____

Personal Year Numbers:

1988 _____   1992 _____

1989 _____   1993 _____

1990 _____   1994 _____

1991 _____   1995 _____

Personal Month Numbers:

January _____   July _____

February _____   August _____

March _____   September _____

April _____   October _____

May _____   November _____

June _____   December _____

Challenges:

Major _____

1st Sub-challenge _____

2nd Sub-challenge _____

YOUR PERSONAL CHART

Name _____

Birthdate _____

Birth Sign _____

Birth Number _____

Birth Element _____

> This planetary aspect represents the moral excellence and goodness that the soul has achieved in former lifetimes, virtues which will assist a person in this lifetime.

Birth Colour _____

Birth Musical Note _____

Personal Year Numbers:

1988	_____	1992	_____
1989	_____	1993	_____
1990	_____	1994	_____
1991	_____	1995	_____

Personal Month Numbers:

January	_____	July	_____
February	_____	August	_____
March	_____	September	_____
April	_____	October	_____
May	_____	November	_____
June	_____	December	_____

Challenges:

Major _____

1st Sub-challenge _____

2nd Sub-challenge _____